Monolith to Microservices
Evolutionary Patterns to Transform
Your Monolith

Sam Newman

Beijing · Boston · Farnham · Sebastopol · Tokyo

Monolith to Microservices

by Sam Newman

Copyright © 2020 Sam Newman. All rights reserved.

Published by O'Reilly Media, Inc., 1005 Gravenstein Highway North, Sebastopol, CA 95472.

O'Reilly books may be purchased for educational, business, or sales promotional use. Online editions are also available for most titles (*http://oreilly.com*). For more information, contact our corporate/institutional sales department: 800-998-9938 or *corporate@oreilly.com*.

Acquisitions Editors: Chris Guzikowski and Ryan Shaw
Developmental Editor: Alicia Young
Production Editor: Nan Barber
Copyeditor: Jasmine Kwityn
Proofreader: Sharon Wilkey
Indexer: Ellen Troutman-Zaig
Interior Designer: David Futato
Cover Designer: Karen Montgomery
Illustrator: Rebecca Demarest

October 2019:   First Edition

Revision History for the First Edition
2019-10-11:   First Release
2019-11-21:   Second Release

See *http://oreilly.com/catalog/errata.csp?isbn=9781492047841* for release details.

978-1-492-04784-1

[LSI]

Table of Contents

Preface

A few years ago, some of us were chatting about microservices being an interesting idea. The next thing you know it's become the default architecture for hundreds of companies around the world (many probably launched as startups aiming to solve the problems microservices cause), and has everyone running to jump on a bandwagon that they are worried is about to disappear over the horizon.

I must admit, I'm partly to blame. Since I wrote my own book on this subject, *Building Microservices* (*https://oreil.ly/building-microservices-2e*), back in 2015, I've made a living working with people to help them understand this type of architecture. What I've always tried to do is to cut through the hype, and help companies decide if microservices are right for them. For many of my clients with existing (non-microservice-oriented) systems, the challenge has been about how to adopt microservice architectures. How do you take an existing system and rearchitect it without having to stop all other work? That is where this book comes in. As importantly, I'll aim to give you an honest appraisal of the challenges associated with microservice architecture, and help you understand whether starting this journey is even right for you.

What You Will Learn

This book is designed as a deep dive into how you think about, and execute, breaking apart existing systems into a microservice architecture. We will touch on many topics related to microservice architecture, but the focus is on the decomposition side of things. For a more general guide to microservice architectures, my previous book *Building Microservices* would be a good place to start. In fact, I strongly recommend that you consider that book to be a companion to this one.

Chapter 1 contains an overview of what microservices are, and explores further the ideas that led us to these sorts of architectures. It should work well for people who are new to microservices, but I also strongly urge those of you with more experience to not skip this chapter. I feel that in the flurry of technology, some of the important core ideas of microservices often get missed: these are concepts that the book will return to again and again.

Understanding more about microservices is good, but knowing if they are right for you is something else. In Chapter 2, I walk you through how to go about assessing whether or not microservices are right for you, and also give you some really important guidelines for how to manage a transition from a monolith to a microservice architecture. Here we'll touch on everything from domain-driven design to organizational change models—vital underpinnings that will stand you in good stead even if you decide not to adopt a microservice architecture.

In Chapters 3 and 4 we dive deeper into the technical aspects associated with decomposing a monolith, exploring real-world examples and extracting out migration patterns. Chapter 3 focuses on application decomposition aspects, where Chapter 4 is a deep dive on data issues. If you really want to move from a monolithic system to a microservice architecture, we'll need to pull some databases apart!

Finally, Chapter 5 looks at the sorts of challenges you will face as your microservice architecture grows. These systems can offer huge benefits, but they come with a lot of complexity and problems you won't have had to face before. This chapter is my attempt at helping you spot these problems as they start to occur, and at offering ways to deal with the growing pains associated with microservices.

Conventions Used in This Book

The following typographical conventions are used in this book:

Italic
> Indicates new terms, URLs, email addresses, filenames, and file extensions.

`Constant width`
> Used for program listings, as well as within paragraphs to refer to program elements such as variable or function names, databases, data types, environment variables, statements, and keywords.

`Constant width bold`
> Shows commands or other text that should be typed literally by the user.

`Constant width italic`
> Shows text that should be replaced with user-supplied values or by values determined by context.

This element signifies a tip or suggestion.

 This element signifies a general note.

 This element indicates a warning or caution.

O'Reilly Online Learning

 For more than 40 years, *O'Reilly Media* has provided technology and business training, knowledge, and insight to help companies succeed.

Our unique network of experts and innovators share their knowledge and expertise through books, articles, conferences, and our online learning platform. O'Reilly's online learning platform gives you on-demand access to live training courses, in-depth learning paths, interactive coding environments, and a vast collection of text and video from O'Reilly and 200+ other publishers. For more information, please visit *http://oreilly.com*.

How to Contact Us

Please address comments and questions concerning this book to the publisher:

O'Reilly Media, Inc.
1005 Gravenstein Highway North
Sebastopol, CA 95472
800-998-9938 (in the United States or Canada)
707-829-0515 (international or local)
707-829-0104 (fax)

We have a web page for this book, where we list errata, examples, and any additional information. You can access this page at *https://oreil.ly/monolith-to-microservices*.

Email *bookquestions@oreilly.com* to comment or ask technical questions about this book.

For more information about our books, courses, conferences, and news, see our website at *http://www.oreilly.com*.

Find us on Facebook: *http://facebook.com/oreilly*

Follow us on Twitter: *http://twitter.com/oreillymedia*

Watch us on YouTube: *http://www.youtube.com/oreillymedia*

Acknowledgments

Without the help and understanding of my wonderful wife, Lindy Stephens, this book would not have been possible. This book is for her. Lindy, sorry for being so grouchy when various deadlines came and went. I'd also like to thank the lovely Gillman Staynes clan for all their support—I'm lucky to have such a great family.

This book benefited hugely from people who kindly volunteered their time and energy to read various drafts and provide valuable insights. I especially want to call out Chris O'Dell, Daniel Bryant, Pete Hodgson, Martin Fowler, Stefan Schrass, and Derek Hammer for their efforts in this area. There were also people who directly contributed in numerous ways, so I'd also like to thank Graham Tackley, Erik Doernenberg, Marcin Zasepa, Michael Feathers, Randy Shoup, Kief Morris, Peter Gillard-Moss, Matt Heath, Steve Freeman, Rene Lengwinat, Sarah Wells, Rhys Evans, and Berke Sokhan. If you find errors in this book, the mistakes are mine, not theirs.

The team at O'Reilly has also been incredibly supportive, and I would like to highlight my editors Eleanor Bru and Alicia Young, in addition to Christopher Guzikowski, Mary Treseler, and Rachel Roumeliotis. I also want to say a big thanks to Helen Codling and her colleagues elsewhere in the world for continuing to drag my books to various conferences, Susan Conant for keeping me sane while navigating the changing world of publishing, and Mike Loukides for initially getting me involved with O'Reilly. I know there are many more people behind the scenes who have helped, so thanks as well to you all.

Beyond those who directly contributed to this book, I also want to call out others who, whether they realized it or not, helped this book come about. So I would like to thank (in no particular order) Martin Kelppmann, Ben Stopford, Charity Majors, Alistair Cockburn, Gregor Hohpe, Bobby Woolf, Eric Evans, Larry Constantine, Leslie Lamport, Edward Yourdon, David Parnas, Mike Bland, David Woods, John Allspaw, Alberto Brandolini, Frederick Brooks, Cindy Sridharan, Dave Farley, Jez Humble, Gene Kim, James Lewis, Nicole Forsgren, Hector Garcia-Molina, Sheep & Cheese, Kenneth Salem, Adrian Colyer, Pat Helland, Kresten Thorup, Henrik

Kniberg, Anders Ivarsson, Manuel Pais, Steve Smith, Bernd Rucker, Matthew Skelton, Alexis Richardson, James Governor, and Kane Stephens.

As is always the case with these things, it seems highly likely that I've missed someone who has materially contributed to this book. To those people, all I can say is I'm very sorry for forgetting to thank you by name, and that I hope you can forgive me.

Finally, some people ask me from time to time about the tools I used to write this book. I wrote in AsciiDoc using Visual Studio Code along with João Pinto's AsciiDoc plug-in. The book was source controlled in Git, using O'Reilly's Atlas system. I wrote mostly on my laptop, using an external Razer mechanical keyboard, but toward the end also made heavy use of an iPad Pro running Working Copy to finish off the last few things. This enabled me to write while traveling, allowing me on one memorable occasion to write about database refactoring on a ferry to the Orkneys. The resulting seasickness was totally worth it.

CHAPTER 1

Just Enough Microservices

Well, that escalated quickly, really got out of hand fast!

—Ron Burgundy, *Anchorman*

Before we dive into how to work with microservices, it is important that we have a common, shared understanding about what microservice architectures are. I'd like to address some common misconceptions I see on a regular basis, as well as nuances that are often missed. You'll need this firm foundation of knowledge to get the most out of what follows in the rest of the book. As such, this chapter will provide an explanation of microservice architectures, look briefly at how microservices developed (which means, naturally, taking a look at monoliths), and examine some of the advantages and challenges of working with microservices.

What Are Microservices?

Microservices are independently deployable services modeled around a business domain. They communicate with each other via networks, and as an architecture choice offer many options for solving the problems you may face. It follows that a microservice architecture is based on multiple collaborating microservices.

They are a *type* of service-oriented architecture (SOA), albeit one that is opinionated about how service boundaries should be drawn, and that independent deployability is key. Microservices also have the advantage of being technology agnostic.

From a technology viewpoint, microservices expose the business capabilities that they encapsulate via one or more network endpoints. Microservices communicate with each other via these networks—making them a form of distributed system. They also encapsulate data storage and retrieval, exposing data, via well-defined interfaces. So databases are hidden inside the service boundary.

There is a lot to unpack in all of that, so let's dig a bit deeper into some of these ideas.

Independent Deployability

Independent deployability is the idea that we can make a change to a microservice and deploy it into a production environment without having to utilize any other services. More importantly, it's not just that we *can* do this; it's that this is *actually* how you manage deployments in your system. It's a discipline you practice for the bulk of your releases. This is a simple idea that is nonetheless complex in execution.

 If there is only one thing you take out of this book, it should be this: ensure you embrace the concept of independent deployability of your microservices. Get into the habit of releasing changes to a single microservice into production without having to deploy anything else. From this, many good things will follow.

To guarantee independent deployability, we need to ensure our services are *loosely coupled*—in other words, we need to be able to change one service without having to change anything else. This means we need explicit, well-defined, and stable contracts between services. Some implementation choices make this difficult—the sharing of databases, for example, is especially problematic. The desire for loosely coupled services with stable interfaces guides our thinking about how we find service boundaries in the first place.

Modeled Around a Business Domain

Making a change across a process boundary is expensive. If you need to make a change to two services to roll out a feature, and orchestrate the deployment of these two changes, that takes more work than making the same change inside a single service (or, for that matter, a monolith). It therefore follows that we want to find ways of ensuring we make cross-service changes as infrequently as possible.

Following the same approach I used in *Building Microservices*, this book uses a fake domain and company to illustrate certain concepts when it isn't possible to share real-world stories. The company in question is Music Corp, a large multi-national organization that somehow remains in business, despite it focusing almost entirely on selling CDs.

We've decided to move Music Corp kicking and screaming into the 21st century, and as part of that we're assessing the existing system architecture. In Figure 1-1, we see a simple three-tiered architecture. We have a web-based user interface, a business logic layer in the form of a monolithic backend, and data storage in a traditional database. These layers, as is common, are owned by different teams.

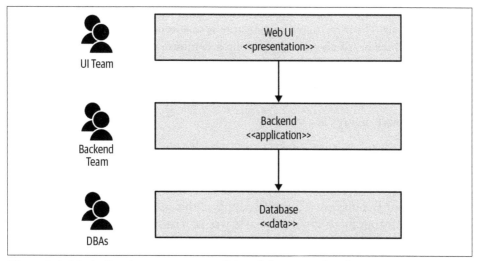

Figure 1-1. Music Corp's systems as a traditional three-tiered architecture

We want to make a simple change to our functionality: we want to allow our customers to specify their favorite genre of music. This change requires us to change the user interface to show the genre choice UI, the backend service to allow for the genre to be surfaced to the UI and for the value to be changed, and the database to accept this change. These changes will need to be managed by each team, as outlined in Figure 1-2, and those changes will need to be deployed in the correct order.

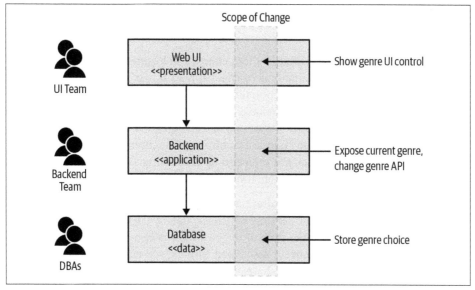

Figure 1-2. Making a change across all three tiers is more involved

Now this architecture isn't bad. All architecture ends up getting optimized around some set of goals. The three-tiered architecture is so common partly because it is universal—everyone's heard about it. So picking a common architecture you may have seen elsewhere is often one reason we keep seeing this pattern. But I think the biggest reason we see this architecture again and again is because it is based on how we organize our teams.

The now famous Conway's law states

> Any organization that designs a system…will inevitably produce a design whose structure is a copy of the organization's communication structure.
>
> —Melvin Conway, *How Do Committees Invent?*

The three-tiered architecture is a good example of this in action. In the past, the primary way IT organizations grouped people was in terms of their core competency: database admins were in a team with other database admins; Java developers were in a team with other Java developers; and frontend developers (who nowadays know exotic things like JavaScript and native mobile application development) were in yet another team. We group people based on their core competency, so we create IT assets that can be aligned to those teams.

So that explains why this architecture is so common. It's not bad; it's just optimized around one set of forces—how we traditionally grouped people, around familiarity. But the forces have changed. Our aspirations around our software have changed. We now group people in poly-skilled teams, to reduce hand-offs and silos. We want to ship software much more quickly than ever before. That is driving us to make different choices about how we organize our teams, and therefore in terms of how we break our systems apart.

Changes in functionality are primarily about changes in business functionality. But in Figure 1-1 our business functionality is in effect spread across all three tiers, increasing the chance that a change in functionality will cross layers. This is an architecture in which we have high cohesion of related technology, but low cohesion of business functionality. If we want to make it easier to make changes, instead we need to change how we group code—we choose cohesion of business functionality, rather than technology. Each service may or may not then end up containing a mix of these three layers, but that is a local service implementation concern.

Let's compare this with a potential alternative architecture illustrated in Figure 1-3. We have a dedicated Customer service, which exposes a UI to allow customers to update their information, and the state of the customer is also stored within this service. The choice of a favorite genre is associated with a given customer, so this change is much more localized. In Figure 1-3 we also show the list of available genres being fetched from a Catalog service, likely something that would already be in place. We also see a new Recommendation service accessing our favorite genre information, something that could easily follow in a subsequent release.

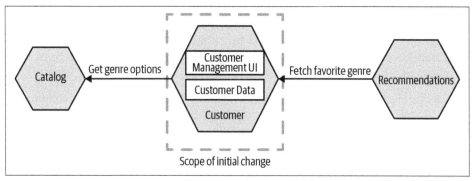

Figure 1-3. A dedicated Customer service may make it much easier to record the favorite musical genre of a customer

In such a situation, our Customer service encapsulates a thin slice of each of the three tiers—it has a bit of UI, a bit of application logic, and a bit of data storage—but these layers are all encapsulated in the single service.

Our business domain becomes the primary force driving our system architecture, hopefully making it easier to make changes, and making it easier for us to organize our teams around our business domain. This is so important that before we finish this chapter, we'll revisit the concept of modeling software around a domain, so I can share some ideas around domain-driven design that shape how we think about our microservice architecture.

Own Their Own Data

One of the things I see people having the hardest time with is the idea that microservices should not share databases. If one service wants to access data held by another service, then it should go and ask that service for the data it needs. This gives the service the ability to decide what is shared and what is hidden. It also allows the service to map from internal implementation details, which can change for various arbitrary reasons, to a more stable public contract, ensuring stable service interfaces. Having stable interfaces between services is essential if we want independent deployability—if the interface a service exposes keeps changing, this will have a ripple effect causing other services to need to change as well.

Don't share databases, unless you really have to. And even then do everything you can to avoid it. In my opinion, it's one of the worst things you can do if you're trying to achieve independent deployability.

As we discussed in the previous section, we want to think of our services as end-to-end slices of business functionality, that where appropriate encapsulate the UI, application logic, and data storage. This is because we want to reduce the effort needed to change business-related functionality. The encapsulation of data and behavior in this way gives us high cohesion of business functionality. By hiding the database that backs our service, we also ensure we reduce coupling. We'll be coming back to coupling and cohesion in a moment.

This can be hard to get your head around, especially when you have an existing monolithic system that has a giant database you have to deal with. Luckily, Chapter 4 is entirely dedicated to moving away from monolithic databases.

What Advantages Can Microservices Bring?

The advantages of microservices are many and varied. The independent nature of the deployments opens up new models for improving the scale and robustness of systems, and allows you to mix and match technology. As services can be worked on in parallel, you can bring more developers to bear on a problem without them getting in each other's way. It can also be easier for those developers to understand their part of the system, as they can focus their attention on just one part of it. Process isolation also makes it possible for us to vary the technology choices we make, perhaps mixing different programming languages, programming styles, deployment platforms, or databases to find the right mix.

Perhaps, above all, microservice architectures give you flexibility. They open up many more options regarding how you can solve problems in the future.

However, it's important to note that none of these advantages come for free. There are many ways you can approach system decomposition, and fundamentally what you are trying to achieve will drive this decomposition in different directions. Understanding what you are trying to get from your microservice architecture therefore becomes important.

What Problems Do They Create?

Service-oriented architecture became a thing partly because computers got cheaper, so we had more of them. Rather than deploy systems on single, giant mainframes, it made more sense to make use of multiple cheaper machines. Service-oriented architecture was an attempt to work out how best to build applications that spanned multiple machines. One of the main challenges in all of this is the way in which these computers talk to each other: networks.

Communication between computers over networks is not instantaneous (this apparently has something to do with physics). This means we have to worry about latencies—and specifically, latencies that far outstrip the latencies we see with local, in-process operations. Things get worse when we consider that these latencies will vary, which can make system behavior unpredictable. And we also have to address the fact that networks sometimes fail—packets get lost; network cables are disconnected.

These challenges make activities that are relatively simple with a single-process monolith, like transactions, much more difficult. So difficult, in fact, that as your system grows in complexity, you will likely have to ditch transactions, and the safety they bring, in exchange for other sorts of techniques (which unfortunately have very different trade-offs).

Dealing with the fact that any network call can and will fail becomes a headache, as will the fact that the services you might be talking to could go offline for whatever reason or otherwise start behaving oddly. Adding to all this, you also need to start trying to work out how to get a consistent view of data across multiple machines.

And then, of course, we have a huge wealth of new microservice-friendly technology to take into account—new technology that, if used badly, can help you make mistakes much faster and in more interesting, expensive ways. Honestly, microservices seem like a terrible idea, except for all the good stuff.

It's worth noting that virtually all of the systems we categorize as "monoliths" are also distributed systems. A single-process application likely reads data from a database that runs on a different machine, and presents data on to a web browser. That's at least three computers in the mix there, with communication between them over networks. The difference is the extent to which monolithic systems are distributed compared to microservice architectures. As you have more computers in the mix, communicating over more networks, you're more likely to hit the nasty problems associated with distributed systems. These problems I've briefly discussed may not appear initially, but over time, as your system grows, you'll likely hit most, if not all, of them.

As my old colleague, friend, and fellow microservice-expert James Lewis put it, "Microservices buy you options." James was being deliberate with his words—they *buy* you *options*. They have a cost, and you have to decide if the cost is worth the options you want to take up. We'll explore this topic in more detail in Chapter 2.

User Interfaces

All too often, I see people focus their work in embracing microservices purely on the server side—leaving the user interface as a single, monolithic layer. If we want an architecture that makes it easier for us to more rapidly deploy new features, then leaving the UI as a monolithic blob can be a big mistake. We can, and should, look at breaking apart our user interfaces too, something we'll explore in Chapter 3.

Technology

It can be all too tempting to grab a whole load of new technology to go along with your shiny new microservice architecture, but I strongly urge you not to fall into this temptation. Adopting any new technology will have a cost—it will create some upheaval. Hopefully, that will be worth it (if you've picked the right technology, of course!), but when first adopting a microservice architecture, you have enough going on.

Working out how to properly evolve and manage a microservice architecture involves tackling a multitude of challenges related to distributed systems—challenges you may not have faced before. I think it's much more useful to get your head around these issues as you encounter them, making use of a technology stack you are familiar with, and then consider whether changing your existing technology may help address those problems as you find them.

As we've already touched on, microservices are fundamentally technology agnostic. As long as your services can communicate with each other via a network, everything else is up for grabs. This can be a huge advantage—allowing you to mix and match technology stacks if you wish.

You don't have to use Kubernetes, Docker, containers, or the public cloud. You don't have to code in Go or Rust or whatever else. In fact, your choice of programming language is fairly unimportant when it comes to microservice architectures, over and above how some languages may have a richer ecosystem of supporting libraries and frameworks. If you know PHP best, start building services with PHP![1] There is far too much technical snobbery out there toward some technology stacks that can unfortunately border on contempt for people who work with particular tools.[2] Don't be part of the problem! Choose the approach that works for you, and change things to address problems as and when you see them.

Size

"How big should a microservice be?" is probably the most common question I get. Considering the word "micro" is right there in the name, this comes as no surprise. However, when you get into what makes microservices work as a type of architecture, the concept of size is actually one of the least interesting things.

---

1 For more on this topic, I recommend *PHP Web Services* by Lorna Jane Mitchell (O'Reilly).

2 After reading Aurynn Shaw's "Contempt Culture" blog post (*http://bit.ly/2oeICgL*), I recognized that in the past I have been guilty of showing some degree of contempt toward different technologies, and by extension the communities around them.

How do you measure size? Lines of code? That doesn't make much sense to me. Something that might require 25 lines of code in Java could possibly be written in 10 lines of Clojure. That's not to say Clojure is better or worse than Java, but rather that some languages are more expressive than others.

The closest I think I get to "size" having any meaning in terms of microservices is something fellow microservices expert Chris Richardson once said—that the goal of microservices is to have "as small an interface as possible." That chimes with the concept of information hiding (which we'll discuss in a moment) but does represent an attempt to find meaning after the fact—when we were first talking about these things, our main focus, initially at least, was on these things being really easy to replace.

Ultimately, the concept of "size" is highly contextual. Speak to a person who has worked on a system for 15 years, and they'll feel that their 100K line code system is really easy to understand. Ask the opinion of someone brand-new to the project, and they'll feel it's way too big. Likewise, ask a company that has just embarked on its microservice transition, with perhaps ten of fewer microservices, and you'll get a different answer than you would from a similar-sized company in which microservices have been the norm for many years, and they now have hundreds.

I urge people not to worry about size. When you are first starting out, it's much more important that you focus on two key things. First, how many microservices can you handle? As you have more services, the complexity of your system will increase, and you'll have to learn new skills (and perhaps adopt new technology) to cope with this. It's for this reason I am a strong advocate for incremental migration to a microservice architecture. Second, how do you define microservice boundaries to get the most out of them, without everything becoming a horribly coupled mess? These are topics we'll cover throughout the rest of this chapter.

History of the Term "Microservices"

Back in 2011, when I was still working at a consultancy called ThoughtWorks, my friend and then-colleague James Lewis became really interested in something he was calling "micro-apps." He had spotted this pattern being utilized by a few companies that were using service-oriented architecture—they were optimizing this architecture to make services easy to replace. The companies in question were interested in getting specific functionality deployed quickly, but with a view that it could be rewritten in other technology stacks if and when everything needed to scale.

At the time, the thing that stood out was how small in scope these services were. Some of these services could be written (or rewritten) in a few days. James went on to say that "services should be no bigger than my head." The idea being that the scope of functionality should be easy to understand, and therefore easy to change.

Later, in 2012, James was sharing these ideas at an architectural summit where a few of us were present. In that session, we discussed the fact that really these things weren't self-contained applications, so "micro-apps" wasn't quite right. Instead, "microservices" seemed a more appropriate name.[3]

And Ownership

With microservices modeled around a business domain, we see alignment between our IT artifacts (our independently deployable microservices) and our business domain. This idea resonates well when we consider the shift toward technology companies breaking down the divides between "The Business" and "IT." In traditional IT organizations, the act of developing software is often handled by an entirely separate part of the business from that which actually defines requirements and has a connection with the customer, as Figure 1-4 shows. The dysfunctions of these sorts of organizations are many and varied, and probably don't need to be expanded upon here.

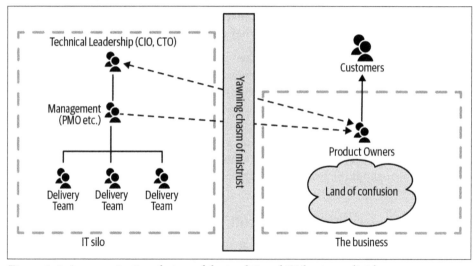

Figure 1-4. An organizational view of the traditional IT/business divide

Instead, we're seeing true technology organizations totally combine these previous disparate organizational silos, as we see in Figure 1-5. Product owners now work directly as part delivery teams, with these teams being aligned around customer-facing product lines, rather than around arbitrary technical groupings. Rather than

---

3 I can't recall the first time we actually wrote down the term, but I vividly recall my insistence, in the face of all logic around grammar, that the term should *not* be hyphenated. In hindsight, it was a hard-to-justify position, which I nonetheless stuck to. I stand by my unreasonable, but ultimately victorious choice.

centralized IT functions being the norm, the existence of any central IT function is to support these customer-focused delivery teams.

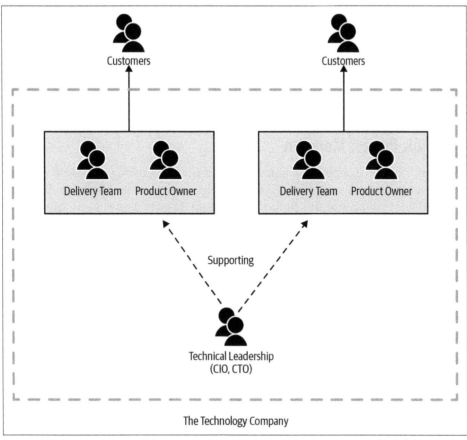

Figure 1-5. An example of how true technology companies are integrating software delivery

While not all organizations have made this shift, microservice architectures make this change much easier. If you want delivery teams aligned around product lines, and the services are aligned around the business domain, then it becomes easier to clearly assign ownership to these product-oriented delivery teams. Reducing services that are shared across multiple teams is key to minimizing delivery contention—business-domain-oriented microservice architectures make this shift in organizational structures much easier.

The Monolith

We've spoken about microservices, but this book is all about moving *from* monoliths *to* microservices, so we also need to establish what is meant by the term *monolith*.

When I talk about the monoliths in this book, I am primarily referring to a unit of deployment. When all functionality in a system had to be deployed together, we consider it a monolith. There are at least three types of monolithic systems that fit the bill: the single-process system, the distributed monolith, and third-party black-box systems.

The Single Process Monolith

The most common example that comes to mind when discussing monoliths is a system in which all of the code is deployed as a *single process*, as in Figure 1-6. You may have multiple instances of this process for robustness or scaling reasons, but fundamentally all the code is packed into a single process. In reality, these single-process systems can be simple distributed systems in their own right, as they nearly always end up reading data from or storing data into a database.

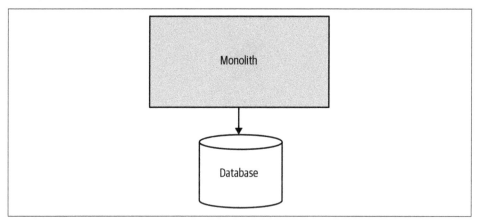

Figure 1-6. A single-process monolith: all code is packaged into a single process

These single-process monoliths probably represent the vast majority of the monolithic systems that I see people struggling with, and hence are the types of monoliths we'll focus most of our time on. When I use the term "monolith" from now on, I'll be talking about these sorts of monoliths unless I say otherwise.

And the modular monolith

As a subset of the single process monolith, the *modular monolith* is a variation: the single process consists of separate modules, each of which can be worked on independently, but which still need to be combined for deployment, as shown in

Figure 1-7. The concept of breaking down software into modules is nothing new; we'll come back to some of the history around this later in this chapter.

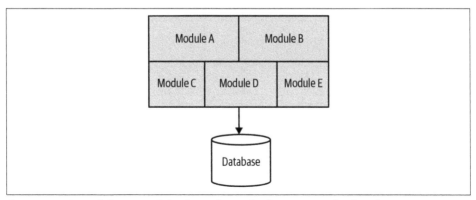

Figure 1-7. A modular monolith: the code inside the process is broken down into modules

For many organizations, the modular monolith can be an excellent choice. If the module boundaries are well defined, it can allow for a high degree of parallel working, but sidesteps the challenges of the more distributed microservice architecture along with much simpler deployment concerns. Shopify is a great example of an organization that has used this technique as an alternative to microservice decomposition, and it seems to work really well for that company.[4]

One of the challenges of a modular monolith is that the database tends to lack the decomposition we find in the code level, leading to significant challenges that can be faced if you want to pull the monolith in the future. I have seen some teams attempt to push the idea of the modular monolith further, having the database decomposed along the same lines as the modules, as shown in Figure 1-8. Fundamentally, making a change like this to an existing monolith can still be very challenging even if you're leaving the code alone—many of the patterns we'll explore in Chapter 4 can help if you want to try to do something similar yourself.

---

4 For an overview of Shopify's thinking behind the use of a modular monolith rather than microservices, Kirsten Westeinde's talk on YouTube (*http://bit.ly/2oauZ29*) has some useful insights.

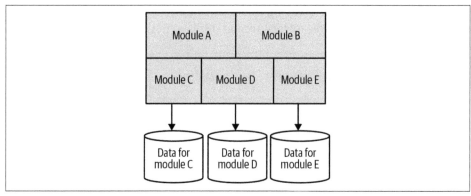

Figure 1-8. A modular monolith with a decomposed database

The Distributed Monolith

> A distributed system is one in which the failure of a computer you didn't even know existed can render your own computer unusable.[5]
>
> —Leslie Lamport

A *distributed monolith* is a system that consists of multiple services, but for whatever reason the entire system has to be deployed together. A distributed monolith may well meet the definition of a service-oriented architecture, but all too often fails to deliver on the promises of SOA. In my experience, distributed monoliths have all the disadvantages of a distributed system, *and* the disadvantages of a single-process monolith, without having enough upsides of either. Encountering distributed monoliths in my work has in large part influenced my own interest in microservice architecture.

Distributed monoliths typically emerge in an environment where not enough focus was placed on concepts like information hiding and cohesion of business functionality, leading instead to highly coupled architectures in which changes ripple across service boundaries, and seemingly innocent changes that appear to be local in scope break other parts of the system.

Third-Party Black-Box Systems

We can also consider some *third-party software* as monoliths that we may want to "decompose" as part of a migration effort. These might include things like payroll systems, CRM systems, and HR systems. The common factor here is that it's software developed by other people, and you don't have the ability to change the code. It could be off-the-shelf software you've deployed on your own infrastructure, or could be a

---

5 Email message sent to a DEC SRC bulletin board at 12:23:29 PDT on May 28, 1987 (see *https://www.micro soft.com/en-us/research/publication/distribution/* for more).

Software-as-a-Service (SaaS) product you are using. Many of the decomposition techniques we'll explore in this book can be used even with systems where you cannot change the underlying code.

Challenges of Monoliths

The monolith, be it a single-process monolith or a distributed monolith, is often more vulnerable to the perils of coupling—specifically, implementation and deployment coupling, topics we'll explore more shortly.

As you have more and more people working in the same place, they get in each other's way. Different developers wanting to change the same piece of code, different teams wanting to push functionality live at different times (or delay deployments). Confusion around who owns what, and who makes decisions. A multitude of studies show the challenges of confused lines of ownership.[6] I refer to this problem as *delivery contention*.

Having a monolith doesn't mean you will definitely face the challenges of delivery contention, any more than having a microservice architecture means that you won't ever face the problem. But a microservice architecture does give you more concrete boundaries in a system around which ownership lines can be drawn, giving you much more flexibility regarding how you reduce this problem.

Advantages of Monoliths

The single-process monolith, though, has a whole host of advantages, too. Its much simpler deployment topology can avoid many of the pitfalls associated with distributed systems. It can result in much simpler developer workflows; and monitoring, troubleshooting, and activities like end-to-end testing can be greatly simplified as well.

Monoliths can also simplify code reuse within the monolith itself. If we want to reuse code within a distributed system, we have to decide whether we want to copy code, break out libraries, or push the shared functionality into a service. With a monolith, our choices are much simpler, and many people like that simplicity—all the code is there, so just use it!

Unfortunately, people have come to view the monolith as something to be avoided—as something that is inherently problematic. I've met multiple people for whom the term *monolith* is synonymous with *legacy*. This is a problem. A monolithic architecture is a choice, and a valid one at that. It may not be the right choice in all

---

6 Microsoft Research has carried out studies in this space, and I recommend all of them. As a starting point, I suggest "Don't Touch My Code! Examining the Effects of Ownership on Software Quality" (*http://bit.ly/2p5RlT1*) by Christian Bird et al.

circumstances, any more than microservices are—but it's a choice nonetheless. If we fall into the trap of systematically denigrating the monolith as a viable option for delivering our software, then we're at risk of not doing right by ourselves or the users of our software. We'll further explore the trade-offs around monoliths and microservices in Chapter 3, and discuss some tools that will help you better assess what is right for your own context.

On Coupling and Cohesion

Understanding the balancing forces between coupling and cohesion is important when defining microservice boundaries. *Coupling* speaks to how changing one thing requires a change in another; *cohesion* talks to how we group related code. These concepts are directly linked. Constantine's law articulates this relationship well:

> A structure is stable if cohesion is high, and coupling is low.
>
> —Larry Constantine

This seems like a sensible and useful observation. If we have two pieces of tightly related code, cohesion is low as the related functionality is spread across both. We also have tight coupling, as when this related code changes, both things need to change.

If the structure of our code system is changing, that will be expensive to deal with, as the cost of change across service boundaries in distributed systems is so high. Having to make changes across one or more independently deployable services, perhaps dealing with the impact of breaking changes for service contracts, is likely to be a huge drag.

The problem with the monolith is that all too often it is the opposite of both. Rather than tend toward cohesion, and keep things together that tend to change together, we acquire and stick together all sorts of unrelated code. Likewise, loose coupling doesn't really exist: if I want to make a change to a line of code, I may be able to do that easily enough, but I cannot deploy that change without potentially impacting much of the rest of the monolith, and I'll certainly have to redeploy the entire system.

We also want system stability because our goal, where possible, is to embrace the concept of independent deployability—that is, we'd like to be able to make a change to our service and deploy that service into production *without having to change anything else*. For this to work, we need stability of the services we consume, and we need to provide a stable contract to those services that consume us.

Given the wealth of information out there about these terms, it would be silly of me to revisit things too much here, but I think a summary is in order, especially to place these ideas in the context of microservice architectures. Ultimately, these concepts of cohesion and coupling influence hugely how we think about microservice architecture. And this is no surprise—cohesion and coupling are concerns regarding modular software, and what is microservice architecture other than modules that communicate via networks and can be independently deployed?

A Brief History of Coupling and Cohesion

The concepts of cohesion and coupling have been around in computing for a long time, with the concepts initially outlined by Larry Constantine in 1968. These twin ideas of coupling and cohesion went on to form the basis of much of how we think about writing computer programs. Books like *Structured Design* by Larry Constantine & Edward Yourdon (Prentice Hall, 1979) subsequently influenced generations of programmers subsequently (this was required reading for my own university degree, almost 20 years after it was first published).

Larry first outlined his concepts of cohesion and coupling in 1968 (an especially auspicious year for computing) at the National Symposium on Modular Programming, the same conference where Conway's law first got its name. That year also gave us two now infamous NATO-sponsored conferences during which software engineering as a concept also rose to prominence (a term previously coined by Margaret H. Hamilton).

Cohesion

One of the most succinct definitions I've heard for describing cohesion is this: "the code that changes together, stays together." For our purposes, this is a pretty good definition. As we've already discussed, we're optimizing our microservice architecture around ease of making changes in business functionality—so we want the functionality grouped in such a way that we can make changes in as few places as possible.

If I want to change how invoice approval is managed, I don't want to have to hunt down the functionality that needs changing across multiple services, and then coordinate the release of those newly changed services in order to roll out our new functionality. Instead, I want to make sure the change involves modifications to as few services as possible to keep the cost of change low.

Coupling

> Information Hiding, like dieting, is somewhat more easily described than done.
>
> —David Parnas, *The Secret History Of Information Hiding*

We like cohesion we like, but we're wary of coupling. The more things are "coupled", the more they have to change together. But there are different types of coupling, and each type may require different solutions.

There has been a lot of prior art when it comes to categorizing types of coupling, notably work done by Meyer, Yourdan, and Constantine. I present my own, not to say that the work done previously is wrong, more than I find this categorization more useful when helping people understand aspects associated to the coupling of distributed systems. As such, it isn't intended to be an exhaustive classification of the different forms of coupling.

Information Hiding

A concept that comes back again and again when it comes to discussions around coupling is the technique called *information hiding*. This concept, first outlined by David Parnas in 1971, came out of his work looking into how to define module boundaries.[7]

The core idea with information hiding is to separate the parts of the code that change frequently from the ones that are static. We want the module boundary to be stable, and it should hide those parts of the module implementation that we expect to change more often. The idea is that internal changes can be made safely as long as module compatibility is maintained.

Personally, I adopt the approach of exposing as little as possible from a module (or microservice) boundary. Once something becomes part of a module interface, it's hard to walk that back. But if you hide it now, you can always decide to share it later.

Encapsulation as a concept in object-oriented (OO) software is related, but depending on whose definition you accept may not be quite the same thing. Encapsulation in OO programming has come to mean the bundling together of one or more things into a container—think of a class containing both fields and the methods that act on those fields. You could then use visibility at the class definition to hide parts of the implementation.

For a longer exploration of the history of information hiding, I recommend Parnas's "The Secret History of Information Hiding."[8]

Implementation coupling

Implementation coupling is typically the most pernicious form of coupling I see, but luckily for us it's often one of the easiest to reduce. With implementation coupling, A

---

7 Although Parnas's well known 1972 paper "On the Criteria to be Used in Decomposing Systems into Modules" is often cited as the source, he first shared this concept in "Information Distributions Aspects of Design Methodology", Proceedings of IFIP Congress '71, 1971.

8 See Parnas, David, "The Secret History of Information Hiding." Published in *Software Pioneers*, eds. M. Broy and E. Denert (Berlin Heidelberg: Springer, 2002).

is coupled to B in terms of how B is implemented—when the implementation of B changes, A also changes.

The issue here is that implementation detail is often an arbitrary choice by developers. There are many ways to solve a problem; we choose one, but we may change our minds. When we decide to change our minds, we don't want this to break consumers (independent deployability, remember?).

A classic and common example of implementation coupling comes in the form of sharing a database. In Figure 1-9, our Order service contains a record of all orders placed in our system. The Recommendation service suggests records to our customers that they might like to buy based on previous purchases. Currently, the Recommendation service directly accesses this data from the database.

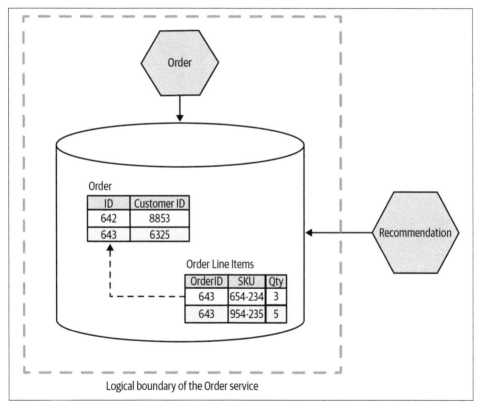

Figure 1-9. The Recommendation service directly accesses the data stored in the Order service

Recommendations require information about which orders have been placed. To an extent, this is unavoidable *domain* coupling, which we'll touch on in a moment. But in this particular situation, we are coupled to a specific schema structure, SQL dialect, and perhaps even the content of the rows. If the Order service changes the name of a column, splits the Customer Order table apart, or whatever else, it conceptually still contains order information, but we break how the Recommendation service fetches this information. A better choice is to hide this implementation detail, as Figure 1-10 shows—now the Recommendation service accesses the information it needs via an API call.

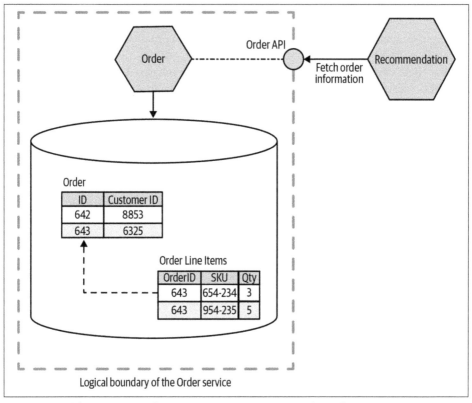

Figure 1-10. The Recommendation service now accesses order information via an API, hiding internal implementation detail

We could also have the Order service publish a dataset, in the form of a database, which is meant to be used for bulk access by consumers—just as we see in Figure 1-11. As long as the Order service can publish data accordingly, any changes made inside the Order service are invisible to consumers, as it maintains the public contract. This also opens up the opportunity to improve the data model exposed for consumers, tuning to their needs. We'll be exploring patterns like this in more detail in Chapters 3 and 4.

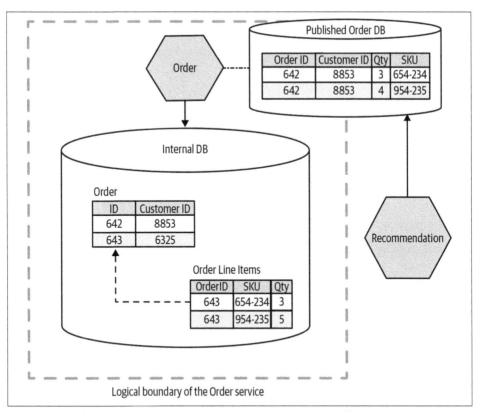

Figure 1-11. The Recommendation service now accesses order information via an exposed database, which is structured differently from the internal database

In effect, with both of the preceding examples, we are making use of information hiding. The act of hiding a database behind a well-defined service interface allows the service to limit the scope of what is exposed, and can allow us to change how this data is represented.

Another helpful trick is to use "outside-in" thinking when it comes to defining a service interface—drive the service interface by thinking of things from the point of the service consumers first, and then work out how to implement that service contract. The alternative approach (which I have observed is all too common, unfortunately) is to do the reverse. The team working on the service takes a data model, or another internal implementation detail, then thinks to expose that to the outside world.

With "outside-in" thinking, you instead first ask, "What do my service consumers need?" And I don't mean you ask *yourself* what your consumers need; I mean you actually ask the people that will call your service!

Treat the service interfaces that your microservice exposes like a user interface. Use outside-in thinking to shape the interface design in partnership with the people who will call your service.

Think of your service contract with the outside world as a user interface. When designing a user interface, you ask the users what they want, and iterate on the design of this with your users. You should shape your service contract in the same way. Aside from the fact it means you end up with a service that is easier for your consumers to use, it also helps keep some separation between the external contract and the internal implementation.

Temporal coupling

Temporal coupling is primarily a runtime concern that generally speaks to one of the key challenges of synchronous calls in a distributed environment. When a message is sent, and how that message is handled is connected in time, we are said to have temporal coupling. That sounds a little odd, so let's take a look at an explicit example in Figure 1-12.

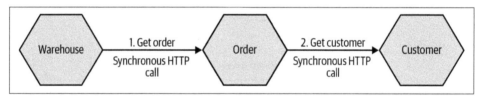

Figure 1-12. Three services making use of synchronous calls to perform an operation can be said to be temporally coupled

Here we see a synchronous HTTP call made from our Warehouse service to a downstream Order service to fetch required information about an order. To satisfy the request, the Order service in turn has to fetch information from the Customer service, again via a synchronous HTTP call. For this overall operation to complete, the Warehouse, Order, and Customer services all needed to be up, and contactable. They are temporally coupled.

We could reduce this problem in various ways. We could consider the use of caching —if the Order service cached the information it needed from the Customer service, then the Order service would be able to avoid temporal coupling on the downstream service in some cases. We could also consider the use of an asynchronous transport to send the requests, perhaps using something like a message broker. This would allow a message to be sent to a downstream service, and for that message to be handled after the downstream service is available.

A full exploration of the types of service-to-service communication is outside the scope of this book, but is covered in more detail in Chapter 4 of *Building Microservices*.

Deployment coupling

Consider a single process, which consists of multiple statically linked modules. A change is made to a single line of code in one of the modules, and we want to deploy that change. In order to do that, we have to deploy the entire monolith—even including those modules that are unchanged. Everything must be deployed together, so we have *deployment coupling*.

Deployment coupling may be enforced, as in the example of our statically linked process, but can also be a matter of choice, driven by practices like a release train. With a release train, preplanned release schedules are drawn up in advance, typically with a repeating schedule. When the release is due, all changes made since the last release train gets deployed. For some people, the release train can be a useful technique, but I strongly prefer to see it as a transitional step toward proper release-on-demand techniques, rather than viewing it as an ultimate goal. I even have worked in organizations that would deploy all services in a system all at once as part of these release train processes, without any thought to whether those services need to be changed.

Deploying something carries risk. There are lots of ways to reduce the risk of deployment, and one of those ways is to change only what needs to be changed. If we can reduce deployment coupling, perhaps through decomposing larger processes into independently deployable microservices, we can reduce the risk of each deployment by reducing the scope of deployment.

Smaller releases make for less risk. There is less to go wrong. If something does go wrong, working out what went wrong and how to fix it is easier because we changed less. Finding ways to reduce the size of release goes to the heart of continuous delivery, which espouses the importance of fast feedback and release-on-demand methods.[9] The smaller the scope of the release, the easier and safer it is to roll out, and the faster feedback we'll get. My own interest in microservices comes from a previous focus on continuous delivery—I was looking for architectures that made adoption of continuous delivery easier.

Reducing deployment coupling doesn't require microservices, of course. Runtimes like Erlang allow for the hot-deployment of new versions of modules into a running

---

9 See Jez Humble and David Farley, *Continuous Delivery: Reliable Software Releases through Build, Test, and Deployment Automation* (Upper Saddle River: Addison Wesley, 2010) for more details.

process. Eventually, perhaps more of us may have access to such capabilities in the technology stacks we use day to day.[10]

Domain coupling

Fundamentally, in a system that consists of multiple independent services, there has to be some interaction between the participants. In a microservice architecture, *domain coupling* is the result—the interactions between services model the interactions in our real domain. If you want to place an order, you need to know what items were in a customer's shopping basket. If you want to ship a product, you need to know where you ship it. In our microservice architecture, by definition this information may be contained in different services.

To give a concrete example, consider Music Corp. We have a warehouse that stores goods. When customers place orders for CDs, the folks working in the warehouse need to understand what items need to be picked and packaged, and where the package needs to be sent. So, information about the order needs to be shared with the people working in the warehouse.

Figure 1-13 shows an example of this: an Order Processing service sends all the details of the order to the Warehouse service, which then triggers the item to be packaged up. As part of this operation, the Warehouse service uses the customer ID to fetch information about the customer from the separate Customer service so that we know how to notify them when the order is sent out.

In this situation, we are sharing the entire order with the warehouse, which may not make sense—the warehouse needs only information about what to package and where to send it. They don't need to know how much the item cost (if they need to include an invoice with the package, this could be passed along as a pre-rendered PDF). We'd also have problems with information that we have to control access to being too widely shared—if we shared the full order, we could end up exposing credit card details to services that don't need it, for example.

---

10 Greenspun's 10th rule states, "Any sufficiently complicated C or Fortran program contains an ad hoc, informally specified, bug-ridden, slow implementation of half of Common Lisp." This has morphed into the newer joke: "Every microservice architecture contains a half-broken reimplementation of Erlang." I think there is a lot of truth to this.

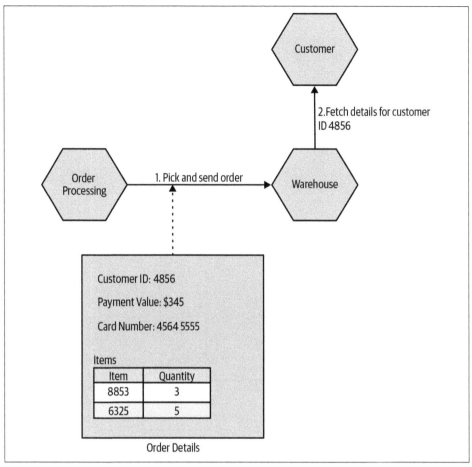

Figure 1-13. An order is sent to the warehouse to allow packaging to commence

So instead, we might come up with a new domain concept of a Pick Instruction containing just the information the Warehouse service needs, as we see in Figure 1-14. This is another example of information hiding.

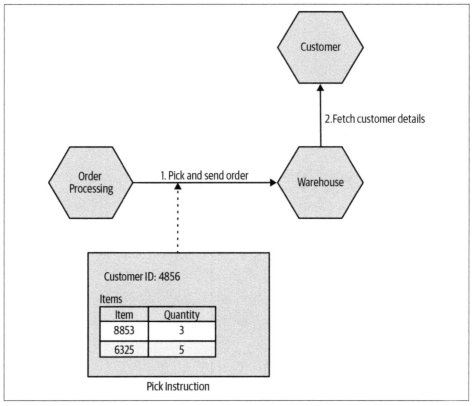

Figure 1-14. Using a Pick Instruction to reduce how much information we send to the Warehouse service

We could further reduce coupling by removing the need for the Warehouse service to even need to know about a customer if we wanted to—we could instead provide all appropriate details via the Pick Instruction, as Figure 1-15 shows.

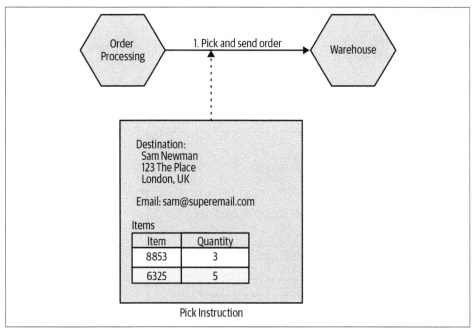

Figure 1-15. Putting more information into the Pick Instruction can avoid the need for a call to the Customer service

For this approach to work, it probably means that at some point Order Processing has to access the Customer service to be able to generate this Pick Instruction in the first place, but it's likely that Order Processing would need to access customer information for other reasons anyway, so this is unlikely to be much of an issue. This process of "sending" a Pick Instruction implies an API call being made from Order Processing to the Warehouse service.

An alternative could be to have Order Processing emit some kind of event that the Warehouse consumes, in Figure 1-16. By emitting an event that the Warehouse consumes, we effectively flip the dependencies. We go from Order Processing depending on the Warehouse service to be able to ensure an order gets sent, to the Warehouse listening to events from the Order Processing service. Both approaches have their merits, and which I would choose would likely depend on a wider understanding of the interactions between the Order Processing logic and the functionality encapsulated in the Warehouse service—that's something that some domain modeling can help with, a topic we'll explore next.

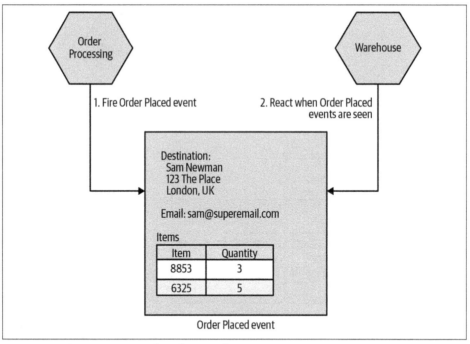

Figure 1-16. Firing an event that the Warehouse service can receive, containing just enough information for the order to be packaged and sent

Fundamentally, some information is needed about an order for the Warehouse service to do any work. We can't avoid that level of domain coupling. But by thinking carefully about what and how we share these concepts, we can still aim to reduce the level of coupling being used.

Just Enough Domain-Driven Design

As we've already discussed, modeling our services around a business domain has significant advantages for our microservice architecture. The question is how to come up with that model—and this is where domain-driven design (DDD) comes in.

The desire to have our programs better represent the real world in which the programs themselves will operate is not a new idea. Object-oriented programming languages like Simula were developed to allow us to model real domains. But it takes more than program language capabilities for this idea to really take shape.

Eric Evans' *Domain-Driven Design*,[11] presented a series of important ideas that helped us better represent the problem domain in our programs. A full exploration of these ideas is outside the scope of this book, but I'll provide a brief overview of the most important ideas involved in considering microservice architectures.

Aggregate

In DDD, an *aggregate* is a somewhat confusing concept, with many different definitions out there. Is it just an arbitrary collection of objects? The smallest unit I should take out of a database? The model that has always worked for me is to first consider an aggregate as a representation of a real domain concept—think of something like an Order, Invoice, Stock Item, etc. Aggregates typically have a life cycle around them, which opens them up to being implemented as a state machine. We want to treat aggregates as self-contained units; we want to ensure that the code that handles the state transitions of an aggregate are grouped together, along with the state itself.

When thinking about aggregates and microservices, a single microservice will handle the life cycle and data storage of one or more different types of aggregates. If functionality in another service wants to change one of these aggregates, it needs to either directly request a change in that aggregate, or else have the aggregate itself react to other things in the system to initiate its own state transitions—examples we see illustrated in Figure 1-17.

The key thing to understand here is that if an outside party requests a state transition in an aggregate, the aggregate can say no. You ideally want to implement your aggregates in such a way that illegal state transitions are impossible.

Aggregates can have relationships with other aggregates. In Figure 1-18, we have a Customer aggregate, which is associated with one or more Orders. We have decided to model Customer and Order as separate aggregates, which could be handled by different services.

---

11 Eric Evans, *Domain-Driven Design: Tackling Complexity in the Heart of Software* (Boston: Addison-Wesley, 2004).

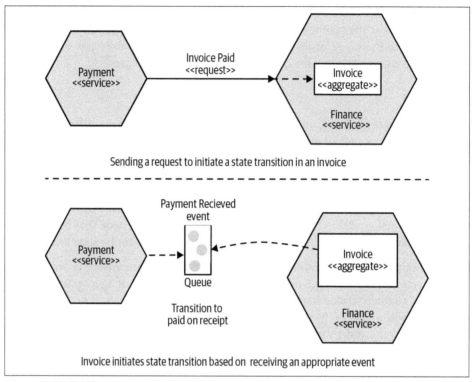

Figure 1-17. Different ways in which our Payment service may trigger a Paid transition in our Invoice aggregate

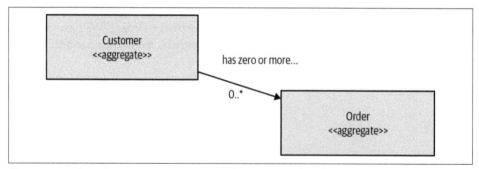

Figure 1-18. One Customer aggregate may be associated with one or more Order aggregates

There are lots of ways to break a system into aggregates, with some choices being highly subjective. You may, for performance reasons or ease of implementation, decide to reshape aggregates over time. To start with, though, I consider implementation concerns to be secondary, initially letting the mental model of the system users be my guiding light on initial design until other factors come into play. In Chapter 2,

I'll introduce Event Storming as a collaborative exercise to help shape these domain models with the help of your nondeveloper colleagues.

Bounded Context

A *bounded context* typically represents a larger organizational boundary inside an organization. Within the scope of that boundary, explicit responsibilities need to be carried out. That's all a bit wooly, so let's look at another specific example.

At Music Corp, our warehouse is a hive of activity—managing orders being shipped out (and the odd return), taking delivery of new stock, having forklift truck races, and so on. Elsewhere, the finance department is perhaps less fun-loving, but still has an important function inside our organization, handling payroll, paying for shipments, and the like.

Bounded contexts hide implementation detail. There are internal concerns—for example, the types of forklift trucks used is of little interest to anyone other than the folks in the warehouse. These internal concerns should be hidden from the outside world—they don't need to know, nor should they care.

From an implementation point of view, bounded contexts contain one or more aggregates. Some aggregates may be exposed outside the bounded context; others may be hidden internally. As with aggregates, bounded contexts may have relationships with other bounded contexts—when mapped to services, these dependencies become inter-service dependencies.

Mapping Aggregates and Bounded Contexts to Microservices

Both the aggregate and the bounded context give us units of cohesion with well-defined interfaces with the wider system. The aggregate is a self-contained state machine that focuses on a single domain concept in our system, with the bounded context representing a collection of associated aggregates, again with an explicit interface to the wider world.

Both can therefore work well as service boundaries. When starting out, as I've already mentioned, I think you want to reduce the number of services you work with. As a result, I think you should probably target services that encompass entire bounded contexts. As you find your feet, and decide to break these services into smaller services, look to split them around aggregate boundaries.

A trick here is that even if you decide to split a service that models an entire bounded context into smaller services later on, you can still hide this decision from the outside world—perhaps by presenting a coarser-grained API to consumers. The decision to decompose a service into smaller parts is arguably an implementation decision, so we might as well hide it if we can!

Further Reading

A thorough exploration of domain-driven design is a worthwhile activity, but outside the scope of this book. If you want to follow this further, I suggest reading either Eric Evans's original *Domain Driven Design* or Vaughn Vernon's *Domain-Driven Design Distilled*.[12]

Summary

As we've discussed in this chapter, microservices are independently deployable services modeled around a business domain. They communicate with each other via networks. We use the principles of information hiding together with domain-driven design to create services with stable boundaries that are easier to work on independently, and we do what we can to reduce the many forms of coupling.

We also looked at a brief history of where they came from, and even found time to look at a small fraction of the huge amount of prior work that they build upon. We also looked briefly at some of the challenges associated with microservice architectures. This is a topic I'll explore in more detail in our next chapter, where I will also discuss how to plan a transition to a microservice architecture—as well as providing guidance to help you decide whether they're even right for you in the first place.

---

12 See Vaughn Vernon, *Domain-Driven Design Distilled* (Boston: Addison-Wesley, 2014).

CHAPTER 2

Planning a Migration

It's all too easy to dive straight into the nitty-gritty technical sides of monolithic decomposition—and this will be the focus of the rest of the book! But first we really need to explore several less technical issues. Where should you start the migration? How should you manage the change? How do you bring others along on the journey? And the important question to be asked early on—should you even use microservices in the first place?

Understanding the Goal

Microservices are not the goal. You don't "win" by having microservices. Adopting a microservice architecture should be a conscious decision, one based on rational decision-making. You should be thinking of migrating to a microservice architecture in order to achieve something that you can't currently achieve with your existing system architecture.

Without having a handle on what you are trying to achieve, how are you going to inform your decision-making process about what options you should take? What you are trying to achieve by adopting microservices will greatly change where you focus your time, and how you prioritize your efforts.

It will also help you avoid becoming a victim of analysis paralysis—being overburdened by choices. You also risk falling into a cargo cult mentality, just assuming that "If microservices are good for Netflix, they're good for us!"

A Common Failing

Several years ago, I was running a microservices workshop at a conference. As I do with all my classes, I like to get a sense of why people are there and what they're hoping to get out of the workshop. In this particular class several people had come from the same company, and I was curious to find out why their company had sent them. "Why are you at the workshop? Why are you interested in using microservices?" I asked one of them. Their answer? "We don't know; our boss told us to come!" Intrigued, I probed further. "So, any idea why your boss wanted you here?" "Well, you could ask him—he's sitting behind us," the attendee responded. I switched my line of questioning to their boss, asking the same question, "So, why are you looking to use microservices?" The boss's response? "Our CTO said we're doing microservices, so I thought we should find out what they are!"

This true story, while at one level funny, is unfortunately all too common. I encounter many teams who have made the decision to adopt a microservice architecture without really understanding why, or what they are hoping to achieve.

The problems with not having a clear view as to why you are using microservices are varied. It can require significant investment, either directly, in terms of adding more people or money, or in terms of prioritizing the transition work over and above adding features. This is further complicated by the fact that it can take a while to see the benefits of a transition. Occasionally this leads to the situation where people are a year or more into a transition but can't remember why they started it in the first place. It's not simply a matter of the sunk cost fallacy; they literally don't know why they're doing the work.

At the same time, I get asked by people to share the return on investment (ROI) of moving to a microservice architecture. Some people want hard facts and figures to back up why they should even consider this approach. The reality is that quite aside from the fact that detailed studies on these sorts of things are few and far between, even when they do exist, the observations from such studies are rarely transferable because of the different contexts people might find themselves in.

So where does that leave us, guess work? Well, no. I am convinced that we can and should have better studies into the efficacy of our development, technology, and architecture choices. Some work is already being done to this end in the form of things like "The State of DevOps Report" (*http://bit.ly/2ojVq5o*), but that looks at architecture only in passing. In lieu of these rigorous studies, we should at least strive to apply more critical thinking to our decision making, and at the same time embrace more of an experimental frame of mind.

You need a clear understanding as to what you are hoping to achieve. No ROI calculation can be done without properly assessing what the return is that you are looking for. We need to focus on the outcomes we hope to achieve, and not slavishly, dogmatically stick to a single approach. We need to think clearly and sensibly about the best way to get what we need, even if it means ditching a lot of work, or going back to the good old-fashioned boring approach.

Three Key Questions

When working with an organization to help them understand if they should consider adopting a microservice architecture, I tend to ask the same set of questions:

What are you hoping to achieve?
> This should be a set of outcomes that are aligned to what the business is trying to achieve, and can be articulated in a way that describes the benefit to the end users of the system.

Have you considered alternatives to using microservices?
> As we'll explore later, there are often many other ways to achieve some of the same benefits that microservices bring. Have you looked at these things? If not, why not? Quite often you can get what you need by using a much easier, more boring technique.

How will you know if the transition is working?
> If you decide to embark on this transition, how will you know if you're going in the right direction? We'll come back to this topic at the end of the chapter.

More than once I've found that asking these questions is enough for companies to think again regarding whether to go any further with a microservice architecture.

Why Might You Choose Microservices?

I can't define the goals you may have for your company. You know better the aspirations of your company and the challenges you are facing. What I can outline are the reasons that often get stated as to why microservices are being adopted by companies all over the world. In the spirit of honesty, I'll also outline other ways you could potentially achieve these same outcomes using different approaches.

Improve Team Autonomy

> Whatever industry you operate in, it is all about your people, and catching them doing things right, and providing them with the confidence, the motivation, the freedom and desire to achieve their true potential.
>
> —John Timpson

Many organizations have shown the benefits of creating autonomous teams. Keeping organizational groups small, allowing them to build close bonds and work effectively together without bringing in too much bureaucracy, has helped many organizations grow and scale more effectively than some of its peers. Gore has found great success by making sure none of their business units ever gets to more than 150, to make sure that everyone knows each other. For these smaller business units to work, they have to be given power and responsibility to work as autonomous units.

Timpsons, a highly successful UK retailer, has achieved massive scale by empowering its workforce, reducing the need for central functions and allowing the local stores to make decisions for themselves, things like giving them power over how much to refund unhappy customers. Now chairman of the company, John Timpson was famous for scrapping internal rules and replacing them with just two:

- Look the part and put the money in the till.
- You can do anything else to best serve customers.

Autonomy works at the smaller scale too, and most modern organizations I work with are looking to create more autonomous teams within their organizations, often trying to copy models from other organizations like Amazon's two-pizza team model, or the Spotify model.[1]

If done right, team autonomy can empower people, help them step up and grow, and get the job done faster. When teams own microservices, and have full control over those services, they increase the amount of autonomy they can have within a larger organization.

How else could you do this?

Autonomy—distribution of responsibility—can play out in many ways. Working out how you can push more responsibility into the team doesn't require a shift in architecture. Essentially, though, it's a process of identifying what responsibilities can be pushed into the teams, and this could play out in many ways. Giving ownership to parts of the codebase to different teams could be one answer (a modular monolith could still benefit you here): this could also be done by identifying people empowered to make decisions for parts of the codebase on functional grounds (e.g., Ryan knows display ads best, so he's responsible for that; Jane knows the most about tuning our query performance, so run anything in that area past her first).

Improving autonomy can also play out in simply not having to wait for other people to do things for you, so adopting self-service approaches to provisioning machines or

---

1 Which famously even Spotify doesn't use anymore.

environments can be a huge enabler, avoiding the need for central operations teams to have to field tickets for day-to-day activities.

Reduce Time to Market

By being able to make and deploy changes to individual microservices, and deploy these changes without having to wait for coordinated releases, we have the potential to release functionality to our customers more quickly. Being able to bring more people to bear on a problem is also a factor—we'll cover that shortly.

How else could you do this?

Well, where do we start? There are so many variables that go into play when considering how to ship software more quickly. I always suggest you carry out some sort of path-to-production modeling exercise, as it may help show that the biggest blocker isn't what you think.

I remember on one project many years ago at a large investment bank, we had been brought in to help speed up delivery of software. "The developers take too long to get things into production!" we were told. One of my colleagues, Kief Morris, took the time to map out all the stages involved in delivering software, looking at the process from the moment a product owner comes up with an idea to the point where that idea actually got into production.

He quickly identified that it took around six weeks on average from when a developer started on a piece of work to it being deployed into a production environment. We felt that we could shave a couple of weeks off of this process through the use of suitable automation, as manual processes were involved. But Kief found a much bigger problem in the path to production—often it took over 40 weeks for the ideas to get from the product owner to the point where developers could even start on the work. By focusing our efforts on improving that part of the process, we'd help the client much more in improving the time to market for new functionality.

So think of all the steps involved with shipping software. Look at how long they take, the durations (both elapsed time and busy time) for each step, and highlight the pain points along the way. After all of that, you may well find that microservices could be part of the solution, but you'll probably find many other things you could try in parallel.

Scale Cost-Effectively for Load

By breaking our processing into individual microservices, these processes can be scaled independently. This means we can also hopefully cost-effectively scale—we need to scale up only those parts of our processing that are currently constraining our ability to handle load. It also follows that we can then scale down those microservices that are under less load, perhaps even turning them off when not required. This is in part why so many companies that build SaaS products adopt microservice architecture—it gives them more control over operational costs.

How else could you do this?

Here we have a huge number of alternatives to consider, most of which are easier to experiment with before committing to a microservices-oriented approach. We could just get a bigger box for a start—if you're on a public cloud or other type of virtualized platform, you could simply provision bigger machines to run your process on. This "vertical" scaling obviously has its limitations, but for a quick short-term improvement, it shouldn't be dismissed outright.

Traditional horizontal scaling of the existing monolith—basically running multiple copies—could prove to be highly effective. Running multiple copies of your monolith behind a load-distribution mechanism like a load balancer or a queue could allow for simple handling of more load, although this may not help if the bottleneck is in the database, which, depending on the technology, may not support such a scaling mechanism. Horizontal scaling is an easy thing to try, and you really should give it a go before considering microservices, as it will likely be quick to assess its suitability, and has far fewer downsides than a full-blown microservice architecture.

You could also replace technology being used with alternatives that can handle load better. This is typically not a trivial undertaking, however—consider the work to port an existing program over to a new type of database or programming language. A shift to microservices may actually make changing technology easier, as you can change the technology being used only inside the microservices that require it, leaving the rest untouched and thereby reducing the impact of the change.

Improve Robustness

The move from single-tenant software to multitenant SaaS applications means the impact of system outages can be significantly more widespread. The expectations of our customers for their software to be available, as well as the importance of software in their lives, has increased. By breaking our application into individual, independently deployable processes, we open up a host of mechanisms to improve the robustness of our applications.

By using microservices, we are able to implement a more robust architecture because functionality is decomposed—that is, an impact on one area of functionality need not bring down the whole system. We also get to focus our time and energy on those parts of the application that most require robustness—ensuring critical parts of our system remain operational.

Resilience Versus Robustness

Typically, when we want to improve a system's ability to avoid outages, handle failures gracefully when they occur, and recover quickly when problems happen, we often talk about *resilience*. Much work has been done in the field of what is now known as *resilience engineering*, looking at the topic as a whole as it applies to all fields, not just computing. The model for resilience pioneered by David Woods looks more broadly at the concept of resilience, and points to the fact that *being resilient* isn't as simple as we might first think, by separating out our ability to deal with known and unknown sources of failure, among other things.[2]

John Allspaw, a colleague of David Woods, helps distinguish between the concepts of robustness and resilience. *Robustness* is the ability to have a system that is able to react to expected variations. *Resilience* is having an organization capable of adapting to things that haven't been thought of, which could well include creating a culture of experimentation through things like chaos engineering. For example, we are aware that a specific machine could die, so we might bring redundancy into our system by load balancing an instance. That is an example of addressing robustness. Resiliency is the process of an organization preparing itself for the fact that it cannot anticipate all potential problems.

An important consideration here is that microservices do not necessarily give you robustness for free. Rather, they open up opportunities to design a system in such a way that it can better tolerate network partitions, service outages, and the like. Just spreading your functionality across multiple separate processes and separate machines does not guarantee improved robustness; quite the contrary—it may just increase your surface area of failure.

How else could you do this?

By running multiple copies of your monolith, perhaps behind a load balancer or another load distribution mechanism like a queue,[3] we add redundancy to our system. We can further improve robustness of our applications by distributing instances of our monolith across multiple failure planes (e.g., don't have all machines in the same rack or same data center).

---

2 See David Woods, "Four Concepts for Resilience and the Implications for the Future of Resilience Engineering." *Reliability Engineering & System Safety* 141 (2015) 5–9.

3 See the competing consumer pattern for one such example, in *Enterprise Integration Patterns* by Gregor Hohpe and Bobby Woolf, page 502.

Investment in more reliable hardware and software could likewise yield benefits, as could a thorough investigation of existing causes of system outages. I've seen more than a few production issues caused by an overreliance on manual processes, for example, or people "not following protocol," which often means an innocent mistake by an individual can have significant impacts. British Airways suffered a massive outage in 2017, causing all of its flights into and out of London Heathrow and Gatwick to be canceled. This problem was apparently inadvertently triggered by a power surge resulting from the actions of one individual. If the robustness of your application relies on human beings never making a mistake, you're in for a rocky ride.

Scale the Number of Developers

We've probably all seen the problem of throwing developers at a project to try to make it go faster—it so often backfires. But some problems do need more people to get them done. As Frederick Brooks outlines in his now seminal book, *The Mythical Man Month*,[4] adding more people will only continue to improve how quickly you can deliver, if the work itself can be partitioned into separate pieces of work with limited interactions between them. He gives the example of harvesting crops in a field—it's a simple task to have multiple people working in parallel, as the work being done by each harvester doesn't require interactions with other people. Software rarely works like this, as the work being done isn't all the same, and often the output from one piece of work is needed as the input for another.

With clearly identified boundaries, and an architecture that has focused around ensuring our microservices limit their coupling with each other, we come up with pieces of code that can be worked on independently. Therefore, we hope we can scale the number of developers by reducing the delivery contention.

To successfully scale the number of developers you bring to bear on the problem requires a good degree of autonomy between the teams themselves. Just having microservices isn't going to be good enough. You'll have to think about how the teams align to the service ownership, and what coordination between teams is required. You'll also need to break up work in such a way that changes don't need to be coordinated across too many services.

How else could you do this?

Microservices work well for larger teams as the microservices themselves become decoupled pieces of functionality that can be worked on independently. An alternative approach could be to consider implementing a modular monolith: different

---

4 See Frederick P. Brooks, *The Mythical Man-Month*, 20th Anniversary Edition (Boston: Addison-Wesley, 1995).

teams own each module, and as long as the interface with other modules remains stable, they could continue to make changes in isolation.

This approach is somewhat limited, though. We still have some form of contention between the different teams, as the software is still all packaged together, so the act of deployment still requires coordination between the appropriate parties.

Embrace New Technology

Monoliths typically limit our technology choices. We normally have one programming language on the backend, making use of one programming idiom. We're fixed to one deployment platform, one operating system, one type of database. With a microservice architecture, we get the option to vary these choices for each service.

By isolating the technology change in one service boundary, we can understand the benefits of the new technology in isolation, and limit the impact if the technology turns out to have issues.

In my experience, while mature microservice organizations often limit how many technology stacks they support, they are rarely homogeneous in the technologies in use. The flexibility in being able to try new technology in a safe way can give them competitive advantage, both in terms of delivering better results for customers and in helping keep their developers happy as they get to master new skills.

How else could you do this?

If we still continue to ship our software as a single process, we do have limits on which technologies we can bring in. We could safely adopt new languages on the same runtime, of course—the JVM as one example can happily host code written in multiple languages within the same running process. New types of databases become more problematic, though, as this implies some sort of decomposition of a previously monolithic data model to allow for an incremental migration, unless you're going for a complete, immediate switchover to a new database technology, which is complicated and risky.

If the current technology stack is considered a "burning platform," you may have no choice other than to replace it with a newer, better-supported technology stack.[5] Of course, there is nothing to stop you from incrementally replacing your existing monolith with the new monolith—patterns like the strangler fig approach outlined in Chapter 3 can work well for that.

---

5 The term "burning platform" is typically used to denote a technology that is considered end-of-life. It may be too hard or expensive to get support for the technology, too difficult to hire people with the relevant experience. A common example of a technology most organizations consider a burning platform is a COBOL mainframe application.

Reuse?

Reuse is one of the most oft-stated goals for microservice migration, and in my opinion is a poor goal in the first place. Fundamentally, reuse is *not* a direct outcome people want. Reuse is something people hope will lead to other benefits. We hope that through reuse, we may be able to ship features more quickly, or perhaps reduce costs, but if those things are your goals, track those things instead, or you may end up optimizing the wrong thing.

To explain what I mean, let's take a deeper look into one of the usual reasons reuse is chosen as an objective. We want to ship features more quickly. We think that by optimizing our development process around reusing existing code, we won't have to write as much code—and with less work to do, we can get our software out the door more quickly, right? But let's take a simple example. The Customer Services team in Music Corp needs to format a PDF in order to provide customer invoices. Another part of the system already handles PDF generation: we produce PDFs for printing purposes in the warehouse, to produce packing slips for orders shipped to customers and to send order requests to suppliers.

Following the goal of reuse, our team may be directed to use the existing PDF generation capability. But that functionality is currently managed by a different team, in a different part of the organization. So now we have to coordinate with them to make the required changes to support our features. This may mean we have to ask them to do the work for us, or perhaps we have to make the changes ourselves and submit a pull request (assuming our company works like that). Either way, we have to coordinate with another part of the organization to make the change.

We could spend the time to coordinate with other people and get the changes made, all so we could roll out our change. But we work out that we could actually just write our own implementation much faster and ship the feature to the customer more quickly than if we spend the time to adapt the existing code. If your actual goal is faster time to market, this may be the right choice. But if you optimize for reuse hoping you get faster time to market, you may end up doing things that slow you down.

Measuring reuse in complex systems is difficult, and as I've outlined, it is typically something we're doing to achieve something else. Spend your time focusing on the actual objective instead, and recognize that reuse may not always be the right answer.

When Might Microservices Be a Bad Idea?

We've spent ages exploring the potential benefits of microservice architectures. But in a few situations I recommend that you not use microservices at all. Let's look at some of those situations now.

Unclear Domain

Getting service boundaries wrong can be expensive. It can lead to a larger number of cross-service changes, overly coupled components, and in general could be worse than just having a single monolithic system. In *Building Microservices*, I shared the experiences of the SnapCI product team at ThoughtWorks. Despite knowing the domain of continuous integration really well, their initial stab at coming up with service boundaries for their hosted-CI solution wasn't quite right. This led to a high cost of change and high cost of ownership. After several months fighting this problem, the team decided to merge the services back into one big application. Later, when the feature-set of the application had stabilized somewhat and the team had a firmer understanding of the domain, it was easier to find those stable boundaries.

SnapCI was a hosted continuous integration and continuous delivery tool. The team had previously worked on another similar tool, Go-CD, a now open source continuous delivery tool that can be deployed locally rather than being hosted in the cloud. Although there was some code reuse early on between the SnapCI and Go-CD projects, in the end SnapCI turned out to be a completely new codebase. Nonetheless, the previous experience of the team in the domain of CD tooling emboldened them to move more quickly in identifying boundaries, and building their system as a set of microservices.

After a few months, though, it became clear that the use cases of SnapCI were subtly different enough that the initial take on the service boundaries wasn't quite right. This led to lots of changes being made across services, and an associated high cost of change. Eventually, the team merged the services back into one monolithic system, giving them time to better understand where the boundaries should exist. A year later, the team was then able to split the monolithic system into microservices, whose boundaries proved to be much more stable. This is far from the only example of this situation I have seen. Prematurely decomposing a system into microservices can be costly, especially if you are new to the domain. In many ways, having an existing codebase you want to decompose into microservices is much easier than trying to go to microservices from the beginning.

If you feel that you don't yet have a full grasp of your domain, resolving that before committing to a system decomposition may be a good idea. (Yet another reason to do some domain modeling! We'll discuss that more shortly.)

Startups

This might seem a bit controversial, as so many of the organizations famous for their use of microservices are considered startups, but in reality many of these companies including Netflix, Airbnb, and the like moved toward microservice architecture only later in their evolution. Microservices can be a great option for "scale-ups"—startup companies that have established at least the fundamentals of their product/market fit, and are now scaling to increase (or likely simply achieve) profitability.

Startups, as distinct from scale-ups, are often experimenting with various ideas in an attempt to find a fit with customers. This can lead to huge shifts in the original vision for the product as the space is explored, resulting in huge shifts in the product domain.

A real startup is likely a small organization with limited funding, which needs to focus all its attention on finding the right fit for its product. Microservices primarily solve the sorts of problems startups have once they've found that fit with their customer base. Put a different way, microservices are a great way of solving the sorts of problems you'll get once you have initial success as a startup. So focus initially on being a success! If your initial idea is bad, it doesn't matter whether you built it with microservices or not.

It is much easier to partition an existing, "brownfield" system than to do so up front with a new, greenfield system that a startup would create. You have more to work with. You have code you can examine, and you can speak to people who use and maintain the system. You also know what *good* looks like—you have a working system to change, making it easier for you to know when you may have made a mistake or been too aggressive in your decision-making process.

You also have a system that is actually running. You understand how it operates and how it behaves in production. Decomposition into microservices can cause some nasty performance issues, for example, but with a brownfield system you have a chance to establish a healthy baseline before making potentially performance-impacting changes.

I'm certainly not saying *never do microservices for startups*, but I am saying that these factors mean you should be cautious. Only split around those boundaries that are clear at the beginning, and keep the rest on the more monolithic side. This will also give you time to assess how mature you are from an operational point of view—if you struggle to manage two services, managing ten is going to be difficult.

Customer-Installed and Managed Software

If you create software that is packaged and shipped to customers who then operate it themselves, microservices may well be a bad choice. When you migrate to a microservice architecture, you push a lot of complexity into the operational domain. Previous techniques you used to monitor and troubleshoot your monolithic deployment may well not work with your new distributed system. Now teams who undertake a migration to microservices offset these challenges by adopting new skills, or perhaps adopting new technology—these aren't things you can typically expect of your end customers.

Typically, with customer-installed software, you target a specific platform. For example, you might say "requires Windows 2016 Server" or "needs macOS 10.12 or above." These are well-defined target deployment environments, and you are quite possibly packaging your monolithic software using mechanisms that are well understood by people who manage these systems (e.g., shipping Windows services, bundled up in a Windows Installer package). Your customers are likely familiar with purchasing and running software in this way.

Imagine the trouble you have if you go from giving them one process to run and manage, to then giving them 10 or 20? Or perhaps even more aggressively, expecting them to run your software on a Kubernetes cluster or similar?

The reality is that you cannot expect your customers to have the skills or platforms available to manage microservice architectures. Even if they do, they may not have the same skills or platform that you require. There is a large variation between Kubernetes installs, for example.

Not Having a Good Reason!

And finally, we have the biggest reason not to adopt microservices, and that is if you don't have a clear idea of what exactly it is that you're trying to achieve. As we'll explore, the outcome you are looking for from your adoption of microservices will define *where* you start that migration and *how* you decompose the system. Without a clear vision of your goals, you are fumbling around in the dark. Doing microservices just because everyone else is doing it is a terrible idea.

Trade-Offs

So far, I've outlined the reasons people may want to adopt microservices in isolation, and laid out (however briefly) the case for also considering other options. However, in the real world, it's common for people to be trying to change not one thing, but many things, all at once. This can lead to confusing priorities that can quickly increase the amount of change needed and delay seeing any benefits.

It all starts innocently enough. We need to rearchitect our application to handle a significant increase in traffic, and decide microservices are the way forward. Someone else comes up and says, "Well, if we're doing microservices, we can make our teams more autonomous at the same time!" Another person chimes in, "And this gives us a great chance to try out Kotlin as a programming language!" Before you know it, you have a massive change initiative that is attempting to roll out team autonomy, scale the application, and bring in new technology all at once, along with other things people have tacked on to the program of work for good measure.

Moreover, in this situation, microservices become locked in as *the* approach. If you focus on just the scaling aspect, during your migration you may come to realize that you'd be better off just horizontally scaling out your existing monolithic application. But doing that won't help the new secondary goals of improving team autonomy or bringing in Kotlin as a programming language.

It is important, therefore, to separate the core driver behind the shift from any secondary benefits you might also like to achieve. In this case, handling improved scale of the application is the most important thing—work done to make progress on the other secondary goals (like improving team autonomy) may be useful, but if they get in the way or detract from the key objective, they should take a back seat.

The important thing here is to recognize that some things *are* more important than others. Otherwise, you can't properly prioritize. One exercise I like here is to think of each of your desired outcomes as a slider. Each slider starts in the middle. As you make one thing more important, you have to drop the priority of another—you can see an example of this in Figure 2-1. This clearly articulates, for example, that while you'd like to make polyglot programming easier, it's not *as* important as ensuring the application has improved resiliency. When it comes to working out how you're going to move forward, having these outcomes clearly articulated and ranked can make decision-making much easier.

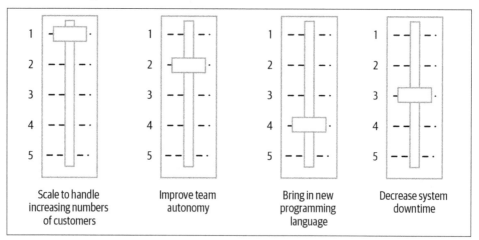

Figure 2-1. Using sliders to balance the competing priorities you may have

These relative priorities can change (and should change as you learn more). But they can help guide decision-making. If you want to distribute responsibility, pushing more power into newly autonomous teams, simple models like this can help inform their local decision-making and help them make better choices that line up with what you're trying to achieve across the company.

Taking People on the Journey

I am frequently asked, "How can I sell microservices to my boss?" This question typically comes from a developer—someone who has seen the potential of microservice architecture and is convinced it's the way forward.

Often, when people disagree about an approach, it's because they may have different views of what you are trying to achieve. It's important that you and the other people you need to bring on the journey with you have a shared understanding about *what* you're trying to achieve. If you're on the same page about that, then at least you know you are disagreeing only about *how* to get there. So it comes back to the goal again— if the other folks in the organization share the goal, they are much more likely to be onboard for making a change.

In fact, it's worth exploring in more detail about how you can both help sell the idea, and make it happen, by looking for inspiration at one of the better-known models for helping make organizational change. Let's take a look at that next.

Changing Organizations

Dr. John Kotter's eight-step process for implementing organizational change is a staple of change managers the world over, partly as it does a good job of distilling the required activities into discrete, comprehensible steps. It's far from the only such model out there, but it's the one I find the most helpful.

A wealth of content out there describes the process, outlined in Figure 2-2, so I won't dwell on it too much here.[6] However, it is worth briefly outlining the steps and thinking about how they may help us if we're considering adopting a microservice architecture.

Before I outline the process here, I should note that this model for change is typically used to institute large-scale organizational shifts in behavior. As such, it may well be huge overkill if all you're trying to do is bring microservices to a team of 10 people. Even in these smaller-scoped settings, though, I've found this model to be useful, especially the earlier steps.

---

6 Kotter's change model is laid out in detail in his book *Leading Change* (Harvard Business Review Press, 1996).

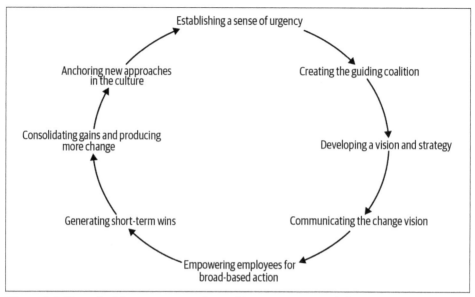

Figure 2-2. Kotter's eight-step process for making organizational change

Establishing a Sense of Urgency

People may think your idea of moving to microservices is a good one. The problem is that your idea is just one of many good ideas that are likely floating around the organization. The trick is to help people understand that *now* is the time to make this particular change.

Looking for "teachable" moments here can help. Sometimes the right time to bolt the stable door is *after* the horse has bolted, because people suddenly realize that horses running off is a thing they need to think about, and now they realize they even have a door, and "Oh look, it can be closed and everything!" In the moments after a crisis has been dealt with, you have a brief moment in people's consciousness where pushing for change can work. Wait too long, and the pain—and causes of that pain—will diminish.

Remember, what you're trying to do is not say, "We should do microservices now!" You're trying to share a sense of urgency about what you want to achieve—and as I've stated, microservices are not the goal!

Creating the Guiding Coalition

You don't need everyone on board, but you need enough to make it happen. You need to identify the people inside your organization who can help you drive this change forward. If you're a developer, this probably starts with your immediate colleagues in your team, and perhaps someone more senior—it might be a tech lead, an architect, or a delivery manager. Depending on the scope of the change, you may not need loads of people involved. If you're just changing how your team does something, then ensuring you have enough air cover may be enough. If you're trying to transform the way software is developed in your company, you may need someone at the exec level to be championing this (perhaps a CIO or CTO).

Getting people on board to help make this change may not be easy. No matter how good you think the idea is, if the person has never heard of you, or never worked with you, why should they back your idea? Trust is earned. Someone is much more likely to back your big idea if they've already worked with you on smaller, quick wins.

It's important here that you have involvement of people outside software delivery. If you are already working in an organization where the barriers between "IT" and "The Business" have been broken down, this is probably OK. On the other hand, if these silos still exist, you may need to reach across the aisle to find a supporter elsewhere. Of course, if your adoption of microservice architecture is focused on solving problems the business is facing, this will be a much easier sell.

The reason you need involvement from people outside the IT silo is that many of the changes you make can potentially have significant impacts on how the software works and behaves. You'll need to make different trade-offs around how your system behaves during failure modes, for example, or how you tackle latency. For example, caching data to avoid making a service call is a good way to ensure you reduce the latency of key operations in a distributed system, but the trade-off is that this can result in users of your system seeing stale data. Is that the right thing to do? You'll probably have to discuss that with your users—and that will be a tough discussion to have if the people who champion the cause of your users inside your organization don't understand the rationale behind the change.

Developing a Vision and Strategy

This is where you get your folks together and agree on what change you're hoping to bring (the *vision*) and how you're going to get there (the *strategy*). Visions are tricky things. They need to be realistic yet aspirational, and finding the balance between the two is key. The more widely shared the vision, the more work will need to go into packaging it up to get people onboard. But a vision can be a vague thing and still work with smaller teams ("We've got to reduce our bug count!").

The vision is mostly about the goal—*what* it is you're aiming for. The strategy is about the *how*. Microservices are going to achieve that goal (you hope; they'll be part of your strategy). Remember that your strategy may change. Being committed to a vision is important, but being overly committed to a specific strategy in the face of contrary evidence is dangerous, and can lead to significant sunk cost fallacy.

Communicating the Change Vision

Having a big vision can be great, but don't make it so big that people won't believe it's possible. I saw a statement put out by the CEO of a large organization recently that said (paraphrasing somewhat)

> In the next 12 months, we will reduce costs and deliver faster by moving to microservices and embracing cloud-native technologies.
>
> —Unnamed CEO

None of the staff in the company I spoke to believed anything of the sort was possible. Part of the problem in the preceding statement is the potentially contradictory goals that are outlined—a wholesale change of how software is delivered may help you deliver faster, but doing that in 12 months isn't going to reduce costs, as you'll likely have to bring in new skills, and you'll probably suffer a negative impact in productivity until the new skills are bedded in. The other issue is the time frame outlined here. In this particular organization, the speed of change was slow enough that a 12-month goal was considered laughable. So whatever vision you share has to be somewhat believable.

You can start small when it comes to sharing a vision. I was part of a program called the "Test Mercenaries" to help roll out test automation practices at Google many years ago. The reason that program even got started was because of previous endeavors by what we would now call a community of practice (a "Grouplet" in Google nomenclature) to help share the importance of automated testing. One of the program's early efforts in sharing information about testing was an initiative called "Testing on the Toilet." It consisted of brief, one-page articles pinned to the back of the toilet doors so folks could read them "at their leisure"! I'm not suggesting this technique would work everywhere, but it worked well at Google—and it was a really effective way of sharing small, actionable advice.[7]

One last note here. There is an increasing trend away from face-to-face communication in favor of systems like Slack. When it comes to sharing important messages of this sort, face-to-face communication (ideally in person, but perhaps by video) will be significantly more effective. It makes it easier to understand people's reaction to hearing these ideas, and helps to calibrate your message and avoid misunderstandings. Even if you may need other forms of communication to broadcast your vision across a larger organization, do as much face to face as possible first. This will help you refine your message much more efficiently.

---

7 For a more detailed history of the change initiative to roll out testing at Google, Mike Bland has an excellent write-up (*http://bit.ly/2omkxVy*) that is well worth a read. Mike wrote up a detailed history (*http://bit.ly/2ojpWwm*) of Testing on the Toilet as well.

Empowering Employees for Broad-Based Action

"Empowering employees" is management consultancy speak for helping them do their job. Most often this means something pretty straightforward—removing road-blocks.

You've shared your vision and built up excitement—and then what happens? Things get in the way. One of the most common problems is that people are too busy doing what they do now to have the bandwidth to change—this is often why companies bring new people into an organization (perhaps through hires or as consultants) to give teams extra bandwidth and expertise to make a change.

As a concrete example, when it comes to microservice adoption, the existing pro-cesses around provisioning of infrastructure can be a real problem. If the way your organization handles the deployment of a new production service involves placing an order for hardware six months in advance, then embracing technology that allows for the on-demand provisioning of virtualized execution environments (like virtual machines or containers) could be a huge boon, as could the shift to a public cloud vendor.

I do want to echo my advice from the previous chapter, though. Don't throw new technology into the mix for the sake of it. Bring it in to solve concrete problems you see. As you identify obstacles, bring in new technology to fix those problems. Don't fall into the trap of spending a year defining The Perfect Microservice Platform only to find that it doesn't actually solve the problems you have.

As part of the Test Mercenaries program at Google, we ended up creating frameworks to make test suite creation and management easier, promoted visibility of tests as part of the code review system, and even ended up driving the creation of a new company-wide CI tool to make test execution easier. We didn't do this all at once, though. We worked with a few teams, saw the pain points, learned from that, and then invested time in bringing in new tools. We also started small—making test suite creation easier was a pretty simple process, but changing the company-wide code review system was a much bigger ask. We didn't try that until we'd had some successes elsewhere.

Generating Short-Term Wins

If it takes too long for people to see progress being made, they'll lose faith in the vision. So go for some quick wins. Focusing initially on small, easy, low-hanging fruit will help build momentum. When it comes to microservice decomposition, function-ality that can easily be extracted from our monolith should be high on your list. But as we've already established, microservices themselves aren't the goal—so you'll need to balance the ease of extraction of some piece of functionality versus the benefit that will bring. We'll come back to that idea later in this chapter.

Of course, if you choose something you think is easy and end up having huge problems with making it happen, that could be valuable insight into your strategy, and may make you reconsider what you're doing. This is totally OK! The key thing is that if you focus something easy first, you're likely to gain this insight *early*. Making mistakes is natural—all we can do is structure things to make sure we learn from those mistakes as quickly as possible.

Consolidating Gains and Producing More Change

Once you've got some success, it becomes important not to sit on your laurels. Quick wins might be the only wins if you don't continue to push on. It's important you pause and reflect after successes (and failures) so you can think about how to keep driving the change. You may need to change your approach as you reach different parts of the organization.

With a microservice transition, as you cut deeper, you may find it harder going. Handling decomposition of a database may be something you put off initially, but it can't be delayed forever. As we'll explore in Chapter 4, you have many techniques at your disposal, but working out which is the right approach will take careful consideration. Just remember that decomposition technique that worked for you in one area of your monolith may not work somewhere else—you'll need to be constantly trying new ways of making forward progress.

Anchoring New Approaches in the Culture

By continuing to iterate, roll out changes, and share the stories of successes (and failures), the new way of working will start to become business as usual. A large part of this is about sharing stories with your colleagues, with other teams and other folks in the organization. It's all too often that once we've solved a hard problem, we just move on to the next. For change to scale—and stick—continually finding ways to share information inside your organization is essential.

Over time, the new way of doing something becomes *the* way that things are done. If you look at companies that are a long way down the road of adopting microservice architectures, whether or not it's the right approach has ceased to be a question. This is the way things are now done, and the organization understands how to do them well.

This, in turn, can create a new problem. Once the Big New Idea becomes the Established Way of Working, how can you make sure that future, better approaches have space to emerge and perhaps displace how things are done?

Importance of Incremental Migration

If you do a big-bang rewrite, the only thing you're guaranteed of is a big bang.
—Martin Fowler

If you get to the point of deciding that breaking apart your existing monolithic system is the right thing to do, I strongly advise you to chip away at these monoliths, extracting a bit at a time. An incremental approach will help you learn about microservices as you go, and will also limit the impact of getting something wrong (and you will get things wrong!). Think of our monolith as a block of marble. We could blow the whole thing up, but that rarely ends well. It makes much more sense to just chip away at it incrementally.

The issue is that the cost of an experiment to move a nontrivial monolithic system over to a microservice architecture can be large, and if you're doing everything at once, it can be difficult to get good feedback about what is (or isn't) working well. It's much easier to break such a journey into smaller stages; each one can be analyzed and learned from. It's for this reason that I have been a huge fan of iterative software delivery since even before the advent of agile—accepting that I will make mistakes, and therefore need a way to reduce the size of those mistakes.

Any transition to a microservice architecture should bear these principles in mind. Break the big journey into lots of little steps. Each step can be carried out and learned from. If it turns out to be a retrograde step, it was only a small one. Either way, you learn from it, and the next step you take will be informed by those steps that came before.

As we discussed earlier, breaking things into smaller pieces also allows you to identify quick wins and learn from them. This can help make the next step easier and can help build momentum. By splitting out microservices one at a time, you also get to unlock the value they bring incrementally, rather than having to wait for some big bang deployment.

All of this leads to what has become almost stock advice for people looking at microservices. If you think it's a good idea, start somewhere small. Choose one or two areas of functionality, implement them as microservices, get them deployed into production, and reflect on whether it worked. I'll take you through a model for identifying which microservices you should start with later in the chapter.

It's Production That Counts

It is *really* important to note that the extraction of a microservice can't be considered complete until it is in production and being actively used. Part of the goal of incremental extraction is to give us chances to learn from and understand the impact of the decomposition itself. The vast majority of the important lessons will not be learned until your service hits production.

Microservice decomposition can cause issues with troubleshooting, tracing flows, latency, referential integrity, cascading failures, and a host of other things. Most of those problems are things you'll notice only after you hit production. In the next couple of chapters, we will look at techniques that allow you to deploy into a production environment but limit the impact of issues as they occur. If you make a small change, it's much easier to spot (and fix) a problem you create.

Cost of Change

There are many reasons why, throughout the book, I promote the need to make small, incremental changes, but one of the key drivers is to understand the impact of each alteration we make and change course if required. This allows us to better mitigate the cost of mistakes, but doesn't remove the chance of mistakes entirely. We can—and will—make mistakes, and we should embrace that. What we should also do, though, is understand how best to mitigate the costs of those mistakes.

Reversible and Irreversible Decisions

Jeff Bezos, Amazon CEO, provides interesting insights into how Amazon works in his yearly shareholder letters. The 2015 letter held this gem:

> Some decisions are consequential and irreversible or nearly irreversible—one-way doors—and these decisions must be made methodically, carefully, slowly, with great deliberation and consultation. If you walk through and don't like what you see on the other side, you can't get back to where you were before. We can call these Type 1 decisions. But most decisions aren't like that—they are changeable, reversible—they're two-way doors. If you've made a suboptimal Type 2 decision, you don't have to live with the consequences for that long. You can reopen the door and go back through. Type 2 decisions can and should be made quickly by high judgment individuals or small groups.
>
> —Jeff Bezos, *Letter to Amazon Shareholders (2015)*

Bezos goes on to say that people who don't make decisions often may fall into the trap of treating Type 2 decisions like Type 1 decisions. Everything becomes life or death; everything becomes a major undertaking. The problem is that adopting a microservice architecture brings with it loads of options regarding how you do things—which means you may need to make many more decisions than before. And if you—or your organization—isn't used to that, you may find yourself falling into this trap, and progress will grind to a halt.

The terms aren't terribly descriptive, and it can be hard to remember what Type 1 or Type 2 actually means, so I prefer the names *Irreversible* (for Type 1) or *Reversible* (for Type 2).[8]

While I like this concept, I don't think decisions always fall neatly into either of these buckets; it feels slightly more nuanced than that. I'd rather think in terms of Irreversible and Reversible as being on two ends of a spectrum, as shown in Figure 2-3.

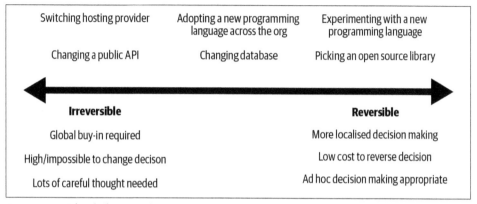

Figure 2-3. The differences between Irreversible and Reversible decisions, with examples along the spectrum

Assessing where you are on that spectrum can be challenging initially, but fundamentally it all comes back to understanding the impact if you decide to change your mind later. The bigger the impact a later course correction will cause, the more it starts to look like an Irreversible decision.

The reality is, the vast number of decisions you will make as part of a microservice transition will be toward the Reversible end of the spectrum. Software has a property where rollbacks or undos are often possible; you can roll back a software change or a software deployment. What you do need to take into account is the cost of changing your mind later.

The Irreversible decisions will need more involvement, careful thought, and consideration, and you should (rightly) take more time over them. The further we get to the right on this spectrum, toward our Reversible decisions, the more we can just rely on our colleagues who are close to the problem at hand to make the right call, knowing that if they make the wrong decision, it's an easy thing to fix later.

8 Hat tip to Martin Fowler for the names here!

Easier Places to Experiment

The cost involved in moving code around within a codebase is pretty small. We have lots of tools that support us, and if we cause a problem, the fix is generally quick. Splitting apart a database, however, is much more work, and rolling back a database change is just as complex. Likewise, untangling an overly coupled integration between services, or having to completely rewrite an API that is used by multiple consumers can be a sizeable undertaking. The large cost of change means that these operations are increasingly risky. How can we manage this risk? My approach is to try to make mistakes where the impact will be lowest.

I tend to do much of my thinking in the place where the cost of change and the cost of mistakes is as low as it can be: the whiteboard. Sketch out your proposed design. See what happens when you run use cases across what you think your service boundaries will be. For our music shop, for example, imagine what happens when a customer searches for a record, registers with the website, or purchases an album. What calls get made? Do you start seeing odd circular references? Do you see two services that are overly chatty, which might indicate they should be one thing?

So Where Do We Start?

OK, so we've spoken about the importance of clearly articulating our goals and understanding the potential trade-offs that might exist. What next? Well, we need a view of what pieces of functionality we may want to extract into services, so that we can start thinking rationally about what microservices we might create next. When it comes to decomposing an existing monolithic system, we need to have some form of logical decomposition to work with, and this is where domain-driven design can come in handy.

Domain-Driven Design

In Chapter 1, I introduced domain-driven design as an important concept in helping define boundaries for our services. Developing a domain model also helps us when it comes to working out how to prioritize our decomposition too. In Figure 2-4, we have an example high-level domain model for Music Corp. What you're seeing is a collection of bounded contexts identified as a result of a domain modeling exercise. We can clearly see relationships between these bounded contexts, which we'd imagine would represent interactions within the organization itself.

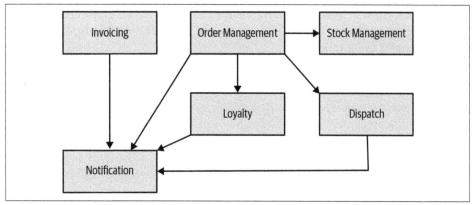

Figure 2-4. The bounded contexts and the relationships between them for Music Corp

Each of these bounded contexts represents a potential unit of decomposition. As we discussed previously, bounded contexts make great starting points for defining microservice boundaries. So already we have our list of things to prioritize. But we have useful information in the form of the relationships between these bounded contexts too—which can help us assess the relative difficulty in extracting the different pieces of functionality. We'll come back to this idea shortly.

I consider coming up with a domain model as a near-essential step that's part of structuring a microservice transition. What can often be daunting is that many people have no direct experience of creating such a view. They also worry greatly about how much work is involved. The reality is that while having experience can greatly help in coming up with a logical model like this, even a small amount of effort exerted can yield some really useful benefits.

How Far Do You Have to Go?

When approaching the decomposition of an existing system, it's a daunting prospect. Many people probably built and continue to build the system, and in all likelihood, a much larger group of people actually use it in a day-to-day fashion. Given the scope, trying to come up with a detailed domain model of the entire system may be daunting.

It's important to understand that what we need from a domain model is *just enough* information to make a reasonable decision about where to start our decomposition. You probably already have some ideas of the parts of your system that are most in need of attention, and therefore it may be enough to come up with a generalized model for the monolith in terms of high-level groupings of functionality, and pick the parts that you want to dive deeper into. There is always a danger that if you look only at part of the system you may miss larger systemic issues that require addressing. But I wouldn't obsess about it—you don't have to get it right first time; you just need enough information to make some informed next steps. You can—and should—continuously refine your domain model as you learn more, and keep it fresh to reflect new functionality as it's rolled out.

Event Storming

Event Storming, created by Alberto Brandolini, is a collaborative exercise involving technical and nontechnical stakeholders who together define a shared domain model. Event Storming works from the bottom up. Participants start by defining the "Domain Events"—things that happen in the system. Then these events are grouped into aggregates, and the aggregates are then grouped into bounded contexts.

It's important to note that Event Storming doesn't mean you have to then build an event-driven system. Instead, it focuses on understanding what (logical) events occur in the system—identifying the facts that you care about as a stakeholder of the system. These domain events can map to events fired as part of an event-driven system, but they could be represented in different ways.

One of the things Alberto is really focusing on with this technique is the idea of the collective defining the model. The output of this exercise isn't just the model itself; it is the *shared understanding* of the model. For this process to work, you need to get the right stakeholders in the room—and often that is the biggest challenge.

Exploring Event Storming in more detail is outside the scope of this book, but it's a technique I've used and like very much. If you want to explore more, you could read Alberto's *Introducing EventStorming* (*https://leanpub.com/introducing_eventstorming*) (currently in progress).

Using a Domain Model for Prioritization

We can gain some useful insights from diagrams like Figure 2-4. Based on the number of upstream or downstream dependencies, we can extrapolate a view regarding which functionality is likely to be easier—or harder—to extract. For example, if we consider extracting Notification functionality, then we can clearly see a number of inbound dependencies, as indicated in Figure 2-5—lots of parts of our system require the use of this behavior. If we want to extract out our new Notification service, we'd therefore have a lot of work to do with the existing code, changing calls from being local calls to the existing notification functionality and making them service calls instead. We'll be looking at multiple techniques regarding these sorts of changes in Chapter 3.

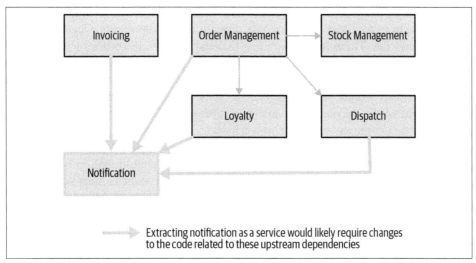

Figure 2-5. Notification functionality seems logically coupled from our domain model point of view, so may be harder to extract

So Notification may not be a good place to start. On the other hand, as highlighted in Figure 2-6, Invoicing may well represent a much easier piece of system behavior to extract; it has no in-bound dependencies, which would reduce the required changes we'd need to make to the existing monolith. A pattern like the strangler fig could be effective in these cases, as we can easily proxy these inbound calls before they hit the monolith. We'll explore that pattern, and many others, in the next chapter.

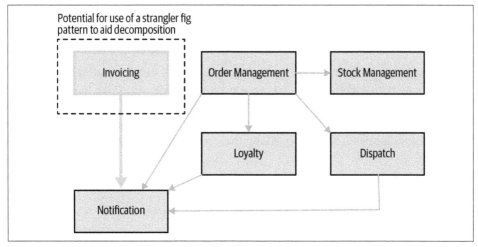

Figure 2-6. Invoicing appears to be easier to extract

When assessing likely difficulty of extraction, these relationships are a good way to start, but we have to understand that this domain model represents a *logical* view of an existing system. There is no guarantee that the underlying code structure of our monolith is structured in this way. This means that our logical model can help guide us in terms of pieces of functionality that are likely to be more (or less) coupled, but we may still need to look at the code itself to get a better assessment of the degree of entanglement of the current functionality. A domain model like this won't show us which bounded contexts store data in a database. We might find for that Invoicing manages lots of data, meaning we'd need to consider the impact of database decomposition work. As we'll discuss in Chapter 4, we can and should look to break apart monolithic datastores, but this may not be something we want to start off with for our first couple of microservices.

So we can look at things through a lens of what looks easy and what looks hard, and this is a worthwhile activity—we want to find some quick wins after all! However, we have to remember that we're looking at microservices as a way of achieving something specific. We may identify that Invoicing does, in fact, represent an easy first step, but if our goal is to help improve time to market, and the Invoicing functionality is hardly ever changed, then this may not be a good use of our time.

We need, therefore, to combine our view of what is easy and what is hard, together with our view of what benefits microservice decomposition will bring.

A Combined Model

We want some quick wins to make early progress, to build a sense of momentum, and to get early feedback on the efficacy of our approach. This will push us toward wanting to choose easier things to extract. But we also need to gain some benefits from the decomposition—so how do we factor that into our thinking?

Fundamentally, both forms of prioritization make sense, but we need a mechanism for visualizing both together and making appropriate trade-offs. I like to use a simple structure for this, as shown in Figure 2-7. For each candidate service to be extracted, you place it along the two axes displayed. The x-axis represents the value that you think the decomposition will bring. Along the y-axis, you order things based on their difficulty.

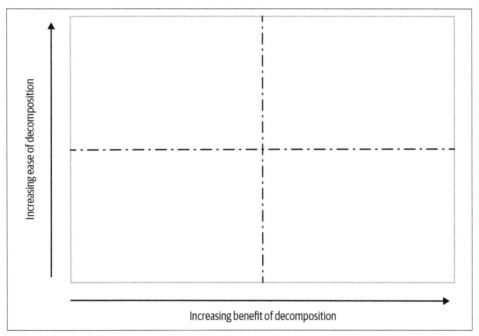

Figure 2-7. A simple two-axis model for prioritizing service decomposition

By working through this process as a team, you can come up with a view of what could be good candidates for extraction—and like every good quadrant model, it's the stuff in the top right we like, as Figure 2-8 shows. Functionality there, including Invoicing, represents functionality we think should be easy to extract, and will also deliver some benefit. So, choose one (or maybe two) services from this group as your first services to extract.

As you start to make changes, you'll learn more. Some of the things you thought were easy will turn out to be hard. Some of the things you thought would be hard turn out to be easy. This is natural! But it does mean that it's important to revisit this prioritization exercise and replan as you learn more. Perhaps as you chip away, you realize that Notifications might be easier to extract than you thought.

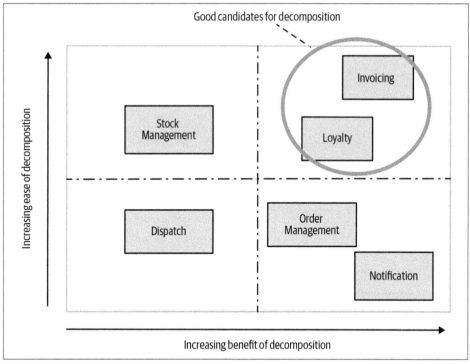

Figure 2-8. An example of the prioritization quadrant in use

Reorganizing Teams

After this chapter, we'll mostly be focusing on the changes that you'll need to make to your architecture and code to create a successful transition to a microservices. But as we've already explored, aligning architecture and organization can be key to getting the most out of a microservice architecture.

However, you might be in a situation where your organization needs to change to take advantage of these new ideas. While an in-depth study of organizational change is outside the scope of this book, I want to leave you with a few ideas before we dive into the deeper technical side of things.

Shifting Structures

Historically, IT organizations were structured around core competency. Java developers were in a team with other Java developers. Testers were in a team with other testers. The DBAs were all in a team by themselves. When creating software, people from these teams would be assigned to work on these often-short lived initiatives.

The act of creating software therefore required multiple hand-offs between teams. The business analyst would speak to a customer and find out what they wanted. The analyst then write up a requirement and hand it to the development team to work on. A developer would finish some work and hand that to the test team. If the test team found an issue, it would be sent back. If it was OK, it might proceed to the operations team to be deployed.

This siloing seems quite familiar. Consider the layered architectures we discussed in the previous chapter. Layered architectures could require multiple services to need to be changed when rolling out simple changes. The same applies with organizational silos: the more teams that need to be involved in creating or changing a piece of software, the longer it can take.

These silos have been breaking down. Dedicated test teams are now a thing of the past for many organizations. Instead, test specialists are becoming an integrated part of delivery teams, enabling developers and testers to work more closely together. The DevOps movement has also led in part to many organizations shifting away from centralized operations teams, instead pushing more responsibility for operational considerations onto the delivery teams.

In situations where the roles of these dedicated teams have been pushed into the delivery teams, the roles of these centralized teams have shifted. They've gone from doing the work themselves to helping the delivery teams do the work instead. This can involve embedding specialists with the teams, creating self-service tooling, providing training, or a whole host of other activities. Their responsibility has shifted from doing to enabling.

Increasingly, therefore, we're seeing more independent, autonomous teams, able to be responsible for more of the end-to-end delivery cycle than ever before. Their focus is on different areas of the product, rather than a specific technology or activity—just in the same way that we're switching from technical-oriented services toward services modeled around vertical slices of business functionality. Now, the important thing to understand is that while this shift is a definite trend that has been evident for many years, it isn't universal, nor is such a shift a quick transformation.

It's Not One Size Fits All

We started this chapter by discussing how your decision about whether to use microservices should be rooted in the challenges you are facing, and the changes you want to bring about. Making changes in your organizational structure is just as important. Understanding if and how your organization needs to change needs to be based on your context, your working culture, and your people. This is why just copying other people's organizational design can be especially dangerous.

Earlier, we touched very briefly on the Spotify model. Interest grew in how Spotify organized itself in the well-known 2012 paper "Scaling Agile @ Spotify" (*http://bit.ly/2ogAz3d*) by Henrik Kniberg and Anders Ivarsson. This is the paper that popularized the notion of Squads, Chapters, and Guilds, terms that are now commonplace (albeit misunderstood) in our industry. Ultimately, this led to people christening this "the Spotify model," even though this was never a term used by Spotify.

Subsequently, there was a rush of companies adopting this structure. But as with microservices, many organizations gravitated to the Spotify model without sufficient thought as to the context in which Spotify operates, their business model, the challenges they are facing, or the culture of the company. It turns out that an organizational structure that worked well for a Swedish music streaming company may not work for an investment bank. In addition, the original paper showed a snapshot of how Spotify worked in 2012 and things have changed since. It turns out not even Spotify uses the Spotify model.

The same needs to apply to you. Take inspiration from what other organizations have done, absolutely, but don't assume that what worked for someone else will work in your context. As Jessica Kerr once put it, in relation to the Spotify model, "Copy the questions, not the answers" (*http://bit.ly/2AKTaXP*). The snapshot of Spotify's organizational structure reflected changes its had carried out to solve its problems. Copy that flexible, questioning attitude in how you do things, and try new things, but make sure the changes you apply are rooted in an understanding of your company, its needs, its people, and its culture.

To give a specific example, I see a lot of companies saying to their delivery teams, "Right, now you all need to deploy your software and run 24/7 support." This can be incredibly disruptive and unhelpful. Sometimes, making big, bold statements can be a great way to get things moving, but be prepared for the chaos it can bring. If you're working in an environment where the developers are used to working 9–5, not being on call, have never worked in a support or operations environment, and wouldn't know their SSH from their elbow, then this is a great way to alienate your staff and lose a lot of people. If you think that this is the right move for your organization, then great! But talk about it as an aspiration, a goal you want to achieve, and explain why. Then work with your people to craft a journey toward that goal.

If you really want to make a shift toward teams more fully owning the whole life cycle of their software, understand that the skills of those teams need to change. You can provide help and training, add new people to the team (perhaps by embedding people from the current operations team in delivery teams). No matter what change you want to bring about, just as with our software, you can make this happen in an incremental fashion.

DevOps Doesn't Mean NoOps!

There is widespread confusion around DevOps, with some people assuming that it means that developers do all the operations, and that operations people are not needed. This is far from the case. Fundamentally, DevOps is a cultural movement based on the concept of breaking down barriers between development and operations. You may still want specialists in these roles, or you might not, but whatever you want to do, you want to promote common alignment and understanding across the people involved in delivering your software, no matter what their specific responsibilities are.

For more on this, I recommend *Team Topologies*,[9] which explores DevOps organizational structures. Another excellent resource on this topic, albeit broader in scope, is *The Devops Handbook*.[10]

Making a Change

So if you shouldn't just copy someone else's structure, where should you start? When working with organizations that are changing the role of delivery teams, I like to begin with explicitly listing all the activities and responsibilities that are involved in delivering software within that company. Next, map these activities to your existing organizational structure.

If you've already modeled your path to production (something I am a big fan of), you could overlay those ownership boundaries on an existing view. Alternatively, something simple like Figure 2-9 could work well. Just get stakeholders from all the roles involved, and brainstorm as a group all the activities that go into shipping software in your company.

---

9 Manuel Pais and Matthew Skelton, *Team Topologies* (IT Revolution Press, 2019).

10 Gene Kim, Jez Humble, and Patrick Debois, *The DevOps Handbook* (IT Revolution Press, 2016).

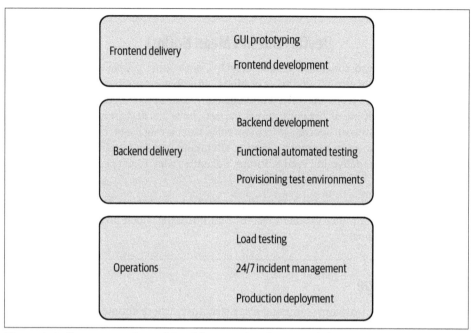

Figure 2-9. Showing a subset of the delivery-related responsibilities, and how they map to existing teams

Having this understanding of the current "as-is" state is very important, as it can help give everyone a shared understanding of all the work involved. The nature of a siloed organization is that you can struggle to understand what one silo does when you're in a different silo. I find that this really helps organizations be honest with themselves as to how quickly things can change. You'll likely find that not all teams are equal too—some may already do a lot for themselves, and others may be entirely dependent on other teams for everything from testing to deployment.

If you find your delivery teams are already deploying software themselves for test and user testing purposes, then the step to production deployments may not be that large. On the other hand, you still have to consider the impact of taking on tier 1 support (carrying a pager), diagnosing production issues, and so on. These skills are built up by people over years of work, and expecting developers to get up to speed with this overnight is totally unrealistic.

Once you have your as-is picture, redraw things with your vision for how things should be in the future, within some sensible timescale. I find that six months to a year is probably as far forward as you'll want to explore in detail. What responsibilities are changing hands? How will you make that transition happen? What is needed to make that shift? What new skills will the teams need? What are the priorities for the various changes you want to make?

Taking our earlier example, in Figure 2-10 we see that we've decided to merge front-end and backend team responsibilities. We also want teams to be able to provision their own test environments. But to do that, the operations team will need to provide a self-service platform for the delivery team to use. We want the delivery team to ultimately handle all support for their software, and so we want to start the teams getting happier with the work involved. Having them owning their own test deployments is a good first step. We've also decided they'll handle all incidents during the working day, giving them a chance to come up to speed with that process in a safe environment, where the existing operations team is on hand to coach them.

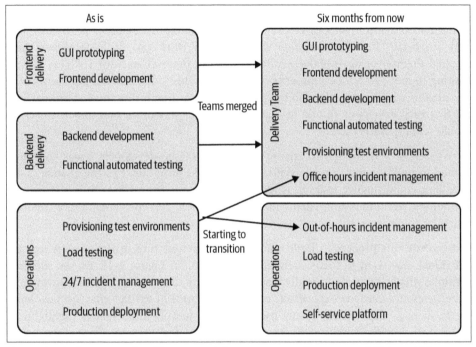

Figure 2-10. One example of how we might want to reassign responsibilities within our organization

The big picture views can really help when starting out with the changes you want to bring, but you'll also need to spend time with the people on the ground to work out whether these changes are feasible, and if so, how to bring them about. By dividing things among specific responsibilities, you can also take an incremental approach to this shift. For you, focusing first on eliminating the need for the operations teams to provision test environments is the right first step.

Changing Skills

When it comes to assessing the skills that people need, and helping them bridge the gap, I'm a big fan of having people self-assess and use that to build a wider understanding of what support the team may need to carry out that change.

A concrete example of this in action is a project I was involved with during my time at ThoughtWorks. We were hired to help *The Guardian* newspaper rebuild its online presence (something we'll come back to in the next chapter). As part of this, they needed to get up to speed with a new programming language and associated technologies.

At the start of the project, our combined teams came up with a list of core skills that were important for *The Guardian* developers to work on. Each developer then assessed themselves against these criteria, ranking themselves from 1 ("This means nothing to me!") to 5 ("I could write a book about this"). Each developer's score was private; this was shared only with the person who was mentoring them. The goal was not that each developer should get each skill to 5; it was more that they themselves should set targets to reach.

As a coach, it was my job to ensure that if one of the developers I was coaching wanted to improve their Oracle skills, I would make sure they had the chance to do that. This could involve making sure they worked on stories that made use of that technology, recommending videos for them to watch, consider attending a training course or conference, etc.

You can use this process to build up a visual representation of the areas where an individual may want to focus their time and effort. In Figure 2-11, we see such an example, which shows that I really want to focus my time and energy in growing my Kubernetes and Lambda experience, perhaps indicative of the fact that I'm now having to manage deployment of my own software. Just as important is highlighting those areas you are happy with—in this example, I feel that my Go coding is not something I need to focus on right now.

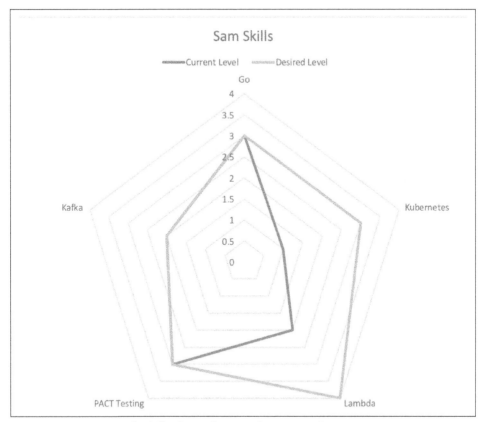

Figure 2-11. An example skills chart, showing those areas that I want to improve

Keeping these sorts of self-assessments private is very important. The point isn't for someone to rate themselves against someone else; it's for people to help guide their own development. Make this public, and you drastically change the parameters of this exercise. Suddenly, people will be worried about giving themselves a low mark as it may impact their performance review, for example.

Although each score is private, you can still use this to build up a picture of the team as a whole. Take the anonymized self-assessment ratings and develop a skill map for the overall team. This can help highlight gaps that may need addressing at a more systemic level. Figure 2-12 shows us that while I might be happy with my level of PACT skill, as a whole the team wants to improve more in that area, while Kafka and Kubernetes is another space that may need some intensive focus. This might highlight the need for some group learning, and perhaps justify a bigger investment such as running an internal training course. Sharing this overall picture with your team can also help individuals understand how they can be part of helping the team as a whole find the balance it needs.

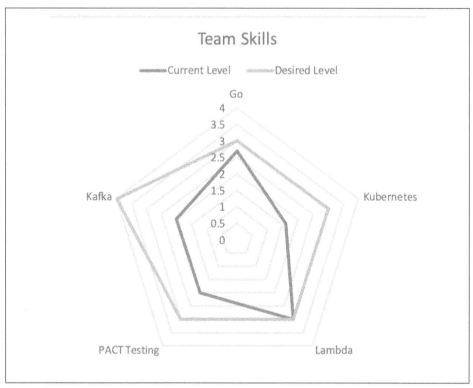

Figure 2-12. Looked at as a whole, the team has a need to improve its Kafka, Kubernetes, and PACT Testing skills

Changing the skill set of the existing team members isn't the only way forward, of course. What we're often aiming for is a delivery team that as a whole takes on more responsibilities. It doesn't necessarily mean that every individual is doing more. The right answer could be to bring new people into the team that have the skills you need. Rather than helping the developers learn more about Kafka, you could hire a Kafka expert to join your team. This could solve the short-term problem, and you then have an in-team expert who can help their colleagues learn more in this area too.

Far more can be explored in this topic, but I hope I've shared enough to get you started. Above all, it starts with understanding your own people and culture, as well as the needs of your users. By all means, be inspired by case studies from other companies, but don't be surprised if slavishly copying someone else's answers to their problems ends up not working out well for you.

How Will You Know if the Transition Is Working?

We all make mistakes. Even if you start the journey toward microservices with all the best intentions, you have to accept that you can't know everything and that sometime down the path you may realize things might not be working out. The questions are these: Do you know if it is working? Have you made a mistake?

Based on the outcomes you are hoping to achieve, you should try defining some measures that can be tracked and can help you answer these questions. We're going to explore some example measures shortly, but I do want to take this opportunity to highlight the fact that we aren't just talking about quantitative metrics here. You also need to take into account qualitative feedback from the people at the coalface.

These measures, quantitative and qualitative, should inform an ongoing review process. You need to establish checkpoints that will allow your team time to reflect on whether you're heading in the right direction. The question to ask yourself during these checkpoints isn't just "Is this working?" but "Should we try something else instead?"

Let's take a look at how you might organize these checkpoint activities, as well as at some example measures we can track.

Having Regular Checkpoints

As part of any transition, it is important to build into your delivery process some time for pause and reflection in order to analyze the available information and determine whether a change of course is required. For small teams, this could be informal, or perhaps folded into regular retrospective exercises. For larger programs of work, they may need to be planned in as explicit activities on a regular cadence—perhaps bringing together the leadership from various activities for monthly sessions to review how things are going.

No matter how frequently you run these exercises, and no matter how formal (or informal) you make them, I suggest making sure you cover the following things:

1. Restate what you are expecting the transition to microservices to achieve. If the business has changed direction such that the direction you're going in no longer makes sense, then stop!

2. Review any quantitative measures you have in place to see whether you're making progress.

3. Ask for qualitative feedback—do people think things are still working out?

4. Decide what, if anything, you're going to change going forward.

Quantitative Measures

The measures you select for tracking progress will depend on the goals you're trying to achieve. If you're focused on improving time to market, for example, measuring cycle time, number of deployments, and failure rates make sense. If you're trying to scale the application to handle more load, reporting back on the latest performance tests would be sensible.

It's worth noting that metrics can be dangerous because lf that old adage "You get what you measure." Metrics can be gamed—inadvertently, or on purpose. I recall my wife telling me of a company she worked at where an external vendor was tracked based on the number of tickets they closed, and paid based on these results. What happened? The vendor would close tickets even if the issue wasn't resolved, getting people to open up new tickets instead.

Other metrics may be hard to change in a short period of time. I'd be surprised if you see much improvement in cycle time as part of a microservice migration in the first few months; in fact, I'd likely expect to see this get worse initially. Introducing a change in how things are done often negatively impacts productivity in the short term, while the team comes up to speed with the new way of working. That's another reason why taking *small* incremental steps is so important: the smaller the change, the smaller the potential negative impacts you'll see, and the faster you can address them when they occur.

Qualitative Measures

> …Software is made of feelings.
>
> —Astrid Atkinson (@shinynew_oz)

Whatever our data shows us, it's people who build the software, and it's important that their feedback is included in measuring success. Are they enjoying the process? Do they feel empowered? Or do they feel overwhelmed? Are they getting the support they need to take on new responsibilities or master new skills?

When reporting up any sort of scorecards to upper management for these sorts of transitions,[11] you should include a sense check of what is coming from your team. If they're loving it, then great! If they aren't, you may need to do something about it. Ignoring what your people are telling you in favor of relying entirely on quantitative metrics is a great way to get yourself into a lot of trouble.

---

11 Yes, this has happened. It's not all fun and games and Kubernetes….

Avoiding the Sunk Cost Fallacy

You need to be aware of sunk cost fallacy, and having a review process is part of keeping you honest and, hopefully, helping you avoid this phenomenon. *Sunk cost fallacy* occurs when people become so invested in a previous approach to doing something that even if evidence shows the approach isn't working, they'll still proceed anyway. Sometimes we justify it to ourselves: "It'll change any minute!" Other times we may have excreted so much political capital within our organization to make a change that we can't backpedal now. Either way, it's certainly arguable that sunk cost fallacy is all about emotional investment: we're so bought into an old way of thinking that we just can't give it up.

In my experience, the bigger the bet, and bigger the accompanying fanfare, the harder it is to pull out when it's going wrong. Sunk cost fallacy is also known as the Concorde fallacy, named for the failed project backed at great expense by the British and French governments to build a supersonic passenger plane. Despite all evidence that the project would never deliver financial returns, more and more money was pumped into the project. Whatever the engineering successes that may have come out of Concorde, it never worked as a viable aircraft for commercial passenger flight.

If you make each step a small one, it becomes easier to avoid the pitfalls of the sunk cost fallacy. It's easier to change direction. Use the checkpoint mechanism discussed previously to reflect on what is happening. You don't need to pull out or change course at the first sign of trouble, but ignoring evidence you are gathering regarding the success (or otherwise) of the change you're trying to bring about is arguably more foolish than not gathering any evidence in the first place.

Being Open to New Approaches

As I hope won't be a surprise to you if you've made it this far, there are several variables involved in breaking apart a monolithic system and multiple different paths we could take. The one certainty is that not everything will go smoothly, and you will need to be open to reverting changes you make, trying new things, or sometimes just letting things settle for a moment to let you see what impact it is having.

If you try to embrace a culture of constant improvement, to always have something new you're trying, then it becomes much more natural to change direction when needed. If you ghettoize the concept of change or process improvements into discrete streams of work, rather than building it into everything you do, then you run the risk of seeing change as one-off transactional activities. Once that work is done, that's it! No more change for us! That way of thinking is how you'll find yourself in another few years way behind all your competitors and with another mountain to climb.

Summary

This chapter has covered a lot of ground. We looked at why you might want to adopt a microservice architecture, and how that decision-making may impact how you prioritize your time. We considered the key questions teams must ask themselves when deciding whether microservices are right for them, and these questions bear repeating:

- What are you hoping to achieve?
- Have you considered alternatives to using microservices?
- How will you know if the transition is working?

In addition, the importance of adopting an incremental approach to extracting microservices cannot be overstated. Mistakes are inevitable, so if accepting that as a given, you should aim to make small mistakes rather than big ones. Breaking a transition to a microservice architecture into small incremental steps ensures that the mistakes we make will be small and easier to recover from.

Most of us also work on systems that have real-world customers. We can't afford to spend months or years on a big bang rewrite of our application, letting the existing application that our customers use lie fallow. The goal should be incremental creation of new microservices, and getting them deployed as part of your production solution so that you start learning from the experience and getting the benefits as soon as possible.

I'm very clear about the idea that when breaking out functionality into a new service, the job isn't done until it's in production and is being used. You learn a huge amount from the process of having your first few services actually *used*. Early on, that needs to be your focus.

All this means we need to develop a series of techniques that allow us to create new microservices and integrate them with our (hopefully) shrinking monolith, and get them shipped to production. What we're looking at next are patterns that show how you can make this work, all while continuing to keep your system up and running, serve your customers, and take on board new functionality.

CHAPTER 3

Splitting the Monolith

In Chapter 2, we explored how to think about migration to a microservice architecture. More specifically, we explored whether it was even a good idea, and if it was, then how you should go about it in terms of rolling out your new architecture and making sure you're going in the right direction.

We've discussed what a good service looks like, and why smaller services may be better for us. But how do we handle the fact that we may already have a large number of applications lying about that don't follow these patterns? How do we go about decomposing these monolithic applications without having to embark on a big bang rewrite?

Throughout the rest of this chapter, we'll explore a variety of migration patterns and tips that can help you adopt a microservice architecture. We'll look at patterns that will work for black-box vendor software, legacy systems, or monoliths that you plan to continue to maintain and evolve. For incremental rollout to work, though, we have to ensure that we can continue to work with, and make use of, the existing monolithic software.

 Remember that we want to make our migration incremental. We want to migrate over to a microservice architecture in small steps, allowing us to learn from the process and change our minds if needed.

To Change the Monolith, or Not?

One of the first things you're going to have to consider as part of your migration is whether or not you plan (or are able) to change the existing monolith.

If you have the ability to change the existing system, this will give you the most flexibility in terms of the various patterns at your disposal. In some situations, however, there will be a hard constraint in place, denying you this opportunity. The existing system may be a vendor product for which you don't have the source code, or it may also be written in a technology that you no longer have the skills for.

There may also be softer drivers that might divert you away from changing the existing system. It's possible that the current monolith is in such a bad state that the cost of change is too high—as a result, you want to cut your losses and start again (although as I detailed earlier, I worry that people reach this conclusion far too easily). Another possibility is that the monolith itself is being worked on by many other people, and you're worried about getting in their way. Some patterns, like the Branch by Abstraction pattern we'll explore shortly, can mitigate these issues, but you may still judge that the impact to others is too great.

In one memorable situation, I was working with some colleagues to help scale a computationally heavy system. The underlying calculations were performed by a C library we were given. Our job was to collect the various inputs, pass them into the library, and retrieve and store the results. The library itself was riddled with problems. Memory leaks and horrendously inefficient API design were just two of the major causes of problems. We asked for many months for the source code for the library so we could fix these issues, but we were rebuffed.

Many years later, I caught up with the project sponsor, and asked why they hadn't let us change the underlying library. It was at that point the sponsor finally admitted they'd lost the source code but were too embarrassed to tell us! Don't let this happen to you.

So, hopefully, we're in a position where we can work with, and change, the existing monolithic codebase. But if we can't, does this mean we're stuck? Quite the contrary —several patterns can help us here. We'll be covering some of those shortly.

Cut, Copy, or Reimplement?

Even if you have access to the existing code in the monolith, when you start migrating functionality to your new microservices, it's not always clear cut as to what to do with the existing code. Should we move the code as is, or re-implement the functionality?

If the existing monolithic codebase is sufficiently well factored, you may be able to save significant time by moving the code itself. The key thing here is to understand that we want to *copy* the code from the monolith, and at this stage, at least, we don't want to remove this functionality from the monolith itself. Why? Because leaving the functionality in the monolith for a period of time gives you more options. It can give us a rollback point, or perhaps the opportunity to run both implementations in parallel. Further down the line, once you're happy that the migration has been successful, you can remove the functionality from the monolith.

Refactoring the Monolith

I've observed that often the biggest barrier to making use of existing code in the monolith in your new microservices is that existing codebases are traditionally not organized around business domain concepts. Technical categorizations are more prominent (think of all the Model, View, Controller package names you've seen, for example). When you're trying to move business domain functionality, this can be difficult: the existing codebase doesn't match that categorization, so even finding the code you're trying to move can be problematic!

If you do go down the route of reorganizing your existing monolith along business domain boundaries, I thoroughly recommend *Working Effectively with Legacy Code* by Michael Feathers (Prentice Hall, 2004). In his book, Michael defines the concept of a *seam*—that is, a place where you can change the behavior of a program without having to edit the existing behavior. Essentially, you define a seam around the piece of code you want to change, work on a new implementation of the seam, and swap it in after the change has been made. He features techniques to work safely with seams as a way of helping clean up codebases.

While generically Michael's concept of seams could be applied at many scopes, the concept does fit very well with bounded contexts, which we discussed in Chapter 1. So while *Working Effectively with Legacy Code* may not refer directly to domain-driven design concepts, you can use the techniques in that book to organize your code along these principles.

A modular monolith?

Once you've started to make sense of your existing codebase, an obvious next step that is worth considering is to take your newly identified seams and start to extract them as separate modules, making your monolith a *modular monolith*. You still have a single unit of deployment, but that deployed unit consists of multiple statically linked modules. The exact nature of these modules depends on your underlying technology stack—for Java, my modular monolith would consist of multiple JAR files; for a Ruby app, it might be a collection of Ruby gems.

As we touched on briefly at the start of the book, having a monolith broken into modules that can be developed independently can deliver many benefits while sidestepping many of the challenges of a microservice architecture, and can be the sweet spot for many organizations. I've spoken to more than one team that has started breaking its monolith apart into a modular monolith, with a view to eventually move to a microservice architecture, only to find that the modular monolith solved most of its problems!

Incremental rewrites

My general inclination is always to attempt to salvage the existing codebase first, before resorting to just reimplementing functionality, and the advice I gave in my previous book, *Building Microservices*, was along these lines. Sometimes teams find that they get enough benefit from this work to not need microservices in the first place!

However, I have to accept that, in practice, I find very few teams take the approach of refactoring their monolith as a precursor to moving to microservices. Instead, what seems more common is that once teams have identified the responsibilities of the newly created microservice, they instead do a new clean-room implementation of that functionality.

But aren't we in danger of repeating the problems associated with big bang rewrites if we start reimplementing our functionality? The key is to ensure you're rewriting only small pieces of functionality at a time, and shipping this reworked functionality to your customers regularly. If the work to reimplement the behavior of the service is a few days or weeks, it's probably fine. If the timelines start looking more like several months, I'd be reexamining my approach.

Migration Patterns

I have seen used many techniques used as part of a microservice migration. For the rest of the chapter, we'll explore these patterns, looking at where they may be useful and how they can be implemented. Remember, as with all patterns, these aren't universally "good" ideas. For each one, I've attempted to give enough information to help you understand whether they make sense in your context.

Make sure you understand the pros and cons of each of these patterns. They are not universally the "right" way to do things.

We'll start with looking at techniques to allow you to migrate and integrate with the monolith; we will deal primarily with where the application code lives. To start with, though, we'll look at one of the most useful and commonly used techniques: the strangler fig application.

Pattern: Strangler Fig Application

A technique that has seen frequent use when doing system rewrites is called the strangler fig application (*http://bit.ly/2p5xMKo*). Martin Fowler first captured this pattern, inspired by a certain type of fig that seeds itself in the upper branches of trees. The fig then descends toward the ground to take root, gradually enveloping the original tree. The existing tree becomes initially a support structure for the new fig, and if taken to the final stages, you may see the original tree die and rot away, leaving only the new, now self-supporting fig in its place.

In the context of software, the parallel here is to have our new system initially be supported by, and wrapping, the existing system. The idea is that the old and the new can coexist, giving the new system time to grow and potentially entirely replace the old system. The key benefit to this pattern, as we'll see shortly, is that it supports our goal of allowing for incremental migration to a new system. Moreover, it gives us the ability to pause and even stop the migration altogether, while still taking advantage of the new system delivered so far.

As we'll see shortly, when we implement this idea for our software, we strive to not only take incremental steps toward our new application architecture, but also ensure that each step is easily reversible, reducing the risk of each incremental step.

How It Works

While the strangler fig pattern has been commonly used to migrate from one monolithic system to another, we will look to migrate from a monolith to a series of microservices. This may involve actually copying the code from the monolith (if possible), or else reimplementing the functionality in question. In addition, if the functionality in question requires the persistence of state, then consideration needs to be given to how that state can be migrated to the new service, and potentially back again. We'll explore aspects related to data in Chapter 4.

Implementing a strangler fig pattern relies on three steps, as outlined in Figure 3-1. First, identify parts of the existing system that you wish to migrate. You'll need to use judgement as to which parts of the system to tackle first, using the sort of trade-off activity we discussed in Chapter 2. You then need to implement this functionality in your new microservice. With your new implementation ready, you need to be able to reroute calls from the monolith over to your shiny new microservice.

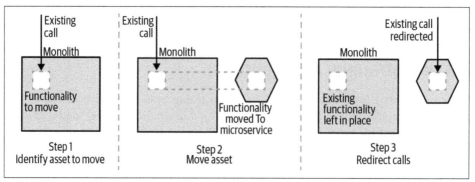

Figure 3-1. An overview of the strangler pattern

It's worth noting that until the call to the moved functionality is redirected, that the new functionality isn't technically live—even if it is deployed into a production environment. This means you could take your time getting that functionality right, working on implementing this functionality over a period of time. You could push these changes into a production environment, safe in the knowledge that it isn't yet being used, allowing us to get happy with the deployment and management aspects of your new service. Once your new service implements the same equivalent functionality as your monolith, you could then consider using a pattern like parallel run (which we explore shortly) to give you confidence that the new functionality is working as intended.

Separating the concepts of *deployment* from *release* is important. Just because software is deployed into a given environment doesn't mean it's actually being used by customers. By treating the two things as separate concepts, you enable the ability to validate your software in the final production environment before it is being used, allowing you to de-risk the rollout of the new software. Patterns like the strangler fig, parallel run, and canary release are among those patterns that make use of the fact that *deployment* and *release* are separate activities.

A key point of this strangler application approach is not just that we can incrementally migrate new functionality to the new system, but that we can also roll back this change very easily if required. Remember, we all make mistakes—so we want techniques that allow us to not only make mistakes as cheaply as possible (hence lots of small steps), but also fix our mistakes quickly.

If the functionality being extracted is also used by other functionality inside the monolith, you need to change how those calls are made as well. We'll cover a few techniques for this later in the chapter.

Where to Use It

The strangler fig pattern allows you to move functionality over to your new services architecture without having to touch or make any changes to your existing system. This has benefits when the existing monolith itself may be being worked on by other people, as this can help reduce contention. It's also very useful when the monolith is in effect a black-box system—such as third-party software or a SaaS service.

Occasionally, you can extract an entire end-to-end slice of functionality in one piece, as we see in Figure 3-2. This simplifies the extraction greatly, aside from concerns around data, which we'll look at later in this book.

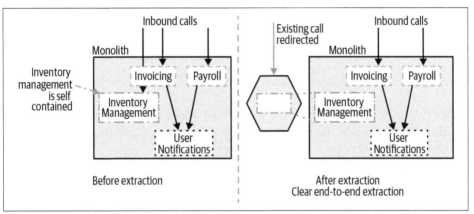

Figure 3-2. Straightforward end-to-end abstraction of Inventory Management functionality

In order to perform a clean end-to-end extraction like this, you might be inclined to extract larger groups of functionality to simplify this process. This can result in a tricky balancing act—by extracting larger slices of functionality, you are taking on more work, but may simplify some of your integration challenges.

If you do want to take a smaller bite, you may have to consider more "shallow" extractions, like those we see in Figure 3-3. Here we are extracting Payroll functionality, despite the fact it makes use of other functionality that remains inside the monolith—in this example, the ability to send User Notifications.

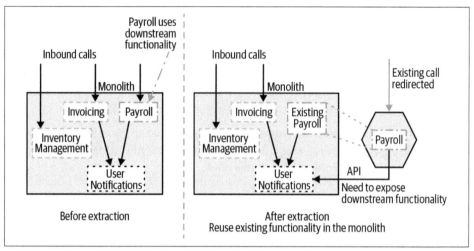

Figure 3-3. Extraction of functionality that still needs to use the monolith

Rather than also reimplementing the User Notifications functionality, we expose this functionality to our new microservice by exposing it from the monolith—something that obviously would require changes to the monolith itself.

For the strangler to work, though, you need to be able to clearly map the inbound call to the functionality you care about to the asset that you want to move. For example, in Figure 3-4, we'd ideally like to move out the ability to send User Notifications to our customers into a new service. However, notifications are fired as a result of multiple inbound calls to the existing monolith. Therefore, we can't clearly redirect the calls from outside the system itself. Instead, we'd need to look at a technique like the one described in the section "Pattern: Branch by Abstraction" on page 104.

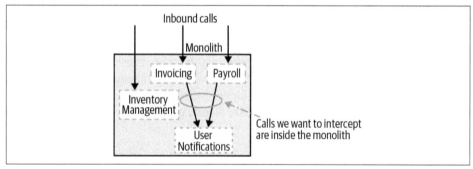

Figure 3-4. The strangler fig pattern doesn't work too well when the functionality to be moved is deeper inside the existing system

You will also need to consider the nature of the calls being made into the existing system. As we explore shortly, a protocol such as HTTP is very amenable to redirection.

HTTP itself has the concepts of transparent redirection built in, and proxies can be used to clearly understand the nature of an inbound request and divert it accordingly. Other types of protocols, such as some RPCs, may be less amenable to redirection. The more work you have to do in the proxy layer to understand and potentially transform the inbound call, the less viable this option becomes.

Despite these restrictions, the strangler fig application has proven itself time and again to be a very useful migration technique. Given the light touch, and easy approach to handle incremental change, it's often my first port of call when exploring how to migrate a system.

Example: HTTP Reverse Proxy

HTTP has some interesting capabilities, among them that it is very easy to intercept and redirect in a way that can be made transparent to the calling system. This means that an existing monolith with an HTTP interface is amenable to migration through use of a strangler fig pattern.

In Figure 3-5, we see an existing monolithic system that exposes an HTTP interface. This application may be headless, or the HTTP interface may, in fact, be being called by an upstream UI. Either way, the goal is the same: to insert an HTTP reverse proxy between the upstream calls and the downstream monolith.

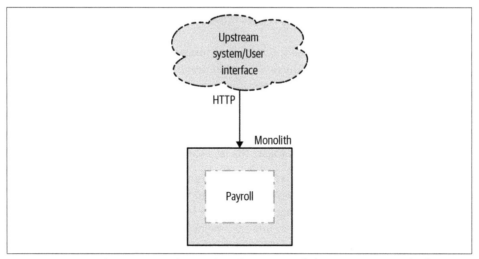

Figure 3-5. A simple overview of an HTTP-driven monolith prior to a strangler being implemented

Step 1: Insert proxy

Unless you already have an appropriate HTTP proxy in place that you can reuse, I suggest getting one in place *first*, as seen in Figure 3-6. In this first step, the proxy will just allow any calls to pass through without change.

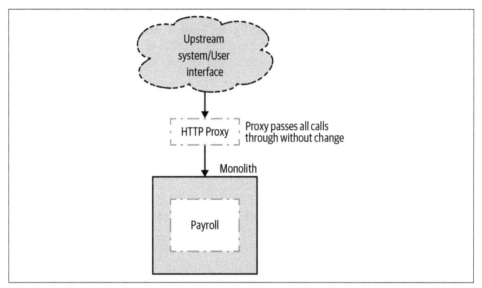

Figure 3-6. Step 1: Inserting a proxy between the monolith and the upstream system

This step will allow you to assess the impact of inserting an additional network hop between the upstream calls and the downstream monolith, set up any required monitoring of your new component, and basically, sit with it a while. From a latency point of view, we will be adding a network hop and a process in the processing path of all calls. With a decent proxy and network, you'd expect a minimal impact on latency (perhaps in the order of a few milliseconds), but if this turns out not to be the case, you have a chance to stop and investigate the issue before you go any further.

If you already have an existing proxy in place in front of your monolith, you can skip this step—although do make sure you understand how this proxy can be reconfigured to redirect calls later on. I suggest at the very least experimenting with the redirection to make sure it will work as intended before assuming that this can be done later on. It would be a nasty surprise to discover that this is impossible just before you plan to send your new service live!

Step 2: Migrate functionality

With our proxy in place, next you can start extracting your new microservice, as we see in Figure 3-7.

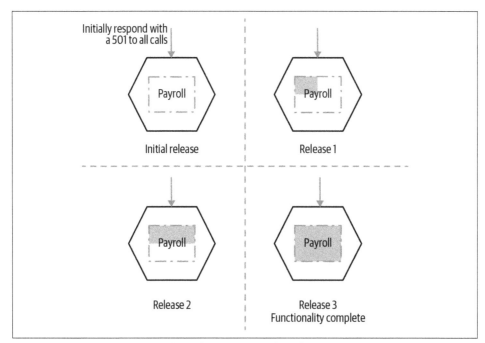

Figure 3-7. Step 2: Incremental implementation of the functionality to be moved

This step itself can be broken into multiple stages. First, get a basic service up and running without any of the functionality being implemented. Your service will need to accept the calls made to the matching functionality, but at this stage you could just return a `501 Not Implemented`. Even at this step, I'd get this service deployed into the production environment. This allows you to get comfortable with the production deployment process, and test the service in situ. At this point, your new service isn't *released*, as you haven't redirected the existing upstream calls yet. Effectively, we are separating the step of software deployment from software release, a common release technique that we'll revisit later on.

Step 3: Redirect calls

It's only once you've completed movement of all the functionality that you reconfigure the proxy to redirect the call, as we see in Figure 3-8. If this fails for whatever reason, then you can switch the redirection back—for most proxies, this is a very quick and easy process, giving you a fast rollback.

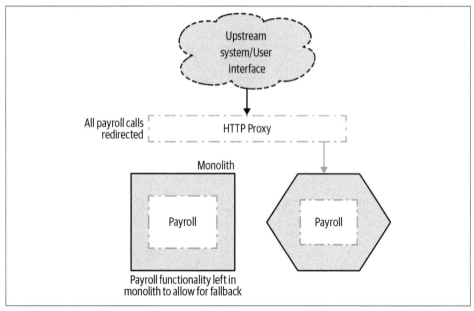

Figure 3-8. Step 3: Redirecting the call to Payroll functionality, completing the migration

You may decide to implement the redirection using something like a feature toggle, which can make your desired configuration state much more obvious. The use of a proxy to redirect the calls is also a great location to consider incremental rollout of the new functionality through a canary rollout, or even a full-blown parallel run, another pattern we discuss in this chapter.

Data?

So far, we haven't talked about data. In Figure 3-8, what happens if our newly migrated Payroll service needs access to data that is currently held in the monolith's database? We'll explore options for this more fully in Chapter 4.

Proxy Options

How you implement the proxy is in part going to depend on the protocol used by the monolith. If the existing monolith uses HTTP, then we're off to a good start. HTTP is such a widely supported protocol that you have a wealth of options out there for managing the redirection. I would probably opt for a dedicated proxy like NGINX, which has been created with exactly these sorts of use cases in mind, and can support a multitude of redirection mechanisms that are tried and tested and likely to perform fairly well.

Some redirections will be simpler than others. Consider redirection around URI paths, perhaps as would be exhibited making use of REST resources. In Figure 3-9, we move the entire Invoice resource over to our new service, and this is easy to parse from the URI path.

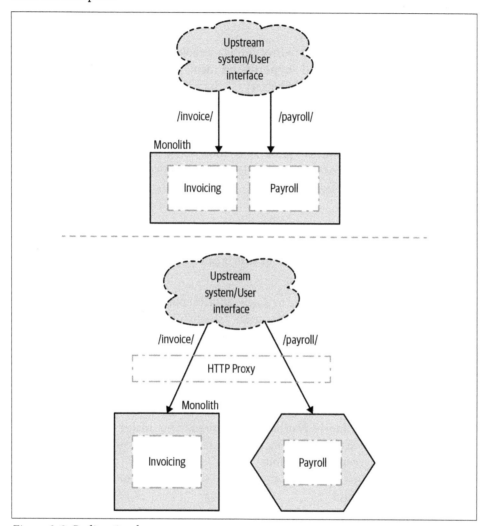

Figure 3-9. Redirection by resources

If, however, the existing system buries information about the nature of the functionality being called somewhere in the request body (perhaps in a form parameter), our redirection rule will need to be able to switch on a parameter in the POST—something that is possible, but more complicated. It is certainly worth checking the proxy options available to you to make sure they are able to handle this if you find yourself in this situation.

If the nature of interception and redirection is more complex, or in situations where the monolith is using a less well-supported protocol, you might be tempted to code something yourself, but you should be very cautious about this approach. I've written a couple of network proxies by hand before (one in Java, the other in Python), and while it may say more about my coding ability than anything else, in both situations the proxies were incredibly inefficient, adding significant lag into the system. Nowadays if I needed more custom behavior, I'd be more likely to consider adding custom behavior to a dedicated proxy—for example, NGINX allows you to use code written in Lua to add custom behavior.

Incremental rollout

As you can see in Figure 3-10, this technique allows for architectural changes to be made via a series of small steps, each of which can be done alongside other work on the system.

You might consider the switchover to a new implementation of the Payroll functionality to still be too big, in which case you can take smaller slices of functionality. You can consider, for example, migrating only part of the Payroll functionality and diverting calls appropriately—having some of the behavior implemented in the monolith, and part in the microservice, as shown in Figure 3-11. This can cause issues if both the functionality in the monolith and in the microservice need to see the same set of data, as this will likely require a shared database and all the problems this can bring.

No big bang, stop-the-line re-platforming required. This makes it much easier to break this work into stages that can be delivered alongside other delivery work. Rather than breaking your backlog into "feature" and "technical" stories, fold all this work together. Get good at making incremental changes to your architecture while still delivering new features!

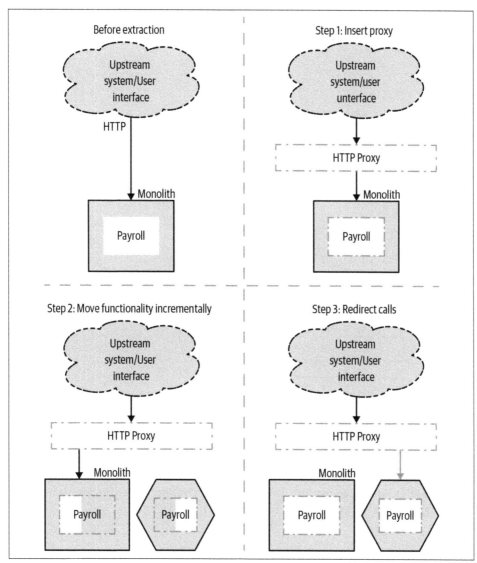

Figure 3-10. An overview of implementing an HTTP-based strangler

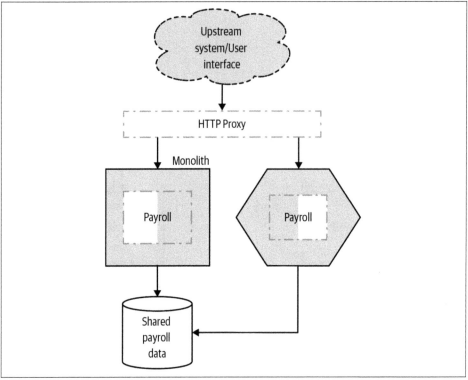

Figure 3-11. An overview of implementing an HTTP-based strangler

Changing Protocols

You could also use your proxy to transform the protocol. For example, you may currently expose a SOAP-based HTTP interface, but your new microservice is going to
support a gRPC interface instead. You could then configure the proxy to transform
requests and responses accordingly, as shown in Figure 3-12.

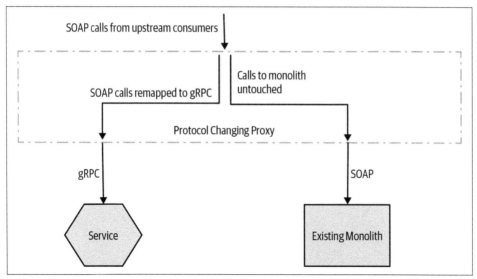

Figure 3-12. Using a proxy to change communication protocol as part of a strangler migration

I do have concerns about this approach, primarily due to the complexity and logic that starts to build up in the proxy itself. For a single service, this doesn't look too bad, but if you start transforming the protocol for multiple services, the work being done in the proxy builds up and up. We're typically optimizing for independent deployability of our services, but if we have a shared proxy layer that multiple teams need to edit, this can slow down the process of making and deploying changes. We need to be careful that we aren't just adding a new source of contention. There is the oft-stated mantra of "Keep the pipes dumb, the endpoints smart" when we discuss microservice architecture. We want to reduce how much functionality gets pushed into shared middleware layers, as this can really slow down feature development.

If you want to migrate the protocol being used, I'd much rather push the mapping into the service itself—with the service supporting both your old communication protocol and the new protocol. Inside the service, calls to our old protocol could just get remapped internally to the new communication protocol, as we see in Figure 3-13. This avoids the need to manage changes in proxy layers used by other services and puts the service in full control over how this functionality changes over time. You can see microservices as a collection of functionality on a network endpoint. You might expose that same functionality in different ways to different consumers; by supporting different message or request formats inside this service, we're basically just supporting the different needs of our upstream consumers.

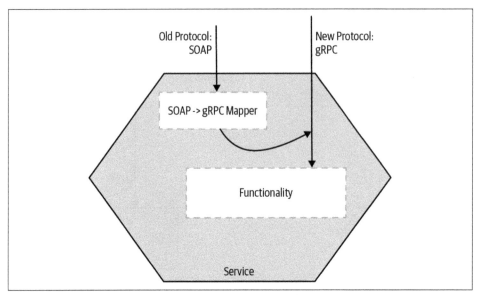

Figure 3-13. If you want to change protocol type, consider having a service expose its capabilities over multiple types of protocol

By pushing service-specific request and response mapping inside the service, this keeps the proxy layer simple and much more generic. Additionally, by a service providing both types of endpoints, you give yourself time to migrate upstream consumers before potentially retiring the old API.

And service meshes

At Square, they adopted a hybrid approach to solve this problem.[1] They had decided to migrate away from their own homegrown RPC mechanism for service-to-service communication, in favor of adopting gRPC, a well-supported open source RPC framework with a very broad ecosystem. To make this as painless as possible, they wanted to reduce the amount of change needed in each service. To do this, they made use of a service mesh.

With a *service mesh*, shown in Figure 3-14, each service instance communicates with other service instances via its own, dedicated local proxy. Each proxy instance can be configured specifically for the service instance it is partnered with. You can also provide centralized control and monitoring of these proxies by using a control plane. As there is no central proxy layer, you avoid the pitfalls regarding having a shared "smart" pipe—effectively, each service can own its own piece of the service-to-service

---

1 For a more thorough explanation, see "The Road to an Envoy Service Mesh" (*https://squ.re/2nts1Gc*) by Snow Pettersen at Square's developer blog.

pipe if needed. It's worth noting that because of the way Square's architecture had evolved, the company ended up having to create its own service mesh specific to its needs, albeit making use of the Envoy open source proxy, rather than being able to use an established solution like Linkerd or Istio.

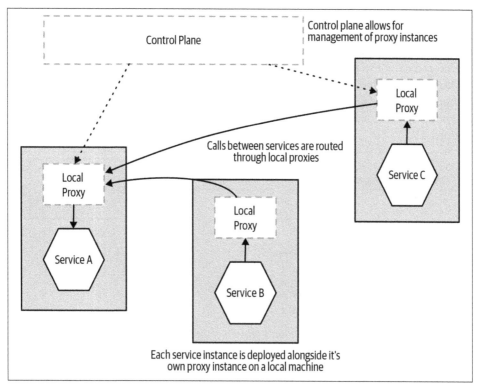

Figure 3-14. An overview of a service mesh

Service meshes are growing in popularity, and conceptually I think the idea is spot on. They can be a great way to handle common service-to-service communication concerns. My worry is that despite a lot of work by some very smart people, it has taken a while for the tooling in this space to stabilize. Istio seems to be the clear leader, but it's far from the only option in this space, and there are new tools emerging on what seems to be a weekly basis. My general advice has been to give the service mesh space a bit more time to stabilize if you can before making your choice.

Example: FTP

Although I've spoken at length regarding the use of the strangler pattern for HTTP-based systems, there is nothing to stop you from intercepting and redirecting other forms of communication protocols. Homegate, a Swiss real estate company, used a variation of this pattern to change how customers uploaded new real estate listings.

Homegate's customers uploaded listings via FTP, with an existing monolithic system handling the uploaded files. The company was keen to move over to microservices, and also wanted to start to support a new upload mechanism that, rather than supporting batch FTP upload, was going to use a REST API that matched a soon-to-be-ratified standard.

The real estate company didn't want to have to change things from the customer point of view—it wanted to make any changes seamless. This means that FTP still needed to be the mechanism by which customers interacted with the system, at least for the moment. In the end, the company intercepted FTP uploads (by detecting changes in the FTP server log), and directed newly uploaded files to an adapter that converted the uploaded files into requests to the new REST API, as shown in Figure 3-15.

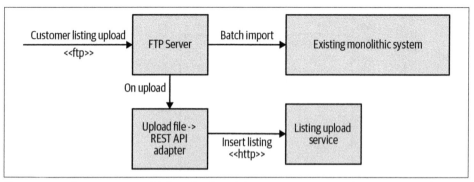

Figure 3-15. Intercepting an FTP upload and diverting it to a new listings service for Homegate

From a customer point of view, the upload process itself didn't change. The benefit came from the fact that the new service that handled the upload was able to publish the new data much more quickly, helping customers get their adverts live much faster. Later on, there is a plan to directly expose the new REST API to customers. Interestingly, during this period, both listing upload mechanisms were enabled. This allowed the team to make sure the two upload mechanisms were working appropriately. This is a great example of a pattern we'll explore later in "Pattern: Parallel Run" on page 113.

Example: Message Interception

So far we've looked at intercepting synchronous calls, but what if your monolith is driven from some other form of protocol, perhaps receiving messages via a message broker? The fundamental pattern is the same—we need a method to intercept the calls, and to redirect them to our new microservice. The main difference is the nature of the protocol itself.

Content-based routing

In Figure 3-16, our monolith receives numerous messages, a subset of which we need to intercept.

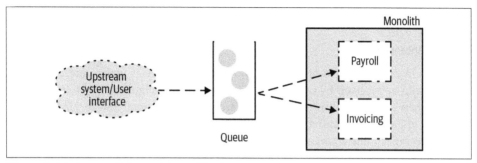

Figure 3-16. A monolith receiving calls via a queue

A simple approach would be to intercept *all* messages intended for the downstream monolith, and filter the messages on to the appropriate location, as outlined in Figure 3-17. This is basically an implementation of the content-based router pattern, as described in *Enterprise Integration Patterns*.[2]

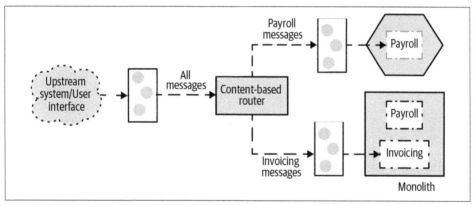

Figure 3-17. Using a content-based router to intercept messaging calls

This technique allows us to leave the monolith untouched, but we're placing another queue on our request path, which could add additional latency and is another thing we need to manage. The other concern is how many "smarts" are we placing into our messaging layer? In Chapter 4 of *Building Microservices*, I spoke about the challenges caused by systems making use of too many smarts in the networks between your services, as this can make systems harder to understand and harder to change.

---

2 Bobby Woolf and Gregor Hohpe, *Enterprise Integration Patterns* (Addison-Wesley, 2003).

Instead I urged you to embrace the mantra of "smart endpoints, dumb pipes," something that I still push for. It's arguable here that the content-based router is us implementing a "smart pipe"—adding complexity in terms of how calls are routed between our systems. In some situations, this is a highly useful technique, but it's up to you find a happy balance.

Selective consumption

An alternative would be to change the monolith and have it ignore messages sent which should be received by our new service, as we see in Figure 3-18. Here, we have both our new service and our monolith share the same queue, and locally they use some sort of pattern-matching process to listen to the messages they care about. This sort of filtering is quite a common requirement in message-based systems and can be implemented using something like a Message Selector in JMS or using equivalent technology on other platforms.

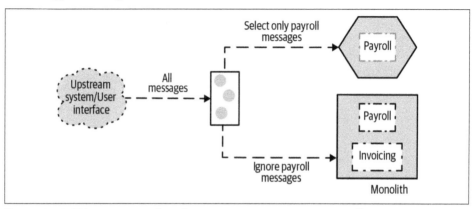

Figure 3-18. Using a content-based router to intercept messaging calls

This filtering approach reduces the need to create an additional queue but has a couple of challenges. First, your underlying messaging technology may or may not let you share a single queue subscription like this (although this is a common feature, so I would be surprised if this was the case). Second, when you want to redirect the calls, it requires two changes to be fairly well coordinated. You need to stop your monolith from reading the calls meant for the new service, and then have the service pick them up. Likewise, reverting the call interception requires two changes to roll back.

The more types of consumers you have for the same queue, and the more complex the filtering rules, the more problematic things can become. It can be easy to imagine a situation in which two consumers start receiving the same message due to overlapping rules, or even the opposite—some messages are being ignored altogether. For this reason, I would likely consider using selective consumption with only a small number of consumers and/or with a simple set of filtering rules. A content-based routing approach is likely to make more sense as the number of types of consumers increases, although beware of the potential downsides cited previously, especially falling into the "smart pipes" problem.

The added complication with either this solution or content-based routing is that if we are using an asynchronous request-response style of communication, we'll need to make sure we can route the request back to the client, hopefully without them realizing anything has changed. There are other options for call routing in message-driven systems, many of which can help you implement strangler fig pattern migrations. I thoroughly recommend *Enterprise Integration Patterns* as a great resource here.

Other Protocols

As I hope you can understand from this example, there are lots of ways to intercept calls into your existing monolith, even if you use different types of protocols. What if your monolith is driven by a batch file upload? Intercept the batch file, extract the calls that you want to intercept, and remove them from the file before you forward it on. True, some mechanisms make this process more complicated, and it's much easier if using something like HTTP, but with some creative thinking the strangler fig pattern can be used in a surprising number of situations.

Other Examples of the Strangler Fig Pattern

The strangler fig pattern is highly useful in any context where you are looking to incrementally re-platform an existing system, and its use isn't limited to teams implementing microservice architectures. The pattern was in use for a long time before Martin Fowler wrote it up in 2004. At my previous employer, ThoughtWorks, we often used it to help rebuild monolithic applications. Paul Hammant has authored a collated nonexhaustive list of projects (*http://bit.ly/2paBpyP*) where we used this pattern over on his blog. They include a trading company's blotter, an airline booking application, a rail ticketing system, and a classified ad portal.

Changing Behavior While Migrating Functionality

Here and elsewhere in the book, I focus on patterns that I chose specifically because they can be used to incrementally migrate an existing system to a microservice architecture. One of the main reasons for this is it lets you mix in migration work with ongoing feature delivery. But there is still a problem that occurs when you want to change or enrich system behavior that is actively being migrated.

Imagine, for example, that we are going to make use of the strangler fig pattern to move our existing Payroll functionality out of the monolith. The strangler fig pattern allows us to do this in multiple steps, with each step theoretically allowing us to roll back. If we'd rolled out a new Payroll service to our customers and found an issue with it, we could divert calls to Payroll functionality back to the old system. This works well if the monolith and microservice Payroll functionality is functionally equivalent, but what if we'd changed how Payroll behaves as part of the migration?

If the Payroll microservice had a few bug fixes applied to how it works that hadn't been back-ported to the equivalent functionality in the monolith, then a rollback would also cause those bugs to reappear in the system. This can get more problematic if you'd added new functionality to the Payroll microservice—a rollback would then require removing features from your customers.

There is no easy fix here. If you allow for changes in functionality you are moving before the migration is complete, then you have to accept that you are making any rollback harder. It's easier if you don't allow for any changes until the migration is complete. The longer the migration takes, the harder it can be to enforce a "feature freeze" in this part of the system—if there is a demand for part of your system to change, that demand is unlikely to go away. The longer it takes you to complete the migration, the more pressure you'll be under to "just slip this feature in while you're at it." The smaller you make each migration, the less pressure you'll be under to change the functionality being migrated before the migration has completed.

 When migrating functionality, try to eliminate any changes in the behavior being moved—delay new features or bug fixes until the migration is complete if you can. Otherwise, you may reduce your ability to roll back changes to your system.

Pattern: UI Composition

With the techniques we've considered so far, we've primarily pushed the work of incremental migration to the server—but the user interface presents us with some useful opportunities to splice together functionality served in part from an existing monolith or new microservice architecture.

Many years ago, I was involved in helping move *The Guardian* (*https://www.guard ian.co.uk/*) online from its existing content management system over to a new, custom Java-based platform. This was going to coincide with the rollout of a whole new look and feel for the online newspaper to tie in with the relaunch of the print edition. As we wanted to embrace an incremental approach, the cut-over from the existing CMS to the new website served from the brand-new was phased in parts, targeting specific verticals (travel, news, culture, etc.). Even within those verticals, we also looked for opportunities to break the migration into smaller chunks.

We ended up using two compositional techniques that were useful. From speaking to other companies, it's become clear to me over the past several years that variations on these techniques are a significant part of how many organizations adopt microservice architectures.

Example: Page Composition

With *The Guardian*, although we started by rolling out a single widget (which we'll discuss shortly), the plan had always been to mostly use a page-based migration in order to allow a brand-new look and feel to go live. This was done on a vertical-by-vertical basis, with Travel being the first we sent live. Visitors to the website during this transition time would have been presented with a different look and feel when they went to the new parts of the site. Great pains were also taken to ensure that all old page links were redirected to the new locations (where URLs had changed).

When *The Guardian* made another change in technology, moving away from the Java monolith some years later, they again used a similar technique of migrating a vertical at a time. At this point, they made use of the Fastly content delivery network (CDN) to implement the new routing rules, effectively using the CDN much as you might use an in-house proxy.[3]

REA Group in Australia, which provides online listings for real estate, has different teams responsible for commercial or residential listings, owning those whole channels. In such a situation, a page-based composition approach makes sense, as a team can own the whole end-to-end experience. REA actually employs subtly different branding for the different channels, which means that page-based decomposition makes even more sense as you can deliver quite different experiences to different customer groups.

Example: Widget Composition

At *The Guardian*, the Travel vertical was the first one identified to be migrated to the new platform. The rationale was partly that it had some interesting challenges around categorization, but also that it wasn't the most high-profile part of the site. Basically, we were looking to get something live, learn from that experience, but also make sure that if something did go wrong, then it wouldn't affect the prime parts of the site.

Rather than go live with the whole travel part of the website, replete with in-depth reportage of glamorous destinations all over the world, we wanted a much more low-key release to test out the system. Instead, we deployed a single widget displaying the top 10 travel destinations, defined using the new system. This widget was spliced into the newspaper's old travel pages, as shown in Figure 3-19. In our case, we made use of

---

3 It was nice to hear from Graham Tackley at *The Guardian* that the "new" system I initially helped implement lasted almost 10 years before being entirely replaced with the current architecture. As a reader of the website, I reflected that I never really noticed anything changing during this period!

a technique called Edge-Side Includes (ESI), using Apache. With ESI, you define a template in your web page, and a web server splices in this content.

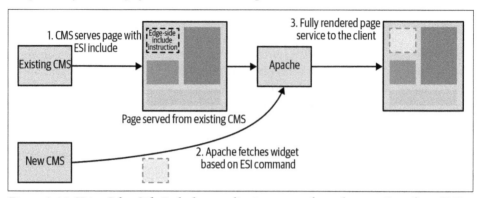

Figure 3-19. Using Edge-Side Includes to splice in content from the new Guardian CMS

Nowadays, splicing in a widget purely on the server side seems less common. This is largely because browser-based technology has become more sophisticated, allowing for much more composition to be done in the browser itself (or in the native app— more on that later). This means for widget-based web UIs, the browser itself is often making multiple calls to load various widgets using a multitude of techniques. This has the further benefit that if one widget fails to load—perhaps because the backing service is unavailable—the other widgets can still be rendered, allowing for only a partial, rather than total, degradation of service.

Although in the end we mostly used page-based composition at *The Guardian*, many other companies make heavy use of widget-based composition with supporting back-end services. Orbitz (now part of Expedia), for example, created dedicated services just to serve up a single widget.[4] Prior to its move to microservices, the Orbitz website was already broken into separate UI "modules" (in Orbitz nomenclature). These modules could represent a search form, booking form, map, etc. These UI modules were initially served directly from the Content Orchestration service, as we see in Figure 3-20.

---

4 See Steve Hoffman and Rick Fast, "Enabling Microservices at Orbitz" (*http://bit.ly/2nGNgnI*), YouTube, August 11, 2016.

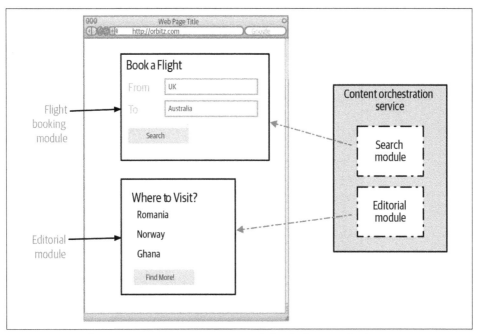

Figure 3-20. Before migration to microservices, Orbitz's Content Orchestration service served up all modules

The Content Orchestration service was in effect a large monolith. Teams that owned these modules all had to coordinate changes being made inside the monolith, causing significant delays in rolling out changes. This is a classic example of the Delivery Contention problem I highlighted in Chapter 1—whenever teams have to coordinate to roll out a change, the cost of change goes up. As part of a drive toward faster release cycles, when Orbitz decided to try microservices, they focused their decomposition along these module lines—starting with the editorial module. The Content Orchestration service was changed to delegate responsibility for transitioned modules to downstream services, as we see in Figure 3-21.

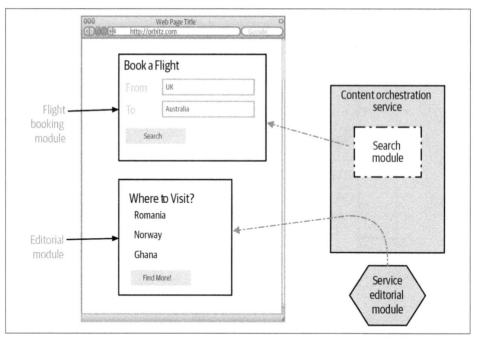

Figure 3-21. Modules were migrated one at a time, with the Content Orchestration service delegating to the new backing services

The fact that the UI was already decomposed visually along these lines made this work easier to do in an incremental fashion. This transition was further helped as the separate modules already had clean lines of ownership, making it easier to perform migrations without interfering with other teams.

It's worth noting that not all user interfaces suit decomposition into clean widgets—but when they can, it makes the work of incremental migration to microservices much easier.

And mobile applications

While we've spoken primarily about web-based UIs, some of these techniques can work well for mobile-based clients too. Both Android and iOS, for example, provide the ability to componentize parts of their user interfaces, making it easier for these parts of the UI to be worked on in isolation, or recombined in different ways.

One of the challenges with deploying changes with native mobile applications is that both the Apple App Store and Google Play store require applications to be submitted and vetted prior to new versions being made available. While the times for applications to be signed off by the app stores have in general reduced significantly over the last several years, this still adds time before new releases of software can be deployed.

The app itself is also at this point a monolith: if you want to change one single part of a native mobile application, the whole application still needs to be deployed. You also have to consider the fact that users have to download the new app to see the new features—something you typically don't have to deal with when using a web-based application, as changes are seamlessly delivered to the users' browser.

Many organizations have dealt with this by allowing them to make dynamic changes to an existing native mobile application without having to resort to deploying a new version of a native application. By deploying changes on the server side, client devices can immediately see the new functionality without necessarily having to deploy a new version of the native mobile application. This can be achieved simply using things like embedded web views, although some companies use more sophisticated techniques.

Spotify's UI across all platforms is heavily component-oriented, including its iOS and Android applications. Pretty much everything you see is a separate component, from a simple text header, to album artwork, or a playlist.[5] Some of these modules are, in turn, backed by one or more microservices. The configuration and layout of these UI components is defined in a declarative fashion on the server side; Spotify engineers are able to change the views that users see and roll that change quickly, without needing to submit new versions of their application to the app store. This allows them to much more rapidly experiment and try out new features.

Example: Micro Frontends

As bandwidth and the capability of web browsers have improved, so has the sophistication of the code running in browsers improved. Many web-based user interfaces now make use of some form of single-page application framework, which does away with the concept of an application consisting of different web pages. Instead, you have a more powerful user interface, where everything runs in a single pane—effectively in-browser user experiences that previously were available only to those of us working with "thick" UI SDKs like Java's Swing.

By delivering an entire interface in a single page, we obviously can't consider page-based composition, so we have to consider some form of widget-based composition. Attempts have been made to codify common widget formats for the web—most recently, the Web Components specification is attempting to define a standard component model supported across browsers. It has taken a long while, though, for this standard to gain any traction, with browser support (among other things) being a considerable stumbling block.

---

5 See John Sundell, "Building Component-Driven UIs at Spotify" (*http://bit.ly/2nDpJUP*), published August 25, 2016.

People making use of single-page app frameworks like Vue, Angular, or React haven't sat around waiting for Web Components to solve their problems. Instead, many people have tried to tackle the problem of how to modularize UIs built with SDKs that were initially designed to own the whole browser pane. This has led to the push toward what some people have called *Micro Frontends*.

At first glance, Micro Frontends really are just about breaking down a user interface into different components that can be worked on independently. In that, they are nothing new—component-oriented software predates my birth by several years! What is more interesting is that people are working out how to make web browsers, SPA SDKs, and componentization work together. How exactly do you create a single UI out of bits of Vue and React without having their dependencies clash, but still allow them to potentially share information?

Covering this topic in depth is out of scope for this book, partly because the exact way you make this work will vary based on the SPA frameworks being used. But if you find yourself with a single-page application that you want to break apart, you're not alone, and there are many people out there sharing techniques and libraries to make this work.

Where to Use It

UI composition as a technique to allow for re-platforming systems is highly effective, as it allows for whole vertical slices of functionality to be migrated. For it to work, though, you need to have the ability to change the existing user interface to allow for new functionality to be safely inserted. We'll cover compositional techniques later in the book, but it's worth noting that which techniques you can use will often depend on the nature of the technology used to implement the user interface. A good old-fashioned website makes UI composition easy, whereas single-page app technology does add some complexity and an often bewildering array of implementation approaches!

Pattern: Branch by Abstraction

For the useful strangler fig pattern, to work, we need to be able to intercept calls at the perimeter of our monolith. However, what happens if the functionality we want to extract is deeper inside our existing system? Coming back to a previous example, consider the desire to extract the Notification functionality, as seen in Figure 3-4.

In order to perform this extraction, we will need to make changes to the existing system. These changes could be significant, and disruptive to other developers working on the codebase at the same time. We have competing tensions here. On the one hand, we want to make our changes in incremental steps. On the other hand, we want to reduce the disruption to other people working on other areas of the codebase. This will naturally drive us toward wanting to complete the work quickly.

Often, when reworking parts of an existing codebase, people will do that work on a separate source code branch. This allows the changes to be made without disrupting the work of other developers. The challenge is that once the change in the branch has been completed, these changes have to be merged back, which can often cause significant challenges. The longer the branch exists, the bigger these problems are. I won't go into detail now as to the problems associated with long-lived source code branches, other than to say they run contrary to the principles of continuous integration. I could also throw in that data gathered from "The 2017 State of DevOps Report" (*http://bit.ly/2pctNfn*) shows that embracing trunk-based development (where changes are made directly on the main line and branches are avoided) and using short-lived branches contributes to higher performance of IT teams. Let's just say that I am not a fan of long-lived branches, and I'm not alone.

So, we want to be able to make changes to our codebase in an incremental fashion, but also keep disruption to a minimum for developers working on other parts of our codebase. There is another pattern we can use that allows us to incrementally make changes to our monolith without resorting to source code branching. The branch by abstraction pattern instead relies on making changes to the existing codebase to allow the implementations to safely coexist alongside each other, in the same version of code, without causing too much disruption.

How It Works

Branch by abstraction consists of five steps:

1. Create an abstraction for the functionality to be replaced.
2. Change clients of the existing functionality to use the new abstraction.
3. Create a new implementation of the abstraction with the reworked functionality. In our case, this new implementation will call out to our new microservice.
4. Switch over the abstraction to use our new implementation.
5. Clean up the abstraction and remove the old implementation.

Let's take a look at these steps with respect to moving our Notification functionality out into a service, as detailed in Figure 3-4.

Step 1: Create abstraction

The first task is to create an abstraction that represents the interactions between the code to be changed and the callers of that code, as we see in Figure 3-22. If the existing Notification functionality is reasonably well factored, this could be as simple as applying an Extract Interface refactoring in our IDE. If not, you may need to extract a seam, as mentioned earlier. This might have you searching your codebase for calls being made to APIs that send emails, SMSs, or whatever other notification mechanism you might have. Finding this code and creating an abstraction that the other code uses is a required step.

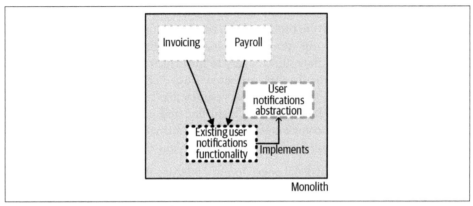

Figure 3-22. Step 1: Create an abstraction

Step 2: Use abstraction

With our abstraction created, we now need to refactor the existing clients of the Notification functionality to use this new abstraction point, as we see in Figure 3-23. It's possible that an Extract Interface refactoring could have done this for us automatically—but in my experience, it's more common that this will need to be an incremental process, involving manually tracking inbound calls to the functionality in question. The nice thing here is that these changes are small and incremental; they're easy to make in small steps without making too much impact on the existing code. At this point, there should be no functional change in system behavior.

Step 3: Create new implementation

With our new abstraction in place, we can now start work on our new service-calling implementation. Inside the monolith, our implementation of the Notification functionality will mostly just be a client calling out to the external service, as in Figure 3-24—the bulk of the functionality will be in the service itself.

The key thing to understand at this point is that although we have two implementations of the abstraction in the codebase at the same time, only one implementation is currently active in the system. Until we're happy that our new service-calling implementation is ready to send live, it is in effect dormant. While we work to implement all the equivalent functionality in our new service, our new implementation of the abstraction could return Not Implemented errors. This doesn't stop us writing tests for the functionality we have written, of course, and this is one of the benefits of getting this work integrated as early as possible.

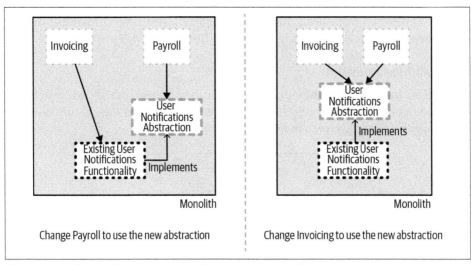

Figure 3-23. Step 2: Change existing clients to use new abstraction

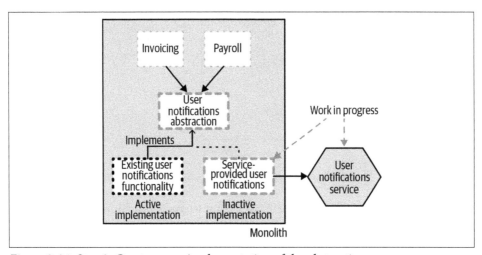

Figure 3-24. Step 3: Create a new implementation of the abstraction

During this process, we can also deploy our work-in-progress User Notification service into production, just as we did with the strangler fig pattern. The fact that it isn't finished is fine—at this point, as our implementation of the Notifications abstraction isn't live, the service isn't actually being called. But we can deploy it, test it in situ, and verify the parts of the functionality we have implemented are working correctly.

This phase could last a significant amount of time. Jez Humble details the use of the branch by abstraction pattern (*http://bit.ly/2p95lv7*) to migrate the database persistence layer used in the continuous delivery application GoCD (at the time called Cruise). The switch from using iBatis to Hibernate lasted several months—during which the application was still being shipped to clients on a twice weekly basis.

Step 4: Switch implementation

Once we are happy that our new implementation is working correctly, we switch our abstraction point so that our new implementation is active, and the old functionality is no longer being used, as seen in Figure 3-25.

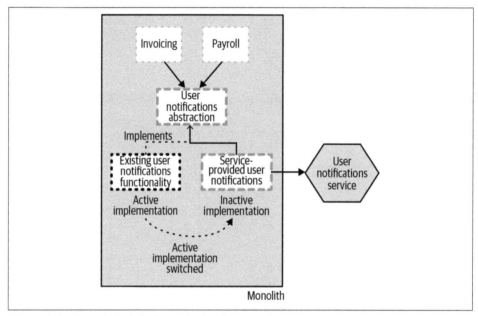

Figure 3-25. Step 4: Switch the active implementation to use our new microservice

Ideally, as with the strangler fig pattern, we'd want to use a switching mechanism that can be toggled easily. This allows us to quickly switch back to the old functionality if we found a problem with it. A common solution to this would be to use feature toggles. In Figure 3-26, we see toggles being implemented using a configuration file, allowing us to change the implementation being used without having to change code. If you want to know more about feature toggles and how to implement them, then Pete Hodgson has an excellent write-up.

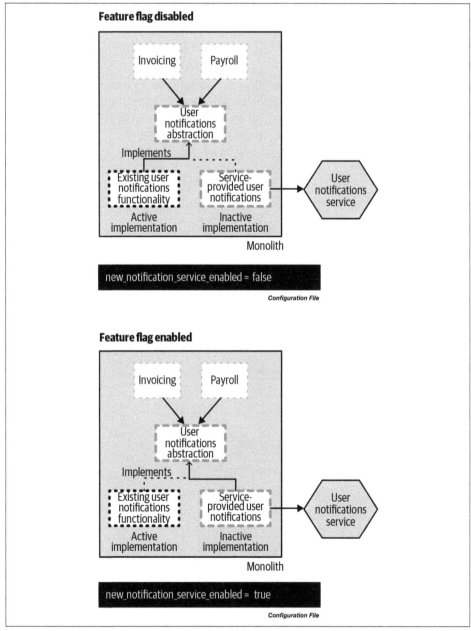

Figure 3-26. Step 5: Using feature toggles to switch between implementations

At this stage, we have two implementations of the same abstraction, which we *hope* should be functionality equivalent. We can use tests to verify equivalency, but we also have the option here to use *both* implementations in production to provide additional verification. This idea is explored further in "Pattern: Parallel Run" on page 113.

Step 5: Clean up

With our new microservice now providing all notifications for our users, we can turn our attention to cleaning up after ourselves. At this point, our old User Notifications functionality is no longer being used, so an obvious step would be to remove it, as shown in Figure 3-27. We are starting to shrink the monolith!

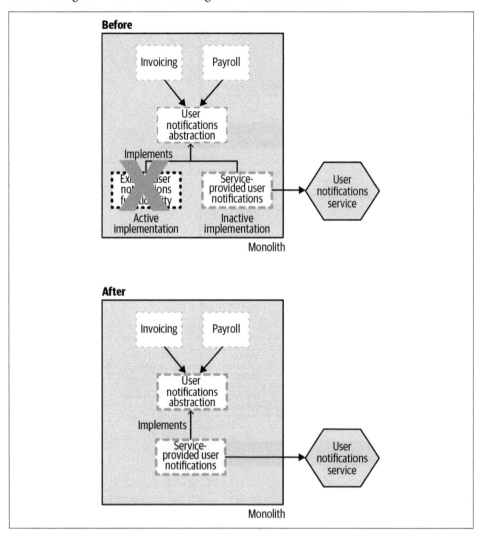

Figure 3-27. Step 6: Remove the old implementation

When removing the old implementation, it would also make sense to remove any feature flag switching we may have implemented. One of the real problems associated with the use of feature flags is leaving old ones lying around—don't do that! Remove flags you don't need anymore to keep things simple.

Finally, with the old implementation gone, we have the option of removing the abstraction point itself, as in Figure 3-28. It's possible, however, that the creation of the abstraction may have improved the codebase to the point where you'd rather keep it in place. If it's something as simple as an interface, retaining it will have minimal impact on the existing codebase.

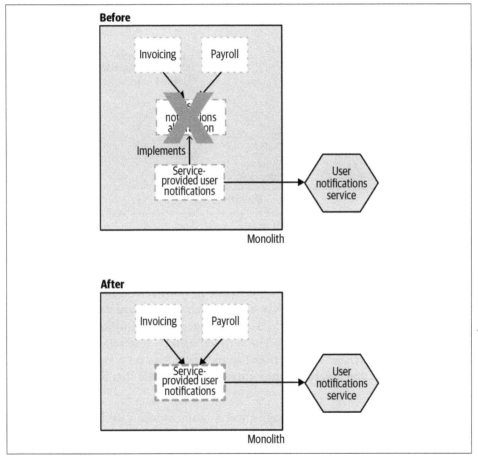

Figure 3-28. Step 7: (Optional) Remove the abstraction point

As a Fallback Mechanism

The ability for us to switch back to our previous implementation if our new service isn't behaving is useful, but is there a way we could do that automatically? Steve Smith details a variation of the branch by abstraction pattern called verify branch by abstraction (*http://bit.ly/2mLVevz*) that also implements a live verification step—we can see an example of this in Figure 3-29. The idea is that if calls to the new implementation fail, then the old implementation could be used instead.

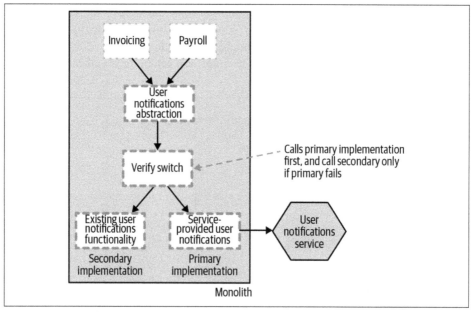

Figure 3-29. Verify branch by abstraction

This clearly adds some complexity, not only in terms of code but also in terms of reasoning about the system. Effectively, both implementations might be active at any given point in time, which can make understanding system behavior more difficult. If the two implementations are in anyway stateful, then we also have data consistency to consider. Although data consistency is a challenge in any situation where we are switching between implementations, The verify branch by abstraction pattern allows for us to switch back and forth between implementations on a request-by-request basis, which means you'll need a consistent shared set of data that both implementations can access.

We'll explore this idea in more detail in just a moment when we look at the more generic parallel run pattern.

Where to Use It

Branch by abstraction is a fairly general-purpose pattern, useful in any situation where changes to the existing codebase are likely going to take time to carry out, but where you want to avoid disrupting your colleagues too much. In my opinion, it is a better option than the use of long-lived code branches in nearly all circumstances.

For migration to a microservice architecture, I'd nearly always look to use a strangler fig pattern first, as it's simpler in many regards. However, there are some situations, as with Notifications here, where that just isn't possible.

This pattern also assumes that you can change the code of the existing system. If you can't, for whatever reason, you may need to look at other options, some of which we explore in the rest of this chapter.

Pattern: Parallel Run

There is only so much testing you can do of your new implementation before you deploy it. You'll do your best to ensure that your prerelease verification of your new microservice is done in as production-like a way as possible as part of a normal testing process, but we all understand that it isn't always possible to think of every scenario that could occur in a production setting. But there are other techniques available to us.

Both the strangler fig pattern and branch by abstraction pattern allow old and new implementations of the same functionality to coexist in production at the same time. Typically, both of these techniques allow us to execute either the old implementation in the monolith or the new microservice-based solution. To mitigate the risk of switching over to the new service-based implementation, these techniques allow us to quickly switch back to the previous implementation.

When using a parallel run, rather than calling either the old or the new implementation, instead we call *both*, allowing us to compare the results to ensure they are equivalent. Despite calling both implementations, only one is considered the source of truth at any given time. Typically, the old implementation is considered the source of truth until the ongoing verification reveals that we can trust our new implementation.

This pattern has been used in different forms for decades, although typically it is used to run two systems in parallel. I'd argue this pattern can be just as useful within a single system, when comparing two implementations of the same functionality.

This technique can be used to verify not just that our new implementation is giving the same answers as the existing implementation, but that it is also operating within acceptable nonfunctional parameters. For example, is our new service responding quickly enough? Are we seeing too many time-outs?

Example: Comparing Credit Derivative Pricing

Many years ago, I was involved in a project to change the platform being used to perform calculations on a type of financial product called *credit derivatives*. The bank I was working at needed to make sure the various derivatives it was offering would be a sensible deal for them. Would we make money on this trade? Was the trade too risky? Once issued, market conditions would also change. So they also needed to assess the value of current trades to make sure they weren't vulnerable to huge losses as market conditions changed.[6]

We were almost entirely replacing the existing system that performed these important calculations. Because of the amount of money involved, and the fact that some people's bonuses were based in part on the value of the trades that had been made, there was a great degree of concern over the changes. We made the decision to run the two sets of calculations side by side and carry out daily comparisons of the results. The pricing events were triggered via events, which were easy to duplicate such that both systems carried out the calculations, as we see in Figure 3-30.

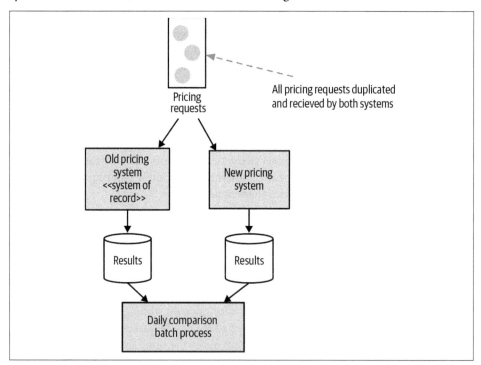

Figure 3-30. An example of a parallel run—both pricing systems are invoked, with the results compared offline

---

6 Turned out we were *terrible* at this as an industry. I recommend Martin Lewis's *The Big Short* (W. W. Norton & Company, 2010) as an excellent overview of the part that credit derivatives played in the global financial crisis of 2007–2008. I often look back at the small part I played in this industry with a great deal of regret. It turns out not knowing what you're doing and doing it anyway can have some pretty disastrous implications.

Each morning, we'd run a batch reconciliation of the results, and would then need to account for any variations in results. We actually wrote a program to perform the reconciliation. We presented the results in an Excel spreadsheet, making it easy to discuss the variations with the experts at the bank.

It turned out we did have a few issues that we had to fix, but we also found a larger number of discrepancies caused by bugs in the existing system. This meant that some of the different results were actually correct, but we had to show our work (made much easier due to surfacing the results in Excel). I remember having to sit down with analysts and explain why our results were correct by working things out from first principles.

Eventually, after a month, we switched over to using our system as the source of truth for the calculations, and some time later we retired the old system (we kept it around for a few more months in case we needed to carry out any auditing of calculations done on the old system).

Example: Homegate Listings

As we discussed earlier in "Example: FTP" on page 93, Homegate ran both its listing import systems in parallel, with the new microservice that handled list imports being compared against the existing monolith. A single FTP upload by a customer would cause both systems to be triggered. Once they had confirmed that the new microservice was behaving in an equivalent fashion, the FTP import was disabled in the old monolith.

N-Version Programming

It could be argued that a variation of parallel run exists in certain safety critical control systems, such as fly-by-wire aircraft. Rather than relying on mechanical controls, airliners increasingly rely on digital control systems. When a pilot uses the controls, rather than this pulling cables to control the rudder, instead fly-by-wire aircraft this sends inputs to control systems that decide how much to turn the rudder by. These control systems have to interpret the signals they are being sent and carry out the appropriate action.

Obviously, a bug in these control systems could be extremely dangerous. To offset the impact of defects, for some situations multiple implementations of the same functionality are used side by side. Signals are sent to all implementations of the same subsystem, which then send their response. These results are compared and the "correct"

---

one selected, normally by looking for a quorum among the participants. This is a technique known as *N-version programming*.[7]

The end goal with this approach is not to replace any of the implementations, unlike the other patterns we have looked at in this chapter. Instead, the alternative implementations will continue to exist alongside each other, with the alternative implementations hopefully reducing the impact of a bug in any one given subsystem.

Verification Techniques

With a parallel run, we want to compare functional equivalence of the two implementations. If we take the example of the credit derivative pricer from before, we can treat both versions as functions—given the same inputs, we expect the same outputs. But we also can (and should) validate the nonfunctional aspects, too. Calls made across network boundaries can introduce significant latency and can be the cause of lost requests due to time-outs, partitions, and the like. So our verification process should also extend to making sure that the calls to the new microservice complete in a timely manner, with an acceptable failure rate.

Using Spies

In the case of our previous notification example, we wouldn't want to send an email to our customer twice. In that situation, a Spy could be handy. A pattern from unit testing, a Spy can stand in for a piece of functionality, and allows us to verify after the fact that certain things were done. The Spy stands in and replaces a piece of functionality, stubbing it out.

So for our Notification functionality, we could use a Spy to replace the low-level code that is used to actually send the email, as shown in Figure 3-31. Our new Notifications service would then use this Spy during the parallel run phase to allow us to verify that this side effect (the sending of the email) would be triggered when the sendNotification call is received by the service.

---

7 See Liming Chen and Algirdas Avizienis, "N-Version Programming: A Fault-Tolerance Approach to Reliability of Software Operation," published in the Twenty-Fifth International Symposium on Fault-Tolerant Computing (1995).

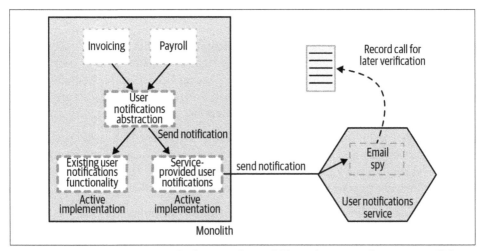

Figure 3-31. Using a Spy to verify that emails would have been sent during a parallel run

Note that we could have decided to use the Spy inside the monolith, and avoid our `RemoteNotification` code ever making a service call. However this is likely not what you want, as you actually do want to take into account the impact of the remote calls being made—to understand if time-outs, failures, or general latency to our new Notifications service is causing us issues.

One added complexity here is the fact that our Spy is running in a separate process, which will complicate when the verification process could be carried out. If we wanted this to happen live, within the scope of the original request, we'd likely need to expose methods on the Notifications service to allow for verification to be carried out after the initial call is sent to our Notifications service. This could be a significant amount of work, and in many cases you don't need live verification. A more likely model for verification of out-of-process spies would be to record the interactions to allow for the verification to be done out of band—perhaps on a daily basis. Obviously, if we did use the Spy to replace the call to the Notifications service, the verification gets easier, but we're testing less! The more functionality you replace with a Spy, the less functionality is actually being tested.

GitHub Scientist

GitHub's Scientist library (*https://github.com/github/scientist*) is a notable library to help implement this pattern at a code level. It's a Ruby library that allows you to run implementations side by side and capture information about the new implementation to help you understand if it is working properly. I've not used it myself, but I can see how having a library like this would really help in verifying your new microservice-based functionality against the existing system—ports now exist for multiple languages including Java, .NET, Python, Node.JS, and many more besides.

Dark Launching and Canary Releasing

It's worth calling out that a parallel run is different from what is traditionally called *canary releasing*. A canary release involves directing some subset of your users to the new functionality, with the bulk of your users seeing the old implementation. The idea is that if the new system has a problem, then only a subset of requests are impacted. With a parallel run, we call *both* implementations.

Another related technique is called *dark launching*. With dark launching, you deploy the new functionality and test it, but the new functionality is invisible to your users. So a parallel run is a way of implementing dark launching, as the "new" functionality is in effect invisible to your users until you've switched over what system is live.

Dark launching, parallel runs, and canary releasing are techniques that can be used to verify that our new functionality is working correctly, and reduce the impact if this turns out not to be the case. All these techniques fall under the banner of what is called *progressive delivery*—an umbrella term coined by James Governor (*http://bit.ly/ 2lZjrxK*) to describe methods to help control how software is rolled out to your users in a more nuanced fashion, allowing you to release software more quickly while validating its efficacy and reducing the impact of problems should they occur.

Where to Use It

Implementing a parallel run is rarely a trivial affair, and is typically reserved for those cases where the functionality being changed is considered to be high risk. We'll examine an example of this pattern being used for medical records in Chapter 4. I'd certainly be fairly selective about where I used this pattern—the work to implement this needs to be traded off against the benefits you gain. I've used this pattern myself only once or twice, but in those situations it has been hugely useful.

Pattern: Decorating Collaborator

What happens if you want to trigger some behavior based on something happening inside the monolith, but you are unable to change the monolith itself? The *decorating collaborator* pattern can help greatly here. The widely known decorator pattern allows you to attach new functionality to something without the underlying thing knowing anything about it. We are going to use a decorator to make it appear that our monolith is making calls to our services directly, even though we haven't actually changed the underlying monolith.

Rather than intercepting these calls before they reach the monolith, we allow the call to go ahead as normal. Then, based on the result of this call, we can call out to our external microservices through whatever collaboration mechanism we choose. Let's explore this idea in detail with an example from Music Corp.

Example: Loyalty Program

Music Corp is all about our customers! We want to add the ability for them to earn points based on orders being placed, but our current order placement functionality is complex enough that we'd rather not change it right now. So the order placement functionality will stay in the existing monolith, but we will use a proxy to intercept these calls, and based on the outcome decide how many points to deliver, as shown in Figure 3-32.

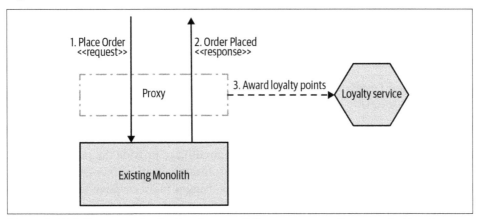

Figure 3-32. When an order is placed successfully, our proxy calls out to the Loyalty service to add points for the customer

With the strangler fig pattern, the proxy was fairly simplistic. Now our proxy is having to embody quite a few more "smarts." It needs to make its own calls out to the new microservice and tunnel responses back to the customer. As before, keep an eye on complexity that sits in the proxy. The more code you start adding here, the more it ends up becoming a microservice in its own right, albeit a technical one, with all the challenges we've discussed previously.

Another potential challenge is that we need enough information from the inbound request to be able to make the call to the microservice. For example, if we want to reward points based on the value of the order, but the value of the order isn't clear from either the Place Order request or response, we may need to look up additional information—perhaps calling back into the monolith to extract the required information as in Figure 3-33.

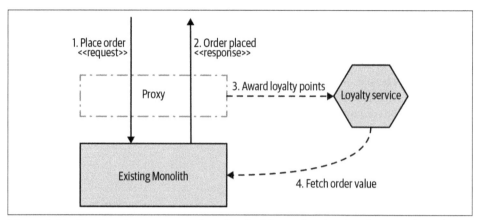

Figure 3-33. Our Loyalty service needs to load additional order details to work out how many points to award

Given that this call could generate additional load, and arguably introduces a circular dependency, it might be better to change the monolith to provide the required information when order placement completes. This, though, would either require changing the code of the monolith, or else perhaps using a more invasive technique like change data capture.

Where to Use It

When kept simple, it is a more elegant and less coupled approach than change data capture. This pattern works best where the required information can be extracted from the inbound request, or the response back from the monolith. Where more information is required for the right calls to be made to your new service, the more complex and tangled this implementation ends up being. My gut feeling is that if the request and response to and from the monolith don't contain the information you need, then think carefully before using this pattern.

Pattern: Change Data Capture

With *change data capture*, rather than trying to intercept and act on calls made into the monolith, we react to changes made in a datastore. For change data capture to work, the underlying capture system has to be coupled to the monolith's datastore. That's really an unavoidable challenge with this pattern.

Example: Issuing Loyalty Cards

We want to integrate some functionality to print out loyalty cards for our users when they sign up. At present, a loyalty account is created when a customer is enrolled. As we can see in Figure 3-34, when enrollment returns from the monolith, we know only that the customer has been successfully enrolled. For us to print a card, we need more details about the customer. This makes inserting this behavior upstream, perhaps using a decorating collaborator, more difficult—at the point where the call returns, we'd need to make additional queries to the monolith to extract the other information we need, and that information may or may not be exposed via an API.

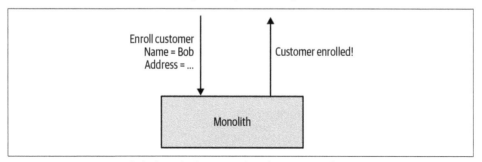

Figure 3-34. Our monolith doesn't share much information when a customer is enrolled

Instead, we decide to use change data capture. We detect any insertions into the LoyaltyAccount table, and on insertion, we make a call to our new Loyalty Card Printing service, as we see in Figure 3-35. In this particular situation, we decide to fire a Loyalty Account Created event. Our printing process works best in batch, so this allows us to build up a list of printing to be done in our message broker.

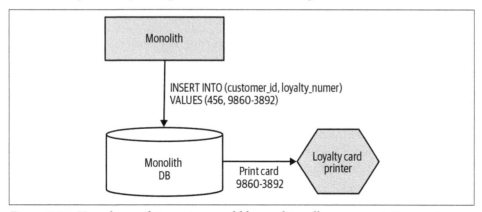

Figure 3-35. How change data capture could be used to call our new printing service

Implementing Change Data Capture

We could use various techniques to implement change data capture, all of which have different trade-offs in terms of complexity, reliability, and timeliness. Let's take a look at a couple of options.

Database triggers

Most relational databases allow you to trigger custom behavior when data is changed. Exactly how these triggers are defined, and what they can trigger varies, but all modern relational databases support these in one way or another. In the example in Figure 3-36, our service is called whenever an INSERT is made into the LoyaltyAccount table.

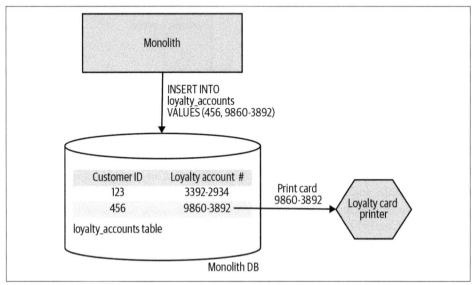

Figure 3-36. Using a database trigger to call our microservice when data is inserted

Triggers need to be installed into the database itself, just like any other stored procedure. There may also be limitations as to what these triggers can do, although at least with Oracle they are quite happy for you to call web services or custom Java code.

At first glance, this can seem like quite a simple thing to do. No need to have any other software running, no need to introduce any new technology. However like stored procedures, database triggers can be a slippery slope.

A friend of mine, Randy Shoup, once said something along the lines of "Having one or two database triggers isn't terrible. Building a whole system off them is a terrible idea." And this is often the problem associated with database triggers. The more of them you have, the harder it can be to understand how your system actually works. The issue is often with the tooling and change management of database triggers—use too many, and your application can become some baroque edifice.

So if you're going to use them, use them *very* sparingly.

Transaction log pollers

Inside most databases, certainly all mainstream transactional databases, there exists a transaction log. This is normally a file, into which is written a record of all the changes that have been made. For change data capture, the most sophisticated tooling tends to make use of this transaction log.

These systems run as a separate process, and their only interaction with the existing database is via this transaction log, as we see in Figure 3-37. It's worth noting here that only committed transactions will show up in the transaction log (which is sort of the point).

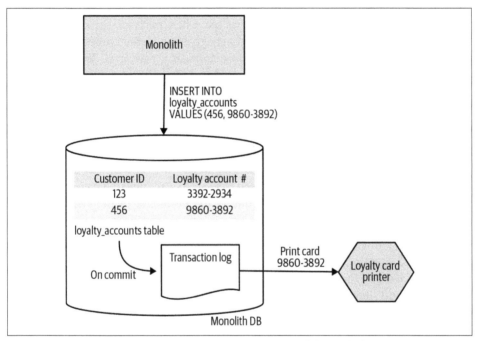

Figure 3-37. A change data capture system making use of the underlying transaction log

These tools will require an understanding of the underlying transaction log format, and this typically varies across different types of databases. As such, exactly what tools you'll have available here will depend on what database you use. A huge array of tools exist in this space, although many of them are used to support data replication. There are also a number of solutions designed to map changes to the transaction log to messages to be placed onto a message broker; this could be very useful if your microservice is asynchronous in nature.

Restrictions aside, in many ways this is the neatest solution for implementing change data capture. The transaction log itself shows only changes to the underlying data, so you aren't worried about working out what has changed. The tooling runs outside the database itself, and can run off a replica of the transaction log, so you have fewer concerns regarding coupling or contention.

Batch delta copier

Probably the most simplistic approach is to write a program that on a regular schedule scans the database in question for what data has changed, and copies this data to the destination. These jobs are often run using tools like `cron` or similar batch scheduling tools.

The main problem is working out what data has actually changed since the batch copier last ran. The schema design might make this obvious, or may not. Some databases allow you to view table metadata to see when parts of the database have changed, but this is far from universal, and may give you change timestamps at only the table level when you'd rather have information at a row level. You could start adding these timestamps yourself, but this could add significant work, and a change data capture system would handle this problem much more elegantly.

Where to Use It

Change data capture is a useful general-purpose pattern, especially if you need to replicate data (something we'll explore more in Chapter 4). In the case of microservice migration, the sweet spot is where you need to react to a change in data in your monolith, but are unable to intercept this either at the perimeter of the system using a strangler or decorator, and cannot change the underlying codebase.

In general, I try to keep the use of this pattern to a minimum because of the challenges around some of the implementations of this pattern. Database triggers have their downsides, and the full-blown change data capture tools that work off transaction logs can add significant complexity to your solution. Nonetheless, if you understand these potential challenges, this can be a useful tool to have at your disposal.

Summary

As we've seen, a vast array of techniques allow for the incremental decomposition of existing codebases, and can help you ease into the world of microservices. In my experience, most folks end up using a mix of approaches; it's rare that one single technique will handle every situation. Hopefully, what I've been able to do so far is give you a variety of approaches and enough information to work out which techniques may work best for you.

We have glossed over one of the bigger challenges in migrating to a microservice architecture—data. We can't put it off any longer! In Chapter 4, we'll explore how to migrate data and break apart the databases.

Decomposing the Database

As we've already explored, there are a host of ways to extract functionality into micro-services. However, we need to address the elephant in the room: namely, what do we do about our data? Microservices work best when we practice information hiding, which in turn typically leads us toward microservices totally encapsulating their own data storage and retrieval mechanisms. This leads us to the conclusion that when migrating toward a microservice architecture, we need to split our monolith's data-base apart if we want to get the best out of the transition.

Splitting a database apart is far from a simple endeavor, however. We need to consider issues of data synchronization during transition, logical versus physical schema decomposition, transactional integrity, joins, latency, and more. Throughout this chapter, we'll take a look at these issues and explore patterns that can help us.

Before we start with splitting things apart, though, we should look at the challenges—and coping patterns—for managing a single shared database.

Pattern: The Shared Database

As we discussed in Chapter 1, we can think of coupling in terms of domain coupling, temporal coupling, or implementation coupling. Of the three, it's implementation coupling that often occupies us most when considering databases, because of the prevalence of people sharing a database among multiple schemas, as we see in Figure 4-1.

On the face of it, there are a number of issues related to sharing a single database among multiple services. The major issue, though, is that we deny ourselves the opportunity to decide what is shared and what is hidden—which flies in the face of our drive toward information hiding. This means it can be difficult to understand what parts of a schema can be changed safely. Knowing an external party can access your database is one thing, but not knowing what part of your schema they use is another. This can be mitigated through the use of views, which we'll discuss shortly, but it's not a total solution.

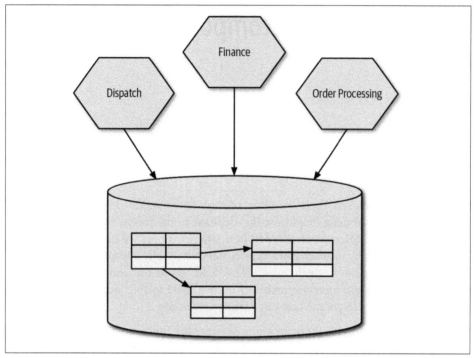

Figure 4-1. Multiple services all directly accessing the same database

Another issue is that it becomes unclear as to who "controls" the data. Where is the business logic that manipulates this data? Is it now spread across services? That in turn implies a lack of cohesion of business logic. As we discussed previously, when thinking about a microservice as being a combination of behavior and state, encapsulating one or more state machines. If the behavior that changes this state is now spread around the system, making sure this state machine can be properly implemented is a tricky issue.

If, as in Figure 4-1, three services can directly change order information, what happens if that behavior is inconsistent across the services? What happens when this behavior does need to change—do I have to apply those changes to all these services? As we spoke about earlier, we're aiming for high cohesion of business functionality, and all too often a shared database implies the opposite.

Coping Patterns

Although it can be a difficult activity, splitting the database apart to allow for each microservice to own its own data is nearly always preferred. If this isn't possible, the use of the database view pattern (see the section "Pattern: Database View" on page 128), or adopting the database wrapping service pattern (see the section "Pattern: Database Wrapping Service" on page 132), can help.

Where to Use It

I think direct sharing of a database is appropriate for a microservice architecture in only two situations. The first is when considering read-only static reference data. We'll explore this topic in more detail shortly, but consider a schema holding country currency code information, postal code or zip code lookup tables, and the like. Here, the data structure is highly stable, and change control of this data is typically handled as an administration task.

The other place where I think multiple services directly accessing the same database can be appropriate is when a service is directly exposing a database as a defined endpoint that is designed and managed in order to handle multiple consumers. We'll expose this idea further when we discuss the database as a service interface pattern (see the section "Pattern: Database-as-a-Service Interface" on page 135).

But It Can't Be Done!

So, ideally, we want our new services to have their own independent schemas. But that's not where we start with an existing monolithic system. Does that mean we should always split these schemas apart? I remain convinced that in most situations this is the appropriate thing to do, but it isn't always feasible initially.

Sometimes, as we'll explore shortly, the work involved will take too long, or involves changing especially sensitive parts of the system. In such cases, it can be useful to use a variety of coping patterns that will at the very least stop things from getting any worse, and at best can be sensible stepping stones toward something better in the future.

Schemas and Databases

I've been guilty in the past of using the terms "database" and "schema" interchangeably. This can sometimes lead to confusion, as there is some ambiguity in these terms. Technically, we can consider a schema to be a logically separated set of tables that hold data, as shown in Figure 4-2. Multiple schemas can then be hosted on a single database engine. Depending on your context, when people say "database," they could be referring to the schema or the database engine ("The database is down!").

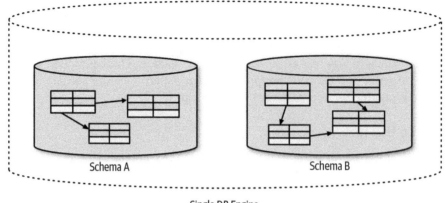

Schema A   Schema B

Single DB Engine

Figure 4-2. A single instance of a database engine can host multiple schemas, each of which provides logical isolation

As this chapter mostly focuses on logical database concepts, and because the term "database" is commonly used in this context to relate effectively to a logically isolated schema, I'll stick to that usage in this chapter. So where I say "database," you can think "logically isolated schema." For the sake of brevity, I'll be omitting the concept of a database engine from our diagrams, unless explicitly called out otherwise.

It's worth noting that the various NoSQL databases out there may or may not have the same concept of logical separation, especially when dealing with databases provided by cloud providers. For example, on AWS, DynamoDB has only the concept of a table, with role-based access controls being used to limit who can see or change the data. This can cause challenges in how we think about logical separation in such situations.

You're going to encounter problems with your current system that seem impossible to deal with right now. Address the problem with the rest of your team so that everyone can come to an agreement that this is a problem you'd like to fix, even if you can't see how right now. Then make sure you at least start doing the right thing *now*. Over time, problems that initially seemed insurmountable will become easier to deal with once you have some new skills and experience.

Pattern: Database View

In a situation where we want a single source of data for multiple services, a view can be used to mitigate the concerns regarding coupling. With a view, a service can be presented with a schema that is a limited projection from an underlying schema. This projection can limit the data that is visible to the service, hiding information it shouldn't have access to.

The Database as a Public Contract

Back in Chapter 3, I discussed my experiences in helping re-platform an existing credit derivative system for a now defunct investment bank. We hit the issue of database coupling in a big way: we had a need to increase the throughput of the system in order to provide faster feedback to the traders who used the system. After some analysis, we found that the bottleneck in the processing was the writes being made into our database. After a quick spike, we realized we could drastically increase the write performance of our system if we restructured the schema.

It was at this point we found that multiple applications outside our control had read access to our database, and in some cases read/write access. Unfortunately, we found that all these external systems had been given the same username and password credentials, so it was impossible to understand who these users were, or what they were accessing. We had an estimate of "over 20" applications as being involved, but that was derived from some basic analysis of the inbound network calls.[1]

 If each actor (e.g., a human or an external system) has a different set of credentials, it becomes much easier to restrict access to certain parties, reduce the impact of revoking and rotating credentials, and better understand what each actor is doing. Managing different sets of credentials can be painful, especially in a microservice system that may have multiple sets of credentials to manage per service. I like the use of dedicated secret stores to solve this problem. HashiCorp's Vault (*https://www.vaultproject.io*) is an excellent tool in this space, as it can generate per-actor credentials for things like databases that can be short lived and limited in scope.

So we didn't know who these users were, but we had to contact them. Eventually, someone had the idea of disabling the shared account they were using, and waiting for people to contact us to complain. This is clearly not a great solution to a problem we shouldn't have had in the first place, but it worked—mostly. However, we soon realized that most of these applications weren't undergoing active maintenance, meaning there was no chance that they would be updated to reflect a new schema

---

1 When you're relying on network analysis to determine who is using your database, you're in trouble.

design.[2] In effect, our database schema had become a public-facing contract that couldn't change: we had to maintain that schema structure going forward.

Views to Present

Our solution was to first resolve those situations where external systems were writing into our schema. Luckily, in our case they were easy to resolve. For all those clients who wanted to read data, though, we created a dedicated schema hosting views that looked like the old schema, and had clients point at that schema instead, as Figure 4-3 shows. That allowed us to make changes in our own schema, as long as we could maintain the view. Let's just say that lots of stored procedures were involved.

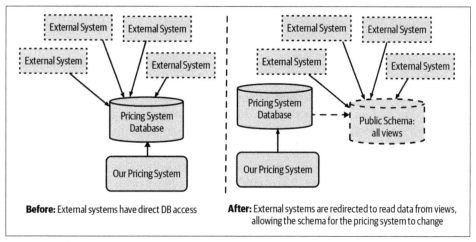

Figure 4-3. Using views to allow the underlying schema to change

In our investment banking example, the view and the underlying schema ended up differing a fair amount. You can, of course, use a view much more simply, perhaps to hide pieces of information you don't want made visible to outside parties. As a simple example, in Figure 4-4, our loyalty service just was a list of loyalty cards in our system. Presently, this information is stored in our customer table as a column. So we define a view that exposes just the customer ID and the loyalty ID mapping in a single table, without exposing any other information in the customer table. Likewise, any other tables that may be in the monolith's database are entirely hidden from the Loyalty service.

---

2 It was rumored that one of the systems using our database was a Python-based neural net that no one understood but "just worked."

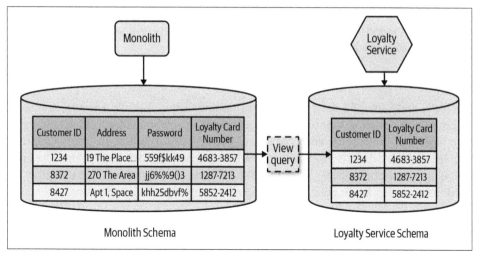

Figure 4-4. A database view projecting a subset of an underlying schema

The ability of a view to project only limited information from the underlying source allows us to implement a form of information hiding. It gives us control over what is shared, and what is hidden. This is not a perfect solution, however-there are restrictions with this approach.

Depending on the nature of the database, you may have the option to create a materialized view. With a materialized view, the view is precomputed—typically, through the use of a cache. This means a read from a view doesn't need to generate a read on the underlying schema, which can improve performance. The trade-off then is around how this pre-computed view is updated; it may well mean you could be reading a "stale" set of data from the view.

Limitations

How views are implemented can vary, but typically they are the result of a query. This means that the view itself is read-only. This immediately limits their usefulness. In addition, while this is a common feature for relational databases, and many of the more mature NoSQL databases support views (both Cassandra and Mongo do, for example), not all do. Even if your database engine does support views, there will likely be other limitations, such as the need for both the source schema and view to be in the same database engine. This could increase your physical deployment coupling, leading to a potential single point of failure.

Ownership

It's worth noting that changes to the underlying source schema may require the view to be updated, and so careful consideration should be given to who "owns" the view. I suggest considering any published database views to be akin to any other service interface, and therefore something that should be kept up-to-date by the team looking after the source schema.

Where to Use It

I typically make use of a database view in situations where I think it is impractical to decompose the existing monolithic schema. Ideally, you should try to avoid the need for a view if possible, if the end goal is to expose this information via a service interface. Instead, it's better to push forward with proper schema decomposition. The limitations of this technique can be significant. Nonetheless, if you feel that the effort of full decomposition is too great, then this can be a step in the right direction.

Pattern: Database Wrapping Service

Sometimes, when something is too hard to deal with, hiding the mess can make sense. With the *database wrapping service pattern*, we do exactly that: hide the database behind a service that acts as a thin wrapper, moving database dependencies to become service dependencies, as we see in Figure 4-5.

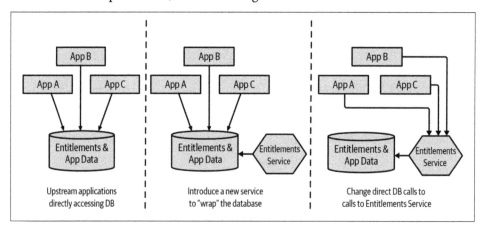

Figure 4-5. Using a service to wrap a database

I was working at a large bank in Australia a few years ago on a short engagement to help one part of the organization implement an improved path to production. On the first day, we set up a few interviews with key people to understand the challenges they were facing and to build up an overview of the current process. Between meetings, someone came up and introduced themselves as the head DBA for that area of the company. "Please" he said, "Stop them from putting things into the database!"

We grabbed a coffee, and the DBA laid out the problems. Over something like a 30-year period, a business banking system, one of the crown jewels of the organization, had taken shape. One of the more important parts of this system was managing what they called "entitlements." In business banking, managing which individuals can access which accounts, and working out what they are allowed to do with those accounts, was very complex. To give you an idea of what these entitlements might look like, consider a bookkeeper who is allowed to view the accounts for companies A, B, and C, but for company B they can transfer up to $500 between accounts, and for company C they can make unlimited transfers between accounts but also withdraw up to $250. The maintenance and application of these entitlements were managed almost exclusively in stored procedures in the database. All data access was gated through this entitlement logic.

As the bank had scaled, and the amount of logic and state had grown, the database had started to buckle under the load. "We've given all the money it's possible to give to Oracle, and it's still not enough." The worry was that given projected growth, and even counting for the improvements in performance of hardware, they would eventually get to a place where the needs of the organization would outstrip the capabilities of the database.

As we explored the problem further, we discussed the idea of splitting out parts of the schema to reduce load. The issue was that the tangled nest in the middle of all of this was this entitlements system. It would be a nightmare to try to untangle, and the risks associated with making mistakes in this area were huge: make a wrong step, and someone could be blocked from accessing their accounts, or worse still, someone could gain access to your money who shouldn't.

We came up with a plan to try to resolve the situation. We accepted that in the near term, we weren't going to be able to make changes to the entitlements system, so it was imperative that we at least not make the problem any worse. So we needed to stop people from putting more data and behavior into the entitlements schema. Once this was in place, we could consider removing those parts of the entitlements schema that were easier to extract, hopefully reducing the load enough that the concerns about the long-term viability were reduced. That would then give some breathing room to consider the next steps.

We discussed introducing a new Entitlements service, which would allow us to "hide" the problematic schema. This service would have very little behavior at first, as the current database already had implemented a lot of behavior in the form of stored procedures. But the goal was to encourage the teams writing the other applications to think of the entitlements schema as someone else's, and encourage them to store their own data locally, as we see in Figure 4-6.

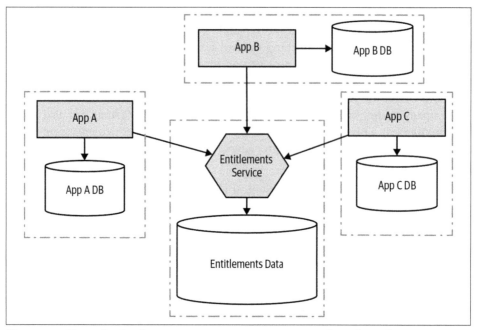

Figure 4-6. Using the database wrapping service pattern to reduce dependence on a central database

Just as with our use of database views, the use of a wrapping service allows us to control what is shared and what is hidden. It presents an interface to consumers that can be fixed, while changes are made under the hood to improve the situation.

Where to Use It

This pattern works really well where the underlying schema is just too hard to consider pulling apart. By placing an explicit wrapper around the schema, and making it clear that the data can be accessed only through that schema, you at the very least can put a brake on the database growing any further. It clearly delineates what is "yours" versus what is "someone else's." I think this approach also works best when you align ownership of both the underlying schema and the service layer to the same team. The service API needs to be properly embraced as a managed interface with appropriate oversight over how this API layer changes. This approach also has benefits for the upstream applications, as they can more easily understand how they are using the downstream schema. This makes activities like stubbing for test purposes much more manageable.

This pattern has advantages over the use of a simple database view. First, you aren't constrained to presenting a view that can be mapped to existing table structures; you can write code in your wrapping service to present much more sophisticated projections on the underlying data. The wrapping service can also take writes (via API calls). Of course, adopting this pattern does require upstream consumers to make changes; they have to shift from direct DB access to API calls.

Ideally, using this pattern would be a stepping stone to more fundamental changes, giving you time to break apart the schema underneath your API layer. It could be argued we're just putting a bandage over the problem, rather than addressing the underling issues. Nonetheless, in the spirit of making incremental improvement, I think this pattern has a lot going for it.

Pattern: Database-as-a-Service Interface

Sometimes, clients just need a database to query. It could be because they need to query or fetch large amounts of data, or perhaps because external parties are already using tool chains that require a SQL endpoint to work against (think about tools like Tableau, which are often used to gain insights into business metrics). In these situations, allowing clients to view data that your service manages in a database can make sense, but we should take care to separate the database we expose from the database we use inside our service boundary.

One approach I have seen work well is to create a dedicated database designed to be exposed as a read-only endpoint, and have this database populated when the data in the underlying database changes. In effect, in the same way that a service could expose a stream of events as one endpoint, and a synchronous API as another endpoint, it could also expose a database to external consumers. In Figure 4-7, we see an example of the Orders service, which exposes a read/write endpoint via an API, and a database as a read-only interface. A mapping engine takes changes in the internal database, and works out what changes need to be made in the external database.

Reporting Database Pattern

Martin Fowler has already documented this under the reporting database pattern (*http://bit.ly/2kWW9Ir*), so why did I use a different name here? As I spoke to more people, I realized that although reporting is a common application of this pattern, it's not the only reason people use this technique. The ability to allow clients to define ad hoc queries has broader scope than traditional batch-oriented workflows. So although this pattern is probably most widely used to support these reporting use cases, I wanted a different name to reflect the fact that it may have wider applicability.

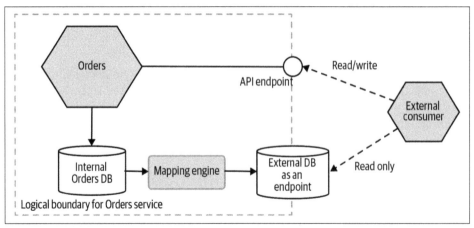

Figure 4-7. Exposing a dedicated database as an endpoint, allowing the internal database to remain hidden

The mapping engine could ignore the changes entirely, expose the change directly, or something in between. The key thing is that the mapping engine acts as an abstraction layer between the internal and external databases. When our internal database changes structure, the mapping engine will need to change to ensure that the public-facing database remains consistent. In virtually all cases, the mapping engine will lag behind writes made to the internal database; typically, the choice of mapping engine implementation will determine this lag. Clients reading from the exposed database need to understand that they are therefore seeing potentially stale data, and you may find it appropriate to programmatically expose information regarding when the external database was last updated.

Implementing a Mapping Engine

The detail here is in working out how to update—namely, how you implement the mapping engine. We've already looked at a change data capture system, which would be an excellent choice here. In fact, that is likely to be the most robust solution while also providing the most up-to-date view. Another option would be to have a batch process just copy the data over, although this can be problematic as it is likely to lead to a longer lag between internal and external databases, and determining which data needs to be copied over can be difficult with some schemas. A third option could be to listen to events fired from the service in question, and use that to update the external database.

In the past, I would have used a batch job to handle this. Nowadays, though, I'd probably utilize a dedicated change data capture system, perhaps something like Debezium (*https://github.com/debezium/debezium*). I've been bitten too many times by batch processes not running or taking too long to run. With the world moving away from batch jobs, and wanting data faster, batch is giving way to real time. Getting a change data capture system in place to handle this makes sense, especially if you are considering using it to expose events outside your service boundary.

Compared to Views

This pattern is more sophisticated than a simple database view. Database views are typically tied to a particular technology stack: if I want to present a view of an Oracle database, both the underlying database and the schema hosting the views both run on Oracle. With this approach, the database we expose can be a totally different technology stack. We could use Cassandra inside our service, but present a traditional SQL database as a public-facing endpoint.

This pattern gives more flexibility than database views, but at an added cost. If the needs of your consumers can be satisfied with a simple database view, this is likely to be less work to implement in the first instance. Just be aware that this may place restrictions on how this interface can evolve. You could start with the use of a database view and consider a shift to a dedicated reporting database later on.

Where to Use It

Obviously, as the database that is exposed as an endpoint is read-only, this is useful only for clients who need read-only access. It fits reporting use cases very well—situations where your clients may need to join across large amounts of data that a given service holds. This idea could be extended to then import this database's data into a larger data warehouse, allowing for data from multiple services to be queried. I discuss this in more detail in Chapter 5 of *Building Microservices*.

Don't underestimate the work required to ensure that this external database projection is kept properly up-to-date. Depending on how your current service is implemented, this might be a complex undertaking.

Transferring Ownership

So far, we've really not tackled the underlying problem. We've just put a variety of different bandages on a big, shared database. Before we start considering the tricky task of pulling data out of the giant monolithic database, we need to consider where the data in question should actually live. As you split services out from the monolith, some of the data should come with you—and some of it should stay where it is.

If we embrace the idea of a microservice encapsulating the logic associated with one or more aggregates, we also need to move the management of their state and associated data into the microservice's own schema. On the other hand, if our new microservice needs to interact with an aggregate that is still owned by the monolith, we need to expose this capability via a well-defined interface. Let's look at these two options now.

Pattern: Aggregate Exposing Monolith

In Figure 4-8, our new Invoicing service needs to access a variety of information that isn't directly related to managing invoicing. At the very least, it needs information on our current Employees to manage approval workflows. This data is currently all inside the monolith database. By exposing information about our Employees via a service endpoint (it could be an API or a stream of events) on the monolith itself, we make explicit what information the Invoice service needs.

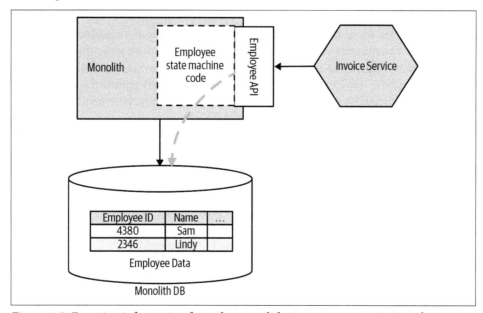

Figure 4-8. Exposing information from the monolith via a proper service interface, allowing our new microservice to access it

We want to think of our microservices as combinations of behavior and state; I've already discussed the idea of thinking of microservices as containing one or more state machines that manage domain aggregates. When exposing an aggregate from the monolith, we want to think in the same terms. The monolith still "owns" the concept of what is and isn't an allowable change in state; we don't want to treat it just like a wrapper around a database.

Beyond just exposing data, we're exposing operations that allow external parties to query the current state of an aggregate, and to make requests for new state transitions. We can still decide to restrict what state of an aggregate is exposed from our service boundary and to limit what state transition operations can be requested from the outside.

As a pathway to more services

By defining the needs of the Invoice service, and explicitly exposing the information needed in a well-defined interface, we're on a path to potentially discovering future service boundaries. In this example, an obvious step might be to next extract an Employee service, as we see in Figure 4-9. By exposing an API to employee-related data, we've already gone a long way to understanding what the needs of the consumers of the new Employee service might be.

Of course, if we do extract those employees from the monolith, and the monolith needs that employee data, it may need to be changed to use this new service!

Where to use it

When the data you want to access is still "owned" by the database, this pattern works well to allow your new services the access they need. When extracting services, having the new service call back to the monolith to access the data it needs is likely little more work than directly accessing the database of the monolith—but in the long term is a much better idea. I'd consider using a database view over this approach only if the monolith in question cannot be changed to expose these new endpoints. In such cases, a database view on the monolith's database could work, as could the previously discussed change data capture pattern (see the section "Pattern: Change Data Capture" on page 120), or creating a dedicated database wrapping service pattern (see the section "Pattern: Database Wrapping Service" on page 132) on top of the monolith's schema, exposing the Employee information we want.

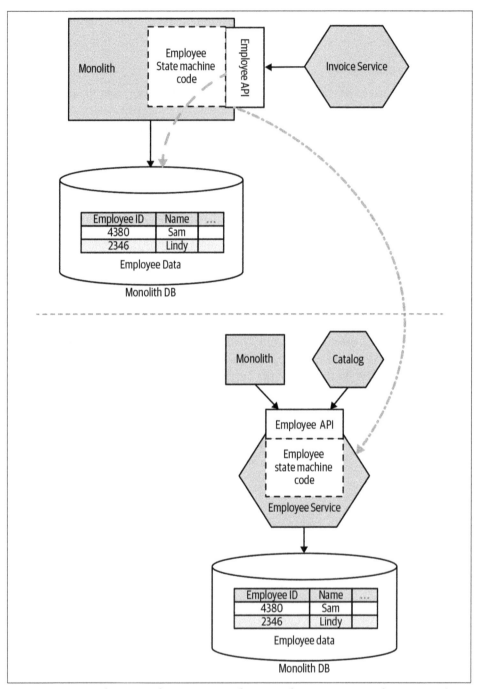

Figure 4-9. Using the scope of an existing endpoint to drive extraction of a new Employee service

Where to use it

When the data you want to access is still "owned" by the database, this pattern works well to allow your new services the access they need. When extracting services, having the new service call back to the monolith to access the data it needs is likely little more work than directly accessing the database of the monolith—but in the long term is a much better idea. I'd consider using a database view over this approach only if the monolith in question cannot be changed to expose these new endpoints. In such cases, a database view on the monolith's database could work, as could the previously discussed change data capture pattern (see the section "Pattern: Change Data Capture" on page 120), or creating a dedicated database wrapping service pattern (see the section "Pattern: Database Wrapping Service" on page 132) on top of the monolith's schema, exposing the Employee information we want.

Pattern: Change Data Ownership

We've looked at what happens when our new Invoice service needs to access data that is owned by other functionality, as in the previous section, where we needed to access Employee data. However, what happens when we consider data that is currently in the monolith that should be under the control of our newly extracted service?

In Figure 4-10, we outline the change that needs to happen. We need to move our invoice-related data out of the monolith and into our new Invoice, as that is where the life cycle of the data should be managed. We'd then need to change the monolith to treat the Invoice service as the source of truth for invoice-related data, and change it such that it called out to the Invoice service endpoint to read the data or request changes.

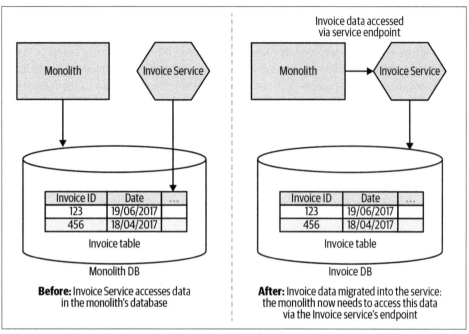

Figure 4-10. Our new Invoice service takes ownership of the related data

Untangling the invoicing data from the existing monolithic database can be a complex problem, however. We may have to consider the impact of breaking foreign-key constraints, breaking transactional boundaries, and more—all topics we'll be coming back to later in this chapter. If the monolith can be changed such that it needs only read access to Invoice-related data, you could consider projecting a view from the Invoice service's database, as Figure 4-11 shows. All the limitations of database views will apply, however; changing the monolith to make calls to the new Invoice service directly is greatly preferred.

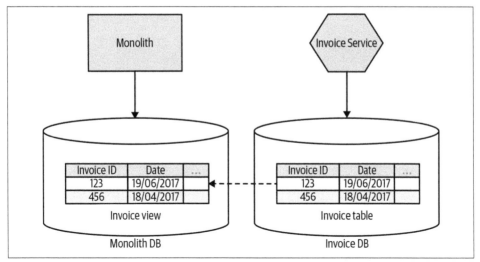

Figure 4-11. Projecting Invoice data back into the monolith as a view

Where to use it

This one is a little more clear-cut. If your newly extracted service encapsulates the business logic that changes some data, that data should be under the new service's control. The data should be moved from where it is, over into the new service. Of course, the process of moving data out of an existing database is far from a simple process. In fact, this will be the focus of the remainder of this chapter.

Data Synchronization

As we discussed in Chapter 3, one of the benefits of something like a strangler fig pattern is that when we switch over to the new service, we can then switch back if there is an issue. The problem occurs when the service in question manages data that will need to be kept in sync between both the monolith and the new service.

In Figure 4-12, we see an example of this. We are in the process of switching over to a new Invoice service. But the new service, and the existing equivalent code in the monolith also manages this data. To maintain the ability to switch between implementations, we need to ensure that both sets of code can see the same data, and that this data can be maintained in a consistent way.

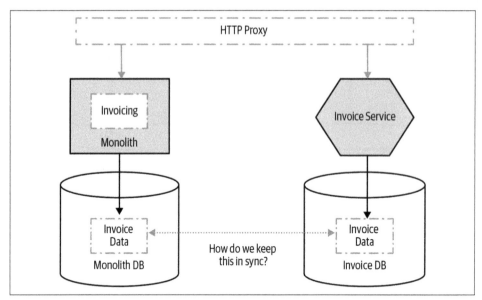

Figure 4-12. We want to use a strangler pattern to migrate to a new Invoice service, but the service manages state

So what are our options here? Well, first, we need to consider the degree to which the data needs to be consistent between the two views. If either set of code needs to always see a totally consistent view of invoice data, one of the most straightforward approaches would be to ensure the data is kept in one place. This would lead us toward probably having our new Invoice service read its data directly from the monolith for a short space of time, perhaps making use of a view, as we explored in the section "Pattern: Database View" on page 128. Once we are happy that the switch has been successful, we can then migrate the data, as we discussed earlier in the section "Pattern: Change Data Ownership" on page 141. However, the concerns about using a shared database cannot be overstated: you should consider this only as a very short-term measure, as part of a more complete extraction; leaving a shared database in place for too long can lead to significant long-term pain.

If we were doing a big-bang switchover (something I'd try to avoid), migrating both the application code and the data at the same time, we could use a batch process to copy the data over in advance of switching to the new microservice. Once the invoice-related data has been copied over into our new microservice, it can start serving traffic. However, what happens if we need to fall back to using the functionality in the existing monolithic system? Data changed in the microservices' schema will not be reflected in the state of the monolithic database, so we could end up losing state.

Another approach could be to consider keeping the two databases in sync via our code. So we would have either the monolith or the new Invoice service make writes to both databases. This involves some careful thought.

Pattern: Synchronize Data in Application

Switching data from one location to another can be a complex undertaking at the best of times, but it can be even more fraught the more valuable the data is. When you start thinking about looking after medical records, thinking carefully about how you migrate data is even more important.

Several years ago, the consultancy Trifork was involved in a project to help store a consolidated view of Danish citizens' medical records.[3] The initial version of this system had stored the data in a MySQL database, but over time it became clear that this may not be suitable for the challenges the system would face. A decision was made to use an alternative database, Riak. The hope was that Riak would allow the system to better scale to handle expected load, but would also offer improved resiliency characteristics.

An existing system stored data in one database, but there were limits to how long the system could be offline, and it was vital that data wasn't lost. So a solution was needed that allowed the company to move the data to a new database, but also build in mechanisms to verify the migration, and have fast rollback mechanisms along the way.

The decision was made that the application itself would perform the synchronization between the two data sources. The idea is that initially the existing MySQL database would remain the source of truth, but for a period of time the application would ensure that data in MySQL and Riak were kept in sync. After a period of time, Riak would move to being the source of truth for the application, prior to MySQL being retired. Let's look at this process in a bit more detail.

Step 1: Bulk Synchronize Data

The first step is to get to the point where you have a copy of the data in the new database. For the medical record project, this involved doing a batch migration of data from the old system into the new Riak database. While the batch import was going on, the existing system was kept running, so the source of data for the import was a snapshot of data taken from the existing MySQL system (Figure 4-13). This causes a challenge, as when the batch import finishes, the data in the source system could well

---

3 For a detailed presentation on this topic, you can view a recording of Kresten Krab Thorup's talk "Riak on Drugs (and the Other Way Around)" (*http://bit.ly/2m1CvLP*).

have changed. In this case, however, it wasn't practical to take the source system offline.

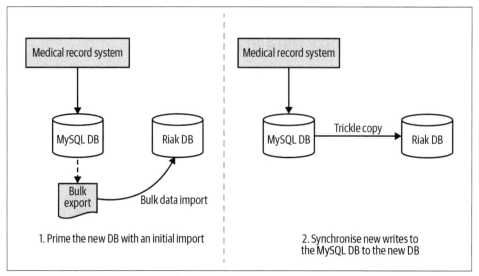

Figure 4-13. Preparing the new datastore for application-based synchronization

Once the batch import completed, a change data capture process was implemented whereby changes since the import could be applied. This allowed Riak to be brought in sync. Once this was achieved, it was time to deploy the new version of the application.

Step 2: Synchronize on Write, Read from Old Schema

With both databases now in sync, a new version of the application was deployed that would write all data to both databases, as we see in Figure 4-14. At this stage, the goal was to ensure that the application was correctly writing to both sources and make sure that Riak was behaving within acceptable tolerances. By still reading all data from MySQL, this ensured that even if Riak fell over in a heap, data could still be retrieved from the existing MySQL database.

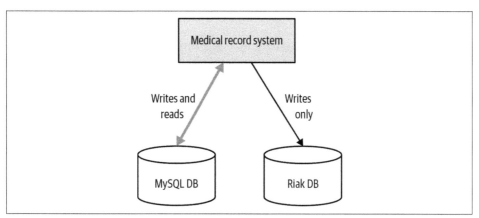

Figure 4-14. The application keeps both databases in sync, but uses one only for reads

Only once enough confidence had been built up in the new Riak system did they move to the next step.

Step 3: Synchronize on Write, Read from New Schema

At this stage, it's been verified that reads to Riak are working fine. The last step is to make sure that reads work too. A simple change to the application now has Riak as being the source of truth, as we see in Figure 4-15. Note that we still write to *both* databases, so if there is an issue, you have a fallback option.

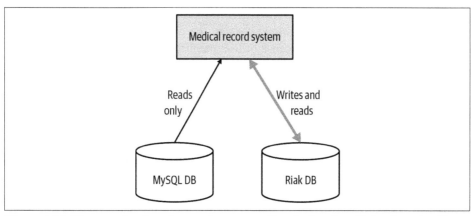

Figure 4-15. The new database is now the source of truth, but the old database is still kept in synchronization

Once the new system has bedded in enough, the old schema could be safely removed.

Where to Use This Pattern

With the Danish medical record system, we had a single application to deal with. But we've been talking about situations where we are looking to split out microservices. So does this pattern really help? The first thing to consider is that this pattern may make a lot of sense if you want to split the schema *before* splitting out the application code. In Figure 4-16, we see exactly such a situation, where we duplicate the invoice-related data first.

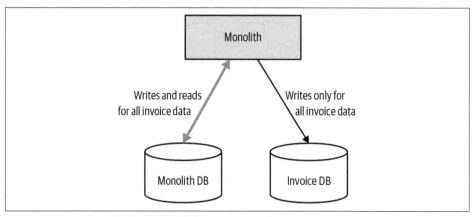

Figure 4-16. Example of a monolith keeping two schemas in sync

If implemented correctly, both data sources should always be in sync, offering us significant benefits in situations where we need fast switching between sources for rollback scenarios, etc. The use of this pattern in the example of the Danish medical records system seems sensible because of the inability to take the application offline for any length of time.

Where to Use It

Now you could consider using this pattern where you have both your monolith and microservice accessing the data, but this gets extremely complicated. In Figure 4-17, we have such a situation. Both the monolith and microservice have to ensure proper synchronization across the databases for this pattern to work. If either one makes a mistake, you could be in trouble. This complexity is greatly mitigated if you can be sure that at any point in time either the Invoice service is making writes, or the monolith's Invoice functionality is—which would work well if using a simple switchover technique, as we discussed with the strangler fig pattern. If, however, requests could hit either the monolith's Invoice functionality *or* the new Invoice functionality, perhaps as part of a canary, then you may not want to use this pattern, as the resulting synchronization will be tricky.

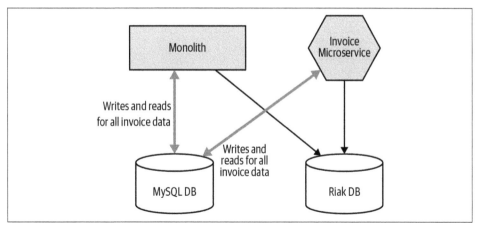

Figure 4-17. Example of a monolith and microservice both trying to keep the same two schemas in sync

Pattern: Tracer Write

The tracer write pattern, outlined in the section Figure 4-18, is arguably a variation of the synchronize data in application pattern (see the section "Pattern: Synchronize Data in Application" on page 145. With a tracer write, we move the source of truth for data in an incremental fashion, tolerating there being two sources of truth during the migration. You identify a new service that will host the relocated data. The current system still maintains a record of this data locally, but when making changes also ensures this data is written to the new service via its service interface. Existing code can be changed to start accessing the new service, and once all functionality is using the new service as the source of truth, the old source of truth can be retired. Careful consideration needs to be given regarding how data is synchronized between the two sources of truth.

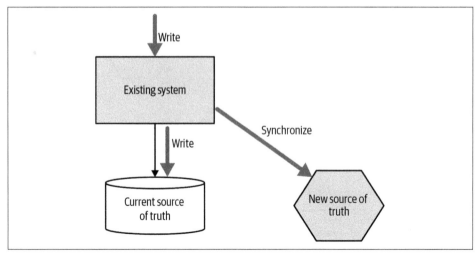

Figure 4-18. A tracer write allows for incremental migration of data from one system to another by accommodating two sources of truth during the migration

Wanting a single source of truth is a totally rational desire. It allows us to ensure consistency of data, to control access to that data, and can reduce maintenance costs. The problem is that if we insist on only ever having one source of truth for a piece of data, then we are forced into a situation that changing where this data lives becomes a single big switchover. Before the release, the monolith is the source of truth. After the release, our new microservice is the source of truth. The issue is that various things can go wrong during this change over. A pattern like the tracer write allows for a phased switchover, reducing the impact of each release, in exchange for being more tolerant of having more than one source of truth.

The reason this pattern is called a tracer write is that you can start with a small set of data being synchronized and increase this over time, while also increasing the number of consumers of the new source of data. If we take the example outlined in Figure 4-12, where invoice-related data was being moved from the monolith over to our new Invoice microservice, we could first synchronize the basic invoice data, then migrate the contact information for the invoice, and finally synchronize payment records, as outlined in Figure 4-19.

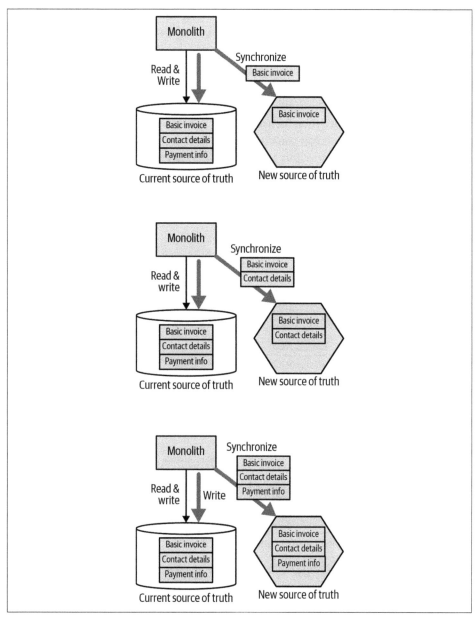

Figure 4-19. Incrementally moving invoice-related information from the monolith over to our Invoice service

Other services that wanted invoice-related information would have a choice to source this from either the monolith or the new service itself, depending on what information they need. If they still needed information available only in the monolith, they would have to wait until that data and the supporting functionality was moved. Once the data and functionality are available in the new microservice, the consumers can switch to the new source of truth.

The goal in our example is to migrate all consumers to use the Invoice service, including the monolith itself. In Figure 4-20, we see an example of a couple of stages during the migration. Initially, we're writing only basic invoice information to both sources of truth. Once we've established that this information is being properly synchronized, the monolith can start to read its data from the new service. As more data is synchronized, the monolith can use the new service as a source of truth for more and more of the data. Once all the data is synchronized, and the last consumer of the old source of truth has been switched over, we can stop synchronizing the data.

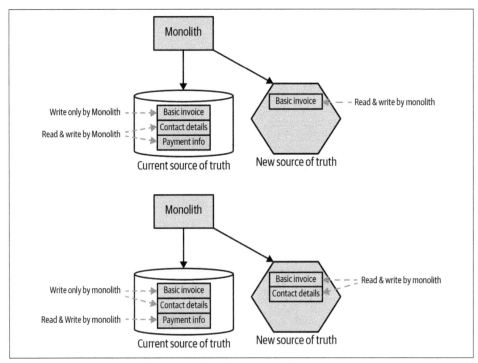

Figure 4-20. Retiring the old source of truth as part of a tracer write

Data Synchronization

The biggest problem that needs to be addressed with the tracer write pattern is the issue that plagues any situation where data is duplicated-inconsistency. To resolve this, you have a few options:

Write to one source

All writes are sent to one of the sources of truth. Data is synchronized to the other source of truth after the write occurs.

Send writes to both sources

All write requests made by upstream clients are sent to both sources of truth. This occurs by making sure the client makes a call to each source of truth itself, or by relying on an intermediary to broadcast the request to each downstream service.

Seed writes to either source

Clients can send write requests to either source of truth, and behind the scenes the data is synchronized in a two-way fashion between the systems.

The two separate options of sending writes to both sources of truth, or sending to one source of truth and relying on some form of background synchronization, seem like workable solutions, and the example we'll explore in a moment uses both of these techniques. However, although it's technically an option, this situation—where writes are made to either one source of truth or the other—should be avoided, as it requires two-way synchronization (something that can be very difficult to achieve).

In all of these cases, there will be some delay in the data being consistent in both sources of truth. The duration of this window of inconsistency will depend on several factors. For example, if you use a nightly batch process to copy updates from one source to another, the second source of truth could contain data that is up to 24 hours out-of-date. If you are constantly streaming updates from one system to another, perhaps using a change data capture system, the windows of inconsistency could be measured in seconds or less.

However long this window of inconsistency is, such synchronization gives us what is called *eventual consistency*—eventually, both sources of truth will have the same data. You will have to understand what period of inconsistency is appropriate in your case, and use that to drive how you implement the synchronization.

 It's important that when maintaining two sources of truth like this that you have some kind of reconciliation process to ensure that the synchronization is working as intended. This may be something as simple as a couple of SQL queries you can run against each database. But without checking that the synchronization is working as expected, you may end up with inconsistencies between the two systems and not realize it until it is too late. Running your new source of truth for a period of time when it has no consumers until you are satisfied with how things are working—which, as we'll explore in the next section, is something that Square did, for example—is very sensible.

Example: Orders at Square

This pattern was originally shared with me by Derek Hammer, a developer at Square, and since then I've found other examples of this pattern being used in the wild.[4] He detailed its usage to help untangle part of Square's domain related to ordering take-out food for delivery. In the initial system, a single Order concept was used to manage multiple workflows: one for customers ordering food, another for the restaurant preparing the food, and a third workflow-managed state related to delivery drivers picking up the food and dropping it off to customers. The needs of the three stakeholders are different, and although all these stakeholders work with the same Order, what that Order means to each of them is different. For the customer, it's something they have chosen to be delivered, and something they need to pay for. For a restaurant it's something that needs to be cooked and picked up. And for the delivery driver, it's something that needs to be taken from the restaurant to the customer in a timely manner. Despite these different needs, the code and associated data for the order was all bound together.

Having all these workflows bundled into this single Order concept was the source of a great degree of what I've previously referred to as *delivery contention*—different developers trying to make changes for different use cases would get in each other's way, as they all needed to make changes in the same part of the codebase. Square wanted to break apart an Order so changes to each workflow could be made in isolation, and also enable different scaling and robustness needs.

Creating the new service

The first step was to create a new Fulfillments service as seen in Figure 4-21, which would manage the Order data associated with restaurant and delivery drivers. This service would become the new source of truth going forward for this subset of the Order data. Initially, this service just exposed functionality to allow for Fulfillments-related entities to be created. Once the new service was live, the company had a background worker copy the Fulfillments-related data from the existing system to the new Fulfillments service. This background worker just made use of an API exposed by the Fulfillments service rather than doing a direct insertion into the database, avoiding the need for direct database access.

---

4 Sangeeta Handa shared how Netflix used this pattern as part of its data migrations at the QCon SF conference, and Daniel Bryant subsequently did a nice write-up (*http://bit.ly/2m1EwHT*) of this.

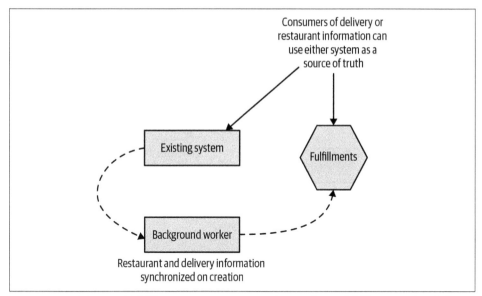

Figure 4-21. The new Fulfillments service was used to replicate fulfillment-related data from the existing system

The background worker was controlled via a feature flag that could be enabled or disabled to stop this copying process. This allowed them to ensure that if the worker caused any issues in production, the process would be easy to turn off. They ran this system in production for sufficient time to be confident that the synchronization was working correctly. Once they were happy that the background worker was working as expected, they removed the feature flag.

Synchronizing the data

One of the challenges with this sort of synchronization is that it is one way. Changes made to the existing system resulted in the fulfillment-related data being written to the new Fulfillments service via its API. Square resolved this by ensuring that all updates were made to both systems, as in Figure 4-22. Not all updates needed to be made to both systems, however. As Derek explained, now that the Fulfillments service represented only a subset of the Order concept, only changes made to the order that delivery or restaurant clients cared about needed to be copied.

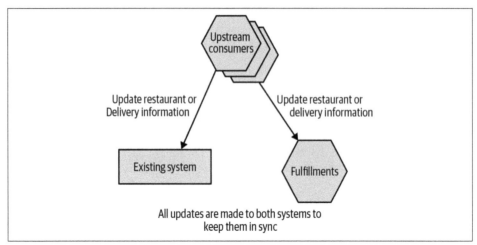

Figure 4-22. Subsequent updates were synchronized by ensuring that all consumers made appropriate API calls to both services

Any code that changed restaurant- or delivery-oriented information needed to be changed to make two sets of API calls—one to the existing system, the other to the same microservice. These upstream clients would also need to handle any error conditions if the write to one worked but the other failed. These changes to the two downstream systems (the existing order system and the new Fulfillments service) were not done in an atomic fashion. This means there could be a brief window in which a change would be visible in one system, but not yet the other. Until both changes have been applied, you can see an inconsistency between the two systems; this is a form of *eventual consistency*, which we discussed earlier.

In terms of the eventual consistent nature of the Order information, this wasn't a problem for this particular use case. Data was synchronized quickly enough between the two systems that it didn't impact the users of the system.

If Square had been using an event-driven system for managing Order updates, rather than making use of API calls, they could have considered an alternative implementation. In Figure 4-23, we have a single stream of messages that could trigger changes in the Order state. Both the existing system and the new Fulfillments service receive the same messages. Upstream clients don't need to know that there are multiple consumers for these messages; this is something that could be handled through the use of a pub-sub style broker.

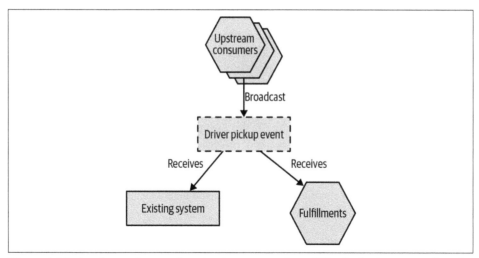

Figure 4-23. An alternative synchronization approach could be for both sources of truth to subscribe to the same events

Retrofitting Square's architecture to be event-based just to satisfy this sort of use case would be a lot of work. But if you are already making use of an event-based system, you may have an easier time managing the synchronization process. It's also worth noting that such an architecture would still exhibit eventually consistent behavior, as you cannot guarantee that both the existing system and Fulfillments service would process the same event at the same time.

Migrating consumers

With the new Fulfillments service now holding all the required information for the restaurant and delivery driver workflows, code that managed those workflows could start switching over to use the new service. During this migration, more functionality can be added to support these consumers' needs; initially, the Fulfillments service needed only to implement an API that enabled creation of new records for the background worker. As new consumers migrate, their needs can be assessed and new functionality can be added to the service to support them.

This incremental migration of both data, as well as changing the consumers to use the new source of truth, proved in the case of Square to be highly effective. Derek said that getting to the point where all consumers had switched over ended up being pretty much a non-event. It was just another small change done during a routine release (another reason I've been advocating for incremental migration patterns so strongly in this book!).

From a domain-driven design point of view, you could certainly argue that the functionality associated with delivery drivers, customers, and restaurants all represented different bounded contexts. From that viewpoint, Derek suggested that he would ideally have considered splitting this Fulfillments service further, into two services—one for Restaurants, and another for the Delivery Drivers. Nonetheless, although there is scope for further decomposition, this migration seemed to be very successful.

In Square's case, it decided to keep the duplicated data. Leaving restaurant- and delivery-related order information in the existing system allowed the company to provide visibility of this information in the event of the Fulfillments service being unavailable. This requires keeping the synchronization in place, of course. I do wonder if this will be revisited over time. Once there is sufficient confidence in the availability of the Fulfillments service, removing the background worker and need for consumers to make two sets of update calls may well help streamline the architecture.

Where to Use It

Implementation of the synchronization is likely to be where most of the work lies. If you can avoid the need for two-way synchronization, and instead use some of the simpler options outlined here, you'll likely find this pattern much easier to implement. If you are already making use of an event-driven system, or have a change data capture pipeline available, then you probably already have a lot of the building blocks available to you to get the synchronization working.

Careful thought does need to be given regarding how long you can tolerate inconsistency between the two systems. Some use cases might not care, others may want the replication to be almost immediate. The shorter the window of acceptable inconsistency, the more difficult this pattern will be to implement.

Splitting Apart the Database

We've already discussed at length the challenges of using databases as a method of integrating multiple services. As should by now be very clear, I am not a fan! This means we need to find seams in our databases too so we can split them out cleanly. Databases, however, are tricky beasts. Before we get into some examples of approaches, we should briefly discuss how logical separation and physical deployment may be related.

Physical Versus Logical Database Separation

When we talk about breaking apart our databases in this context, we're primarily trying to achieve logical separation. A single database engine is perfectly capable of hosting more than one logically separated schema, as we see in Figure 4-24.

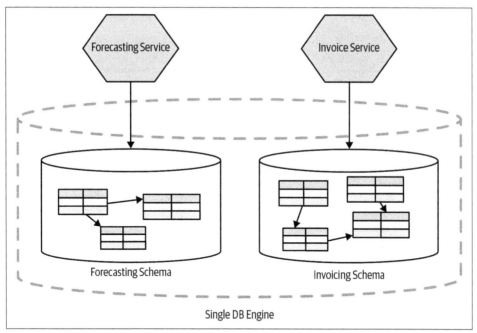

Figure 4-24. Two services making use of separate logical schemas, both running on the same physical database engine

We could take this further, and have each logical schema also on separate database engines, giving us physical separation too, as we see in Figure 4-25.

Why would you want to logically decompose your schemas but still have them on a single database engine? Well, fundamentally, logical and physical decomposition achieve different goals. *Logical decomposition* allows for simpler independent change and information hiding, whereas *physical decomposition* potentially improves system robustness, and could help remove resource contention allowing for improved throughput or latency.

When we logically decompose our database schemas but keep them on the same physical database engine, as in Figure 4-24, we have a potential single point of failure. If the database engine goes down, both services are affected. However, the world isn't that simple. Many database engines have mechanisms to avoid single points of failure, such as multiprimary database modes, warm failover mechanisms, and the like. In fact, significant effort may have been put into creating a highly resilient database cluster in your organization, and it may be hard to justify having multiple clusters because of the time, effort, and cost that may be involved (those pesky license fees can add up!).

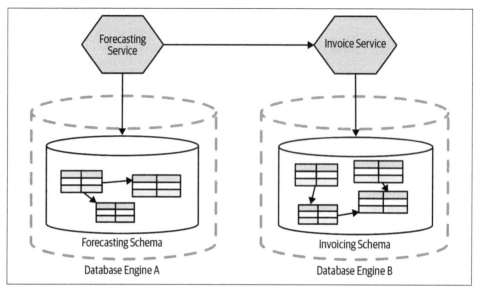

Figure 4-25. Two services making use of separate logical schemas, each running on its own physical database engine

Another consideration is that having multiple schemas sharing the same database engine may be required if you want to expose views of your database. Both the source database and the schemas hosting the views may need to be located on the same database engine.

Of course, for you to even have the option of running separate services on different physical database engines, you need to have already logically decomposed their schemas!

Splitting the Database First, or the Code?

So far, we've spoken about patterns to help work with shared databases, and hopefully move on to less coupled models. In a moment, we need to look in detail at patterns around database decomposition. Before we do that, though, we need to discuss sequencing. Extracting a microservice isn't "done" until the application code is running in its own service, and the data it controls is extracted into its own logically isolated database. But with this being a book largely about enabling incremental change, we have to explore a little how this extraction should be sequenced. We have a few options:

- Split the database first, then the code.
- Split the code first, then the database.

- Split them both at once.

Each has its pros and cons. Let's look at these options now, along with some patterns that may help, depending on the approach you take.

Split the Database First

With a separate schema, we'll be potentially increasing the number of database calls to perform a single action. Whereas before we might have been able to have all the data we wanted in a single SELECT statement, now we may need to pull the data back from two locations and join in memory. Also, we end up breaking transactional integrity when we move to two schemas, which could have significant impact on our applications; we'll be discussing these challenges later in this chapter, as we cover topics like distributed transactions and sagas, and how they might be able to help. By splitting the schemas out but keeping the application code together, as in Figure 4-26, we give ourselves the ability to revert our changes or continue to tweak things without impacting any consumers of our service if we realize we're heading down the wrong path. Once we are satisfied that the DB separation makes sense, we could then think about splitting out the application code into two services.

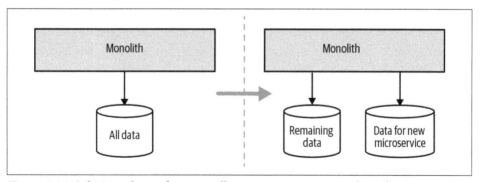

Figure 4-26. Splitting schema first may allow you to spot issues with performance and transactional integrity earlier

The flip side is that this approach is unlikely to yield much short-term benefit. We still have a monolithic code deployment. Arguably, the pain of a shared database is something you feel over time, so we're spending time and effort now to give us return in the long run, without getting enough of the short-term benefit. For this reason, I'd likely go this route only if I'm especially concerned about the potential performance or data consistency issues. We also need to consider that if the monolith itself is a black-box system, like a piece of commercial software, this option isn't available to us.

Pattern: Repository per bounded context

A common practice is to have a repository layer, backed by some sort of framework like Hibernate, to bind your code to the database, making it easy to map objects or data structures to and from the database. Rather than having a single repository layer for all our data access concerns, there is value in breaking down these repositories along the lines of bounded contexts, as shown in Figure 4-27.

Having the database mapping code colocated inside the code for a given context can help us understand what parts of the database are used by what bits of code. Hibernate, for example, can make this very clear if you are using something like a mapping file per bounded context. We can see, therefore, which bounded contexts access which tables in our schema. This can help us greatly understand what tables need to move as part of any future decomposition.

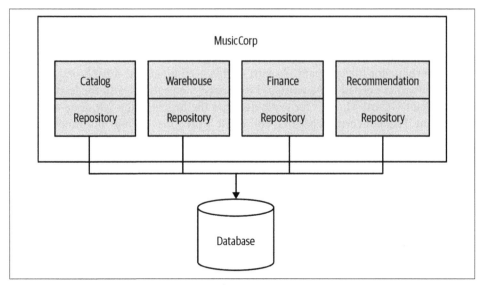

Figure 4-27. Splitting out our repository layers

This doesn't give us the whole story, however. For example, we may be able to tell that the finance code uses the ledger table, and that the catalog code uses the line item table, but it might not be clear that the database enforces a foreign-key relationship from the ledger table to the line item table. To see these database-level constraints, which may be a stumbling block, we need to use another tool to visualize the data. A great place to start is to use a tool like the freely available SchemaSpy (*http://sche maspy.sourceforge.net*), which can generate graphical representations of the relationships between tables.

All this helps you understand the coupling between tables that may span what will eventually become service boundaries. But how do you cut those ties? And what about cases where the same tables are used from multiple bounded contexts? We're going to explore this topic in great length later in this chapter.

Where to use it.　This pattern is really effective in any situation where you are looking to rework the monolith in order to better understand how to split it apart. Breaking down these repository layers along the lines of domain concepts will go a long way to helping you understand where seams for microservices may exist not only in your database, but also in the code itself.

Pattern: Database per bounded context

Once you've clearly isolated data access from the application point of view, it makes sense to continue this approach into the schema. Central to the idea of microservices' independent deployability is the fact that they should own their own data. Before we get to separating out the application code, we can start this decomposition by clearly separating our databases around the lines of our identified bounded contexts.

At ThoughtWorks, we were implementing some new mechanisms to calculate and forecast revenue for the company. As part of this, we'd identified three broad areas of functionality that needed to be written. I discussed the problem with the lead for this project, Peter Gillard-Moss. Peter explained that the functionality felt quite separate, but that he had concerns regarding the extra work that having this functionality would bring if they were put in separate microservices. At this time, his team was small (only three people), and it was felt that the team couldn't justify splitting out these new services. In the end, they settled on a model in which the new revenue functionality was effectively deployed as a single service, containing three isolated bounded contexts (each of which ended up as separate JAR files), as shown in Figure 4-28.

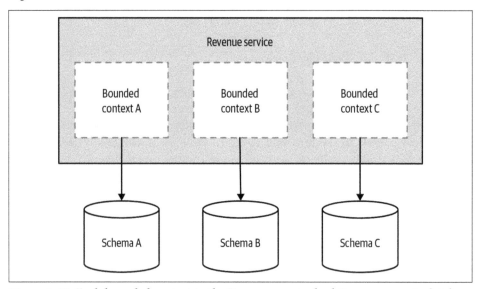

Figure 4-28. Each bounded context in the Revenue service had its own separate database schema, allowing separation later on

Each bounded context had its own, totally separate databases. The idea was that if there was a need to separate them into microservices later, this would be much easier. However, it turned out that this was never needed. Several years later, this revenue service remains as it is, a monolith with multiple associated databases—a great example of a modular monolith.

Where to use it.   At first glance, the extra work in maintaining the separate databases doesn't make much sense if you keep things as a monolith. I view this as a pattern that is all about hedging your bets. It's a bit more work than a single database, but keeps your options open regarding moving to microservices later. Even if you never move to microservices, having the clear separation of schema backing the database can really help, especially if you have lots of people working on the monolith itself.

This is a pattern I nearly always recommend for people building brand-new systems (as opposed to reimplementing an existing system). I'm not a fan of implementing microservices for new products or startups; your understanding of the domain is unlikely to be mature enough to identify stable domain boundaries. With startups especially, the nature of the thing you are building can change drastically. This pattern can be a nice halfway point, though. Keep schema separation where you think you may have service separation in the future. That way, you get some of the benefits of decoupling these ideas, while reducing the complexity of the system.

Split the Code First

In general, I find that most teams split the code first, then the database, as shown in Figure 4-29. They get the short-term improvement (hopefully) from the new service, which gives them confidence to complete the decomposition by separating out the database.

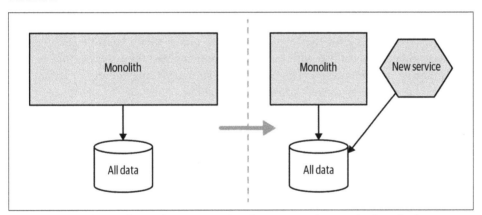

Figure 4-29. Splitting the application tier first leaves us with a single shared schema

By splitting out the application tier, it becomes much easier to understand what data is needed by the new service. You also get the benefit of having an independently deployable code artifact earlier. The concerns I've always had with this approach is that teams may get this far and then stop, leaving a shared database in play on an ongoing basis. If this is the direction you take, you have to understand that you're storing up trouble for the future if you don't complete the separation into the data tier. I've seen teams that have fallen into this trap, but can happily also report speaking to organizations that have done the right thing here. JustSocial is one such organization that used this approach as part of its own microservices migration. The other potential challenge here is that you may be delaying finding out nasty surprises caused by pushing join operations up into the application tier.

If this is the direction you take, be honest with yourself: are you confident that you will be able to make sure that any data owned by the microservice gets split out as part of the next step?

Pattern: Monolith as data access layer

Rather than accessing the data from the monolith directly, we can just move to a model in which we create an API in the monolith itself. In Figure 4-30, the Invoice service needs information about employees in our Customer service, so we create an Employee API allowing for the Invoice service to access them. Susanne Kaiser from JustSocial shared this pattern with me as that company had used successfully as part of its microservices migration. The pattern has so many things going for it that I'm surprised it doesn't seem as well-known as it should be.

Part of the reason this isn't used more widely is likely because people sort of have in their minds the idea that the monolith is dead, and of no use. They want to move away from it. They don't consider making it more useful! But the upsides here are obvious: we don't have to tackle data decomposition (yet) but get to hide information, making it easier to keep our new service isolated from the monolith. I'd be more inclined to adopt this model if I felt that the data in the monolith was going to stay there. But it can work well, especially if you think that your new service will effectively be pretty stateless.

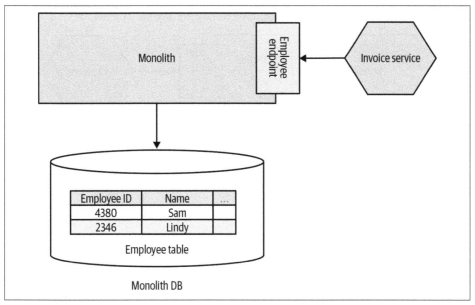

Figure 4-30. Exposing an API on the monolith allows the service to avoid direct data binding

It's not too hard to see this pattern as a way of identifying other candidate services. Extending this idea, we could see the Employee API splitting out from the monolith to become a microservice in its own right, as shown in Figure 4-31.

Where to use it.   This pattern works best when the code managing this data is still in the monolith. As we talked about previously, one way to think of a microservice when it comes to data is the encapsulation of the state and the code that manages the transitions of that state. So if the state transitions of this data are still provided in the monolith, it follows that the microservice that wants to access (or change) that state needs to go via the state transitions in the monolith.

If the data you're trying to access in the monolith's database should really be "owned" by the microservice instead, I'm more inclined to suggest skipping this pattern and instead looking to split the data out.

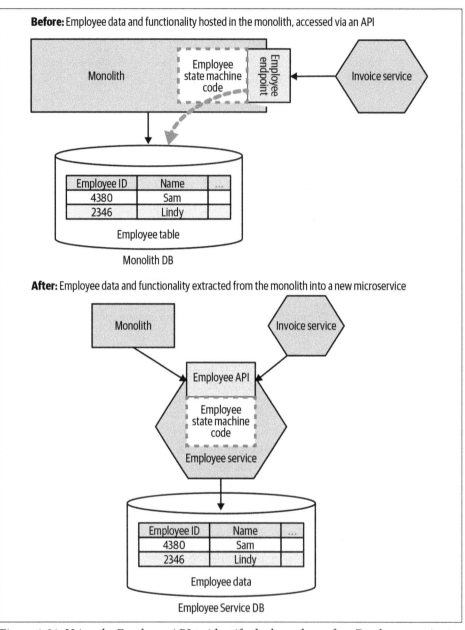

Figure 4-31. Using the Employee API to identify the boundary of an Employee service to be split from the monolith

Pattern: Multischema storage

As we've already discussed, it's a good idea not to make a bad situation any worse. If you are still making direct use of the data in a database, it doesn't mean that *new* data stored by a microservice should go in there too. In Figure 4-32, we see an example of our Invoice service. The invoice core data still lives in the monolith, which is where we (currently) access it from. We've added the ability to add reviews to Invoices; this represents brand-new functionality not in the monolith. To support this, we need to store a table of reviewers, mapping employees to Invoice IDs. If we put this new table in the monolith, we'd be helping grow the database! Instead, we've put this new data in our own schema.

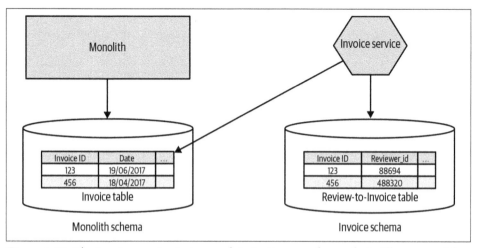

Figure 4-32. The Invoice service puts new data in its own schema, but still accesses old data directly in the monolith

In this example, we have to consider what happens when a foreign-key relationship effectively spans a schema boundary. Later in this chapter, we'll explore this very problem in more depth.

Pulling out the data from a monolithic database will take time, and may not be something you can do in one step. You should therefore feel quite happy to have your microservice access data in the monolithic DB while also managing its own local storage. As you manage to drag clear the rest of the data from the monolith, you can migrate it a table at a time into your new schema.

Where to use it.   This pattern works well when adding brand-new functionality to your microservice that requires the storage of new data. It's clearly not data the monolith needs (the functionality isn't there), so keep it separate from the beginning. This pattern also makes sense as you start moving data out of the monolith into your own schema—a process that may take some time.

If the data you are accessing in the monolith's schema is data that you never planned to move into your schema, I strongly recommend use of the monolith as data access layer pattern (see the section "Pattern: Monolith as data access layer" on page 166) in conjunction with this pattern.

Split Database and Code Together

From a staging point of view, of course, we have the option to just break things apart in one big step as in Figure 4-33. We split both the code and data at once.

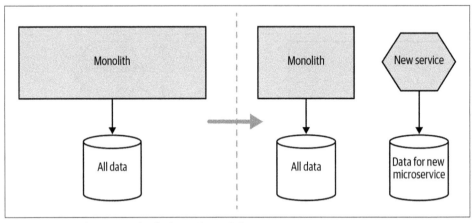

Figure 4-33. Splitting out both the code and data in one step

My concern here is that this is a much bigger step to take, and it will be longer before you can assess the impact of your decision as a result. I strongly suggest avoiding this approach, and instead splitting either the schema or application tier first.

So, Which Should I Split First?

I get it: you're probably tired of all this "It depends" stuff, right? I can't blame you.The problem is, everyone's situation is different, so I'm trying to arm you with enough context and discussion of various pros and cons to help you make up your own mind. However, I know sometimes what people want is a bit of a hot take on these things, so here it is.

If I'm able to change the monolith, and if I am concerned about the potential impact to performance or data consistency, I'll look to split the schema apart first. Otherwise, I'll split the code out, and use that to help understand how that impacts data owner-ship. But it's important that you also think for yourself and take into account any fac-tors that might impact the decision-making process in your particular situation.

Schema Separation Examples

So far, we've looked at schema separation at a fairly high level, but there are complex challenges associated with database decomposition and a few tricky issues to explore. We're going to look at some more low-level data decomposition patterns now and explore the impact they can have.

Relational Databases Versus NoSQL

Many of the example refactorings that I detail in this chapter explore challenges that occur when working with relational schemas. The nature of these types of databases create additional challenges in terms of pulling schemas apart. Many of you may well be using alternative types of nonrelational databases. However, many of the following patterns may still apply. You may have fewer constraints in how the changes can be made, but I hope that the advice is still useful.

Pattern: Split Table

Sometimes you'll find data in a single table that needs to be split across two or more service boundaries, and that can get interesting. In Figure 4-34, we see a single shared table, Item, where we store information about not only the item being sold, but also the stock levels.

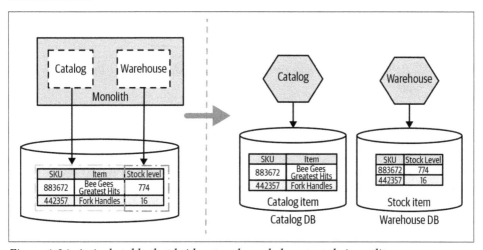

Figure 4-34. A single table that bridges two bounded contexts being split

In this example, we want to split out Catalog and Warehouse as new services, but the data for both is mixed into this single table. So, we need to split this data into two separate tables, as Figure 4-34 shows. In the spirit of incremental migration, it may make sense to split the tables apart in the existing schema, before separating the schemas. If these tables existed in a single schema, it would make sense to declare a foreign-key relationship from the Stock Item SKU column to the Catalog Item table. However, because we plan to move these tables ultimately into separate databases, we may not gain much from this as we won't have a single database enforcing the data consistency (we'll explore this idea in more detail shortly).

This example is fairly straightforward; it was easy to separate ownership of data on a column-by-column basis. But what happens when multiple pieces of code update the same column? In Figure 4-35, we have a Customer table, which contains a Status column.

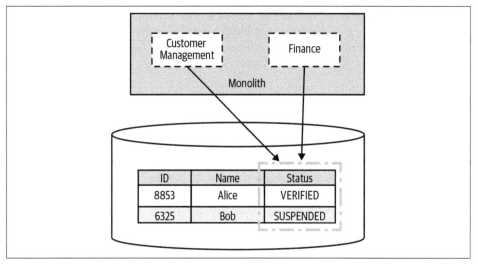

Figure 4-35. Both customer management and finance code can change the status in the Customer table

This column is updated during the customer sign-up process to indicate that a given person has (or hasn't) verified their email, with the value going from NOT_VERI-FIED → VERIFIED. Once a customer is VERIFIED, they are able to shop. Our finance code handles suspending customers if their bills are unpaid, so they will on occasion change the status of a customer to SUSPENDED. In this instance, a customer's Status still feels like it should be part of the customer domain model, and as such it should be managed by the soon-to-be-created Customer service. Remember, we want, where possible, to keep the state machines for our domain entities inside a single service boundary, and updating a Status certainly feels like part of the state machine for a customer! This means that when the service split has been made, our new Finance service will need to make a service call to update this status, as we see in Figure 4-36.

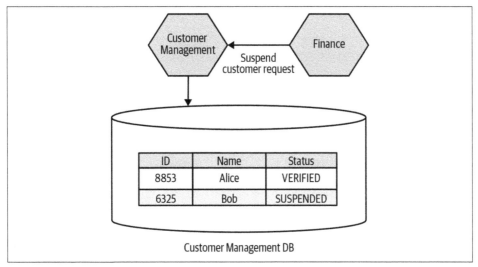

Figure 4-36. The new Finance service has to make service calls to suspend a customer

A big problem with splitting tables like this is that we lose the safety given to us by database transactions. We'll explore this topic in more depth toward the end of this chapter, when we look at "Transactions" on page 187 and "Sagas" on page 193.

Where to Use It

On the face of it, these seem pretty straightforward. When the table is owned by two or more bounded contexts in your current monolith, you need to split the table along those lines. If you find specific columns in that table that seem to be updated by multiple parts of your codebase, you need to make a judgment call as to who should "own" that data. Is it an existing domain concept you have in scope? That will help determine where this data should go.

Pattern: Move Foreign-Key Relationship to Code

We've decided to extract our Catalog service—something that can manage and expose information about artists, tracks, and albums. Currently, our catalog-related code inside the monolith uses an Albums table to store information about the CDs which we might have available for sale. These albums end up getting referenced in our Ledger table, which is where we track all sales. You can see this in Figure 4-37. The rows in the Ledger table just record the amount we receive for a CD, along with an identifier that refers to the item sold; the identifier in our example is called a SKU (a stock keeping unit), a common practice in retail systems.

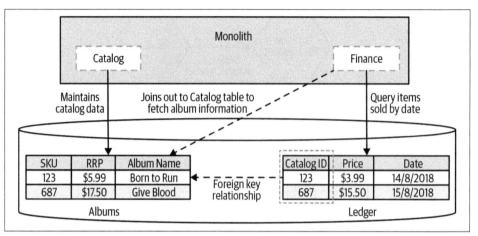

Figure 4-37. Foreign-key relationship

At the end of each month, we need to generate a report outlining our biggest-selling CDs. The Ledger table helps us understand which SKU sold the most copies, but the information about that SKU is over in the Albums table. We want to make the reports nice and easy to read, so rather than saying, "We sold 400 copies of SKU 123 and made $1,596," we'd like to add more information about what was sold, instead saying, "We sold 400 copies of Bruce Springsteen's *Born to Run* and made $1,596." To do this, the database query triggered by our finance code needs to join information from the Ledger table to the Albums table, as Figure 4-37 shows.

We have defined a foreign-key relationship in our schema, such that a row in the Ledger table is identified as having a relationship to a row in the Albums table. By defining such a relationship, the underlying database engine is able to ensure data consistency—namely, that if a row in the Ledger table refers to a row in the Albums table, we know that row exists. In our situation, that means we can always get information about the album that was sold. These foreign-key relationships also let the database engine carry out performance optimizations to ensure that the join operation is as fast as possible.

We want to split out the Catalog and Finance code into their own corresponding services, and that means the data has to come too. The Albums and Ledger tables will end up living in different schemas, so what happens with our foreign-key relationship? Well, we have two key problems to consider. First, when our new Finance service wants to generate this report in the future, how does it retrieve Catalog-related information if it can no longer do this via a database join? The other problem is, what do we do about the fact that data inconsistency could now exist in the new world?

Moving the Join

Let's look at replacing the join first. With a monolithic system, in order to join a row from the Album table with the sales information in the Ledger, we'd have the database perform the join for us. We'd perform a single SELECT query, where we'd join to the Albums table. This would require a single database call to execute the query and pull back all the data we need.

In our new microservice-based world, our new Finance service has the responsibility of generating the best-sellers report, but doesn't have the album data locally. So it will need to fetch this from our new Catalog service, as we see in Figure 4-38. When generating the report, the Finance service first queries the Ledger table, extracting the list of best-selling SKUs for the last month. At this point, all we have is a list of SKUs, and the number of copies sold for each; that's the only information we have locally.

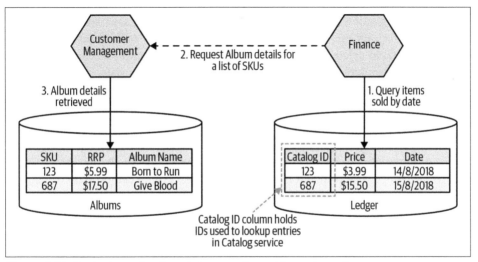

Figure 4-38. Replacing a database join operation with service calls

Next, we need to call the Catalog service, requesting information on each of these SKUs. This request in turn would cause the Catalog service to make its own local SELECT on its own database.

Logically, the join operation is still happening, but it is now happening inside the Finance service, rather than in the database. Unfortunately, it isn't going to be anywhere near as efficient. We've gone from a world where we have a single SELECT statement, to a new world where we have a SELECT query against the Ledger table, followed by a service call to the Catalog service, which in turn triggers a SELECT statement against the Albums table, as we see in Figure 4-38.

In this situation, I'd be very surprised if the overall latency of this operation didn't increase. This may not be a significant problem in this particular case, as this report is generated monthly, and could therefore be aggressively cached. But if this is a frequent operation, that could be more problematic. We can mitigate the likely impact of this increase in latency by allowing for SKUs to be looked up in the Catalog service in bulk, or perhaps even by caching the required album information locally.

Ultimately, whether or not this increase in latency is a problem is something only you can decide. You need to have an understanding of acceptable latency for key operations, and be able to measure what the latency currently is. Distributed systems like Jaeger (*https://www.jaegertracing.io*) can really help here, as they provide the ability to get accurate timing of operations that span multiple services. Making an operation slower may be acceptable if it is still fast enough, especially if as a trade-off you gain some other benefits.

Data Consistency

A trickier consideration is that with Catalog and Finance being separate services, with separate schemas, we may end up with data inconsistency. With a single schema, I wouldn't be able to delete a row in the Albums table if there was a reference to that row in the Ledger table. My schema was enforcing data consistency. In our new world, no such enforcement exists. What are our options here?

Check before deletion

Our first option might be to ensure that when removing a record from the Albums table, we check with the Finance service to ensure that it doesn't already have a reference to the record. The problem here is that guaranteeing we can do this correctly is difficult. Say we want to delete SKU 683. We send a call to Finance saying, "Are you using 683?" It responds that this record is not used. We then delete the record, but while we are doing it, a new reference to 683 gets created in the Finance system. To stop this from happening, we'd need to stop new references being created on record 683 until the deletion has happened—something that would likely require locks, and all the challenges that implies in a distributed system.

Another issue with checking if the record is already in use is that creates a de facto reverse dependency from the Catalog service. Now we'd need to check with any other service that uses our records. This is bad enough if we have only one other service using our information, but becomes significantly worse as we have more consumers.

I strongly urge you not to consider this option, because of the difficulty in ensuring that this operation is implemented correctly as well as the high degree of service coupling that this introduces.

Handle deletion gracefully

A better option is just to have the Finance service handle the fact that the Catalog service may not have information on the Album in a graceful way. This could be as simple as having our report show "Album Information Not Available" if we can't look up a given SKU.

In this situation, the Catalog service could tell us when we request a SKU that used to exist. This would be the good use of a 410 GONE response code if using HTTP, for example. A 410 response code differs from the commonly used 404. A 404 denotes that the requested resource is not found, whereas a 410 means that the requested resource was available but isn't any longer. The distinction can be important, especially when tracking down data inconsistency issues! Even if not using an HTTP-based protocol, consider whether or not you'd benefit from supporting this sort of response.

If we wanted to get really advanced, we could ensure that our Finance service is informed when a Catalog item is removed, perhaps by subscribing to events. When we pick up a Catalog deletion event, we could decide to copy the now deleted Album information into our local database. This feels like overkill in this particular situation, but could be useful in other scenarios, especially if you wanted to implement a distributed state machine to perform something like a cascading deletion across service boundaries.

Don't allow deletion

One way to ensure that we don't introduce too much inconsistency into the system could be to simply not allow records in the Catalog service to be deleted. If in the existing system deleting an item was akin to ensuring it wasn't available for sale or something similar, we could just implement a soft delete capability. We could do this by using a status column to mark that row as being unavailable, or perhaps even moving the row into a dedicated "graveyard" table.[5] The album's record could still be requested by the Finance service in this situation.

So how should we handle deletion?

Basically, we have created a failure mode that couldn't exist in our monolithic system. In looking at ways to solve this, we must consider the needs of our users, as different solutions could impact our users in different ways. Choosing the right solution therefore requires an understanding of your specific context.

Personally, in this specific situation, I'd likely solve this in two ways: by not allowing deletion of album information in the Catalog, and by ensuring that the Finance service can handle a missing record. You could argue that if a record can't be removed from the Catalog service, the lookup from Finance could never fail. However, there is

---

5 Maintaining historical data in a relational database like this can get complicated, especially if you need to programmatically reconstitute old versions of your entities. If you have heavy requirements in this space, exploring event sourcing as an alternative way of maintaining state would be worthwhile.

a possibility that, as a result of corruption, the Catalog service may be recovered to an earlier state, meaning the record we are looking for no longer exists. In that situation, I wouldn't want the Finance service to fall over in a heap. It seems an unlikely set of circumstances, but I'm always looking to build in resiliency, and consider what happens if a call fails; handling this gracefully in the Finance service seems a pretty easy fix.

Where to Use It

When you start considering effectively breaking foreign-key relationships, one of the first things you need to ensure is that you aren't breaking apart two things that really want to be one. If you're worried that you are breaking apart an aggregate, pause and reconsider. In the case of the Ledger and Albums here, it seems clear we have two separate aggregates with a relationship between them. But consider a different case: an Order table, and lots of associated rows in an Order Line table containing details of the items we have ordered. If we split out order lines into a separate service, we'd have data integrity issues to consider. Really, the lines of an order are part of the order itself. We should therefore see them as a unit, and if we wanted to move them out of the monolith, they should be moved together.

Sometimes, by taking a bigger bite out of the monolithic schema, you may be able to move both sides of a foreign-key relationship with you, making your life much easier!

Example: Shared Static Data

Static reference data (which changes infrequently, yet is typically critical) can create some interesting challenges, and I've seen multiple approaches for managing it. More often than not, it finds its way into the database. I have seen perhaps as many country codes stored in databases (shown in Figure 4-39) as I have written my own `String Utils` classes for Java projects.

I've always questioned why small amounts of infrequently changing data like country codes need to exist in databases, but whatever the underlying reason, these examples of shared static data being stored in databases come up a lot. So what do we do in our music shop many parts of our code need the same static reference data? Well, it turns out we have a *lot* of options here.

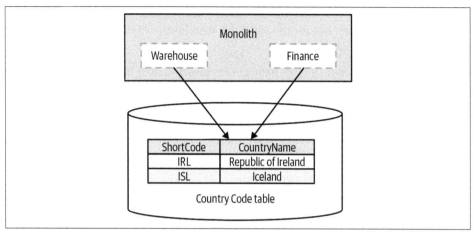

Figure 4-39. Country codes in the database

Pattern: duplicate static reference data

Why not just have each service have its own copy of the data, as in Figure 4-40? This is likely to elicit a sharp intake of breath from many of you. Duplicate data? Am I mad? Hear me out! It's less crazy than you'd think.

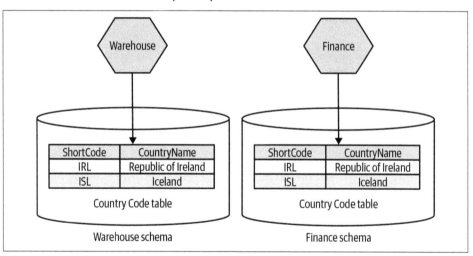

Figure 4-40. Each service has its own Country Code schema

Concerns around duplication of data tend to come down to two things. First, each time I need to change the data, I have to do so in multiple places. But in this situation, how often does the data change? The last time a country was created and officially recognized was in 2011, with the creation of South Sudan (the short code of which is SSD). So I don't think that's much of a concern, is it? The bigger worry is, what happens if the data is inconsistent? For example, the Finance service knows that South Sudan is a country, but inexplicably, the Warehouse service is living in the past and knows nothing about it.

Whether or not inconsistency is an issue comes down to how the data is used. In our example, consider that the Warehouse uses this country code data to record where our CDs are manufactured. It turns out that we don't stock any CDs that are made in South Sudan, so the fact that we're missing this data isn't an issue. On the other hand, the Finance service needs country code information to record information about sales, and we have customers in South Sudan, so we need that updated entry.

When the data is used only locally within each service, the inconsistency is not a problem. Think back to our definition of a bounded context: it's all about information being hidden within boundaries. If, on the other hand, the data is part of the communication between these services, then we have different concerns. If both Warehouse and Finance need the same view of country information, duplication of this nature is definitely something I'd worry about.

We could also consider keeping these copies in sync using some sort of background process, of course. In such a situation, we are unlikely to guarantee that all copies will be consistent, but assuming our background process runs frequently (and quickly) enough, then we can reduce the potential window of inconsistency in our data, and that might be good enough.

 As developers, we often react badly when we see duplication. We worry about the extra cost of managing duplicate copies of information, and are even more concerned if this data diverges. But sometimes duplication is the lesser of two evils. Accepting some duplication in data may be a sensible trade-off if it means we avoid introducing coupling.

Where to use it. This pattern should be used only rarely, and you should prefer some of the options we consider later. It is sometimes useful for large volumes of data, when it's not essential for all services to see the exact same set of data. Something like postal code files in the UK might be a good fit, where you periodically get updates of the mapping from postal codes to addresses. That's a fairly large dataset that would probably be painful to manage in a code form. If you want to join to this data directly, that may be another reason to select this option, but I'll be honest and say I can't remember ever doing it myself!

Pattern: Dedicated reference data schema

If you really want one source of truth for your country codes, you could relocate this data to a dedicated schema, perhaps one set aside for all static reference data, as we can see in Figure 4-41.

We do have to consider all the challenges of a shared database. To an extent, the concerns around coupling and change are somewhat offset by the nature of the data. It changes infrequently, and is simply structured, and therefore we could more easily consider this Reference Data schema to be a defined interface. In this situation, I'd manage the Reference Data schema as its own versioned entity, and ensure that people understood that the schema structure represents a service interface to consumers. Making breaking changes to this schema is likely to be painful.

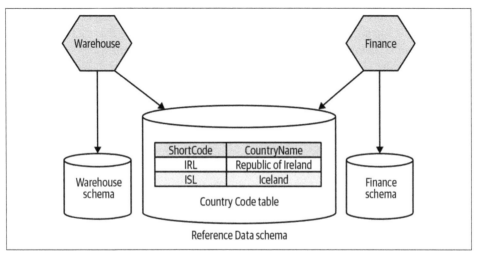

Figure 4-41. Using a dedicated shared schema for reference data

Having the data in a schema does open up the opportunity for services to still use this data as part of join queries on their own local data. For this to happen, though, you'd likely need to ensure that the schemas are located on the same underlying database engine. That adds a degree of complexity in terms of how you map from the logical to the physical world, quite aside from the potential single-point-of-failure concerns.

Where to use it.   This option has a lot of merits. We avoid the concerns around duplication, and the format of the data is highly unlikely to change, so some of our coupling concerns are mitigated. For large volumes of data, or when you want the option of cross-schema joins, it's a valid approach. Just remember, any changes to the schema format will likely cause significant impact across multiple services.

Pattern: Static reference data library

When you get down to it, there aren't many entries in our country code data. Assuming we're using the ISO standard listing, we're looking at only 249 countries being represented.[6] This would fit nicely in code, perhaps as a simple static enumerated type. In fact, storing small volumes of static reference data in code form is something that I've done a number of times, and something I've seen done for microservice architectures.

Of course, we'd rather not duplicate this data if we don't have to, so this leads us to consider placing this data into a library that can be statically linked by any services that want this data. Stitch Fix, a US-based fashion retailer, makes frequent use of shared libraries like this to store static reference data.

Randy Shoup, who was VP of engineering at Stitch Fix said the sweet spot for this technique was for types of data that were small in volume and that changed infrequently or not at all (and if it did change, you had a lot of up-front warning about the change). Consider classic clothes sizing—XS, S, M, L, XL for general sizes, or inseam measurements for trousers.

In our case, we define our country code mappings in a Country enumerated type, and bundle this into a library for use in our services, as shown in Figure 4-42.

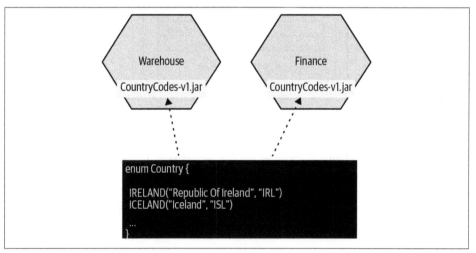

Figure 4-42. Store reference data in a library that can be shared between services

This is a neat solution, but it's not without drawbacks. Obviously, if we have a mix of technology stacks, we may not be able to share a single shared library. Also,

---

6 That's ISO 3166-1 for all you ISO fans out there!

remember the golden rule of microservices? We need to ensure that our microservices are independently deployable. If we needed to update our country codes library, and have all services pick up the new data immediately, we'd need to redeploy all services at the moment the new library is available. This is a classic lock-step release, and exactly what we're trying to avoid with microservice architectures.

In practice, if we need the same data to be available everywhere, then sufficient notice of the change may help. An example Randy gave was the need to add a new color to one of Stitch Fix's datasets. This change needed to be rolled out to all services that made use of this datatype, but they had significant lead time to make sure all the teams pulled in the latest version. If you consider the country codes example, again we'd likely have a lot of advanced notice if a new country needed to be added. For example, South Sudan became an independent state in July 2011 after a referendum six months earlier, giving us a lot of time to roll out our change. New countries are rarely created on a whim!

 If your microservices use shared libraries, remember that you have to accept that you might have different versions of the library deployed in production!

This means that if we need to update our country codes library, we would need to accept that not all microservices can be guaranteed to have the same version of the library, as we see in Figure 4-43. If this doesn't work for you, perhaps the next option may help.

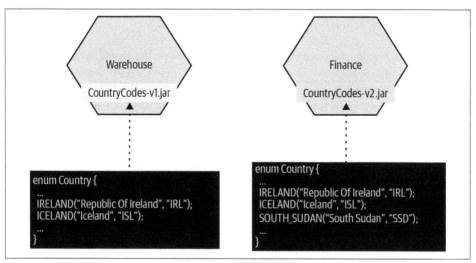

Figure 4-43. Differences between shared reference data libraries may cause issues

In a simple variation of this pattern, the data in question is held in a configuration file, perhaps a standard properties file or, if required, in a more structured JSON format.

Where to use it.   For small volumes of data, where you can be relaxed about different services seeing different versions of this data, this is an excellent but often overlooked option. The visibility regarding which service has what version of data is especially useful.

Pattern: Static reference data service

I suspect you can see where this is ending up. This is a book about creating microservices, so why not consider creating a dedicated service just for country codes, as in Figure 4-44?

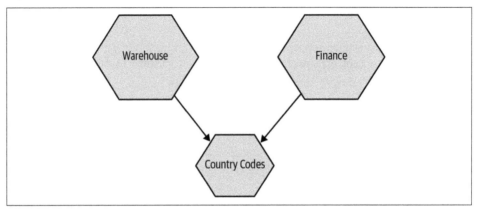

Figure 4-44. Serving country codes from a dedicated service

I've run through this exact scenario with groups all over the world, and it tends to divide the room. Some people immediately think, "That could work!" Typically, though, a larger portion of the group will start shaking their heads and saying something along the lines of, "That looks crazy!" When digging deeper, we get to the heart of their concern; this seems like a lot of work and potential added complexity for not much benefit. The word "overkill" comes up frequently!

So let's explore this a bit further. When I chat to people and try to understand why some people are fine with this idea, and others are not, it typically comes down to a couple of things. People who work in an environment where creating and managing a microservice is low are much more likely to consider this option. If, on the other hand, creating a new service, even one as simple as this, requires days or even weeks of work, then people will understandably push back on creating a service like this.

Ex-colleague and fellow O'Reilly author Kief Morris[7] told me about his experiences at a project for a large international bank based in the UK, where it took nearly a year to get approval for the first release of some software. Over 10 teams inside the bank had to be consulted first before anything could go live—everything from getting designs signed off, to getting machines provisioned for deployment. Such experiences are far from uncommon in larger organizations, unfortunately.

In organizations where deploying new software requires lots of manual work, approvals, and perhaps even the need to procure and configure new hardware, the inherent cost of creating services is significant. In such an environment, I would therefore need to be highly selective in creating new services; they'd have to be delivering a lot of value to justify the extra work. This may make the creation of something like the country code unjustifiable. If, on the other hand, I could spin up a service template and push it to production in the space of a day or less, and have everything done for me, then I'd be much more likely to consider this as a viable option.

Even better, a Country Code service would be a great fit for something like a Function-as-a-Service platform like Azure Cloud Functions or AWS Lambda. The lower operations cost for functions is attractive, and they're a great fit for simple services like the Country Code service.

Another concern cited is that by adding a service for country codes, we'd be adding yet another networked dependency that could impact latency. I think that this approach is no worse, and may be faster, than having a dedicated database for this information. Why? Well, as we've already established, there are only 249 entries in this dataset. Our Country Code service could easily hold this in memory and serve it up directly. Our Country Code service would likely just store these records in code, no baking datastore needed.

This data can, of course, also be aggressively cached at the client side. We don't add new entries to this data often, after all! We could also consider using events to let consumers know when this data has changed, as shown in Figure 4-45. When the data changes, interested consumers can be alerted via events and use this to update their local caches. I suspect that a traditional TTL-based client cache is likely to be good enough in this scenario, given the low change frequency, but I have used a similar approach for a general-purpose Reference Data service many years ago to great effect.

---

7 Kief wrote *Infrastructure as Code: Managing Servers in the Cloud* (Sebastopol: O'Reilly, 2016).

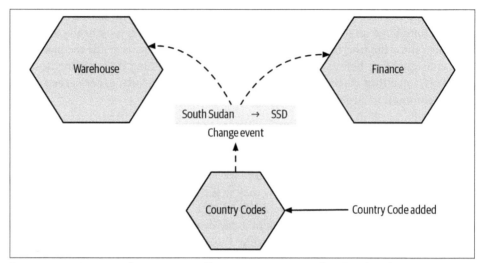

Figure 4-45. Firing update events to allow consumers to update local caches

Where to use it. I'd reach for this option if I was managing the life cycle of this data itself in code. For example, if I wanted to expose an API to update this data, I'd need somewhere for that code to live, and putting that in a dedicated microservice makes sense. At that point, we have a microservice encompassing the state machine for this state. This also makes sense if you want to emit events when this data changes, or just where you want to provide a more convenient contact against which to stub for testing purposes.

The major issue here always seems to come down to the cost of creating yet another microservice. Does it add enough to justify the work, or would one of these other approaches be a more sensible option?

What would I do?

OK, again I've given you lots of options. So what would I do? I suppose I can't sit on the fence forever, so here goes. If we assume that we don't need to ensure that the country codes are consistent across all services at all times, then I'd likely keep this information in a shared library. For this sort of data, it seems to make much more sense than duplicating this data in local service schemas; the data is simple in nature, and small in volume (country codes, dress sizes, and the like). For more complex reference data or for larger volumes, this might tip me toward putting this into the local database for each service.

If the data needs to be consistent between services, I'd look to create a dedicated service (or perhaps serve up this data as part of a larger-scoped static reference service).

I'd likely resort to having a dedicated schema for this sort of data only if it was diffi-cult to justify the work to create a new service.

 What we have covered in the preceding examples are a few data-base refactorings that can help you separate your schemas. For a more detailed discussion of the subject, you may want to take a look at *Refactoring Databases* by Scott J. Ambler and Pramod J. Sadalage (Addison-Wesley).

Transactions

When breaking apart our databases, we've already touched on some of the problems that can result. Maintaining referential integrity becomes problematic, latency can increase, and we can make activities like reporting more complex. We've looked at various coping patterns for some of these challenges, but one big one remains: what about transactions?

The ability to make changes to our database in a transaction can make our systems much easier to reason about, and therefore easier to develop and maintain. We rely on our database ensuring the safety and consistency of our data, leaving us to worry about other things. But when we split data across databases, we lose the benefit of using a database transaction to apply changes in state in an atomic fashion.

Before we explore how to tackle this issue, let's look briefly at what a normal database transaction gives us.

ACID Transactions

Typically, when we talk about database transactions, we are talking about ACID transactions. ACID is an acronym outlining the key properties of database transac-tions that lead to a system we can rely on to ensure the durability and consistency of our data storage. *ACID* stands for *atomicity, consistency, isolation, and durability*, and here is what these properties give us:

Atomicity
Ensures that all operations completed within the transaction either all complete or all fail. If any of the changes we're trying to make fail for some reason, then the whole operation is aborted, and it's as though no changes were ever made.

Consistency
When changes are made to our database, we ensure it is left in a valid, consistent state.

Isolation
> Allows multiple transactions to operate at the same time without interfering. This is achieved by ensuring that any interim state changes made during one transaction are invisible to other transactions.

Durability
> Makes sure that once a transaction has been completed, we are confident the data won't get lost in the event of some system failure.

It's worth noting that not all databases provide ACID transactions. All relational database systems I've ever used do, as do many of the newer NoSQL databases like Neo4j. MongoDB for many years supported ACID transactions around only a single document, which could cause issues if you wanted to make an atomic update to more than one document.[8]

This isn't the book for a detailed, deep dive into these concepts; I've certainly simplified some of these descriptions for the sake of brevity. For those of you who would like to explore these concepts further, I recommend *Designing Data-Intensive Applications*.[9] We'll mostly concern ourselves with atomicity in what follows. That's not to say that the other properties aren't also important, but that atomicity tends to be the first issue we hit when splitting apart transactional boundaries.

Still ACID, but Lacking Atomicity?

I want to be clear that we can still use ACID-style transactions when we split databases apart, but the scope of these transactions is reduced, as is their usefulness. Consider Figure 4-46. We are keeping track of the process involved in onboarding a new customer to our system. We've reached the end of the process, which involves changing the Status of the customer from PENDING to VERIFIED. As the enrollment is now complete, we also want to remove the matching row from the PendingEnrollments table. With a single database, this is done in the scope of a single ACID database transaction—either both the new rows are written, or neither are written.

Compare this with Figure 4-47. We're making exactly the same change, but now each change is made in a different database. This means there are two transactions to consider, each of which could work or fail independently of the other.

---

8 This has now changed with support for multidocument ACID transactions, which was released as part of Mongo 4.0. I haven't used this feature of Mongo myself; I just know it exists!

9 See Martin Kleppmann, *Designing Data-Intensive Applications* (Sebastopol, O'Reilly Media, Inc., 2017).

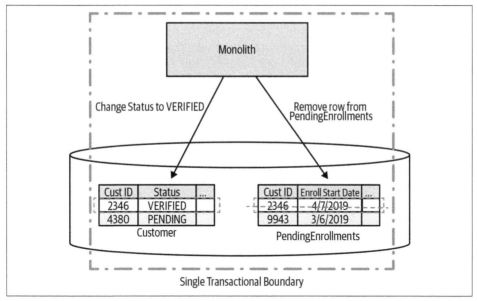

Figure 4-46. Updating two tables in the scope of a single ACID transaction

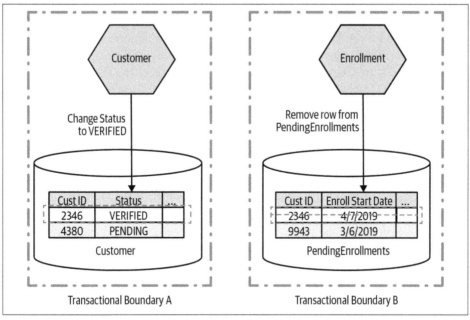

Figure 4-47. Changes made to both Invoice and Order are now done in the scope of two different transactions

We could decide to sequence these two transactions, of course, removing a row from the PendingEnrollments table only if we were able to change the row in the Customer table. But we'd still have to reason about what to do if the deletion from the PendingEnrollments table then failed—all logic that we'd need to implement ourselves. Being able to reorder steps to make handling these use cases can be a really useful idea, though (one we'll come back to when we explore sagas). But fundamentally by decomposing this operation into two separate database transactions, we have to accept that we've lost guaranteed atomicity of the operation as a whole.

This lack of atomicity can start to cause significant problems, especially if we are migrating systems that previously relied on this property. It's at this point that people start to look for other solutions to give them some ability to reason about changes being made to multiple services at once. Normally, the first option that people start considering is distributed transactions. Let's look at one of the most common algorithms for implementing distributed transactions, the two-phase commit, as a way of exploring the challenges associated with distributed transactions as a whole.

Two-Phase Commits

The *two-phase commit algorithm* (sometimes shortened to *2PC*) is frequently used to attempt to give us the ability to make transactional changes in a distributed system, where multiple separate processes may need to be updated as part of the overall operation. I want to let you know up front that 2PCs have limitations, which we'll cover, but they're worth knowing about. Distributed transactions, and two-phased commits more specifically, are frequently raised by teams moving to microservice architectures as a way of solving challenges they face. But as we'll see, they may not solve your problems, and may bring even more confusion to your system.

The algorithm is broken into two phases (hence the name *two-phase commit*): a voting phase and a commit phase. During the *voting phase*, a central coordinator contacts all the workers who are going to be part of the transaction, and asks for confirmation as to whether or not some state change can be made. In Figure 4-48, we see two requests, one to change a customer status to VERIFIED, another to remove a row from our PendingEnrollments table. If all the workers agree that the state change they are asked for can take place, the algorithm proceeds to the next phase. If any workers say the change cannot take place, perhaps because the requested state change violates some local condition, the entire operation aborts.

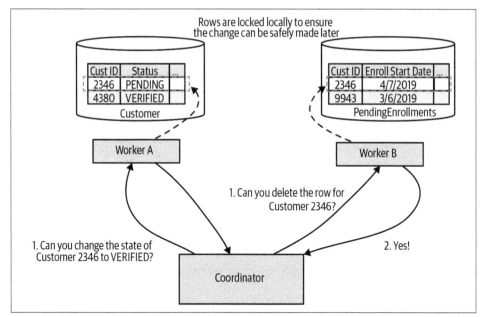

Figure 4-48. In the first phase of a two-phase commit, workers vote to decide if they can carry out some local state change

It's important to highlight that the change does not take effect immediately after a worker indicates that it can make the change. Instead, the worker is guaranteeing that it will be able to make that change at some point in the future. How would the worker make such a guarantee? In Figure 4-48, for example, Worker A has said it will be able to change the state of the row in the Customer table to update that specific customer's status to be VERIFIED. What if a different operation at some later point deletes the row, or makes another smaller change that nonetheless means that a change to VERIFIED later is invalid? To guarantee that this change can be made later, Worker A will likely have to lock that record to ensure that such a change cannot take place.

If any workers didn't vote in factor of the commit, a rollback message needs to be sent to all parties, to ensure that they can clean up locally, which allows the workers to release any locks they may be holding. If all workers agreed to make the change, we move to the commit phase, as in Figure 4-49. Here, the changes are actually made, and associated locks are released.

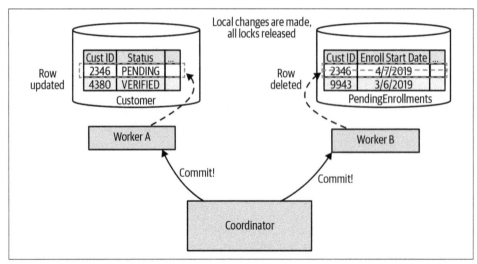

Figure 4-49. In the commit phase of a two-phase commit, changes are actually applied

It's important to note that in such a system, we cannot in any way guarantee that these commits will occur at exactly the same time. The coordinator needs to send the commit request to all participants, and that message could arrive at and be processed at different times. This means it's possible that we could see the change made to Worker A, but not yet see the change to Worker B, if we allow for you to view the states of these workers outside the transaction coordinator. The more latency there is between the coordinator, and the slower it is for the workers to process the response, the wider this window of inconsistency might be. Coming back to our definition of ACID, isolation ensures that we don't see intermediate states during a transaction. But with this two-phase commit, we've lost that.

When two-phase commits work, at their heart they are very often just coordinating distributed locks. The workers need to lock local resources to ensure that the commit can take place during the second phase. Managing locks, and avoiding deadlocks in a single-process system, isn't fun. Now imagine the challenges of coordinating locks among multiple participants. It's not pretty.

There are a host of failure modes associated with two-phase commits that we don't have time to explore. Consider the problem of a worker voting to proceed with the transaction, but then not responding when asked to commit. What should we do then? Some of these failure modes can be handled automatically, but some can leave the system in such a state that things need to be manually unpicked.

The more participants you have, and the more latency you have in the system, the more issues a two-phase commit will have. They can be a quick way to inject huge amounts of latency into your system, especially if the scope of locking is large, or the duration of the transaction is large. It's for this reason two-phase commits are typically used only for very short-lived operations. The longer the operation takes, the longer you've got resources locked for!

Distributed Transactions—Just Say No

For all these reasons outlined so far, I strongly suggest you avoid the use of distributed transactions like the two-phase commit to coordinate changes in state across your microservices. So what else can you do?

Well, the first option could be to just not split the data apart in the first place. If you have pieces of state that you want to manage in a truly atomic and consistent way, and you cannot work out how to sensibly get these characteristics without an ACID-style transaction, then leave that state in a single database, and leave the functionality that manages that state in a single service (or in your monolith). If you're in the process of working out where to split your monolith, and working out what decompositions might be easy (or hard), then you could well decide that splitting apart data that is currently managed in a transaction is just too hard to handle right now. Work on some other area of the system, and come back to this later.

But what happens if you really do need to break this data apart, but you don't want all the pain of managing distributed transactions? How can we carry out operations in multiple services but avoid locking? What if the operation is going to take minutes, days, or perhaps even months? In cases like this, we can consider an alternative approach: sagas.

Sagas

Unlike a two-phase commit, a *saga* is by design an algorithm that can coordinate multiple changes in state, but avoids the need for locking resources for long periods of time. We do this by modeling the steps involved as discrete activities that can be executed independently. It comes with the added benefit of forcing us to explicitly model our business processes, which can have significant benefits.

The core idea, first outlined by Hector Garcia-Molina and Kenneth Salem,[10] reflected on the challenges of how best to handle operations of what they referred to as *long lived transactions* (LLTs). These transactions might take a long time (minutes, hours, or perhaps even days), and as part of that process require changes to be made to a database.

If you directly mapped an LLT to a normal database transaction, a single database transaction would span the entire life cycle of the LLT. This could result in multiple rows or even full tables being locked for long periods of time while the LLT is taking

---

10 See Hector Garcia-Molina and Kenneth Salem, "Sagas," in *ACM Sigmod Record* 16, no. 3 (1987): 249–259.

place, causing significant issues if other processes are trying to read or modify these locked resources.

Instead, the authors of the paper suggest we should break down these LLTs into a sequence of transactions, each of which can be handled independently. The idea is that the duration of each of these "sub" transactions will be shorter lived, and will modify only part of the data affected by the entire LLT. As a result, there will be far less contention in the underlying database as the scope and duration of locks is greatly reduced.

While sagas were originally envisaged as a mechanism to help with LLTs acting against a single database, the model works just as well for coordinating change across multiple services. We can break a single business process into a set of calls that will be made to collaborating services as part of a single saga.

 Before we go any further, you need to understand that a saga does *not* give us atomicity in ACID terms we are used to with a normal database transaction. As we break the LLT into individual transactions, we don't have atomicity at the level of the saga itself. We do have atomicity for each subtransaction inside the LLT, as each one of them can relate to an ACID transactional change if needed. What a saga gives us is enough information to reason about which state it's in; it's up to us to handle the implications of this.

Let's take a look at a simple order fulfillment flow, outlined in Figure 4-50, which we can use to further explore sagas in the context of a microservice architecture.

Here, the order fulfillment process is represented as a single saga, with each step in this flow representing an operation that can be carried out by a different service. Within each service, any state change can be handled within a local ACID transaction. For example, when we check and reserve stock using the Warehouse service, internally the Warehouse service might create a row in its local Reservation table recording the reservation; this change would be handled within a normal transaction.

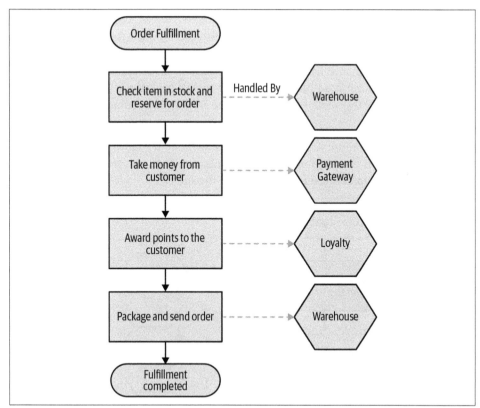

Figure 4-50. An example order fulfillment flow, along with the services responsible for carrying out the operation

Saga Failure Modes

With a saga being broken into individual transactions, we need to consider how to handle failure—or, more specifically, how to recover when a failure happens. The original saga paper describes two types of recovery: backward recovery and forward recovery.

Backward recovery involves reverting the failure, and cleaning up afterwards—a rollback. For this to work, we need to define compensating actions that allow us to undo previously committed transactions. *Forward recovery* allows us to pick up from the point where the failure occurred, and keep processing. For that to work, we need to be able to retry transactions, which in turn implies that our system is persisting enough information to allow this retry to take place.

Depending on the nature of the business process being modeled, you may consider that any failure mode triggers a backward recovery, a forward recovery, or perhaps a mix of the two.

Saga rollbacks

With an ACID transaction, a rollback occurs before a commit. After the rollback, it is like nothing ever happened: the change we were trying to make didn't take place. With our saga, though, we have multiple transactions involved, and some of those may have already committed before we decide to roll back the entire operation. So how can we roll back transactions after they have already been committed?

Let's come back to our example of processing an order, as outlined in Figure 4-50. Consider a potential failure mode. We've gotten as far as trying to package the item, only to find the item can't be found in the warehouse, as shown in Figure 4-51. Our system thinks the item exists, but it's just not on the shelf!

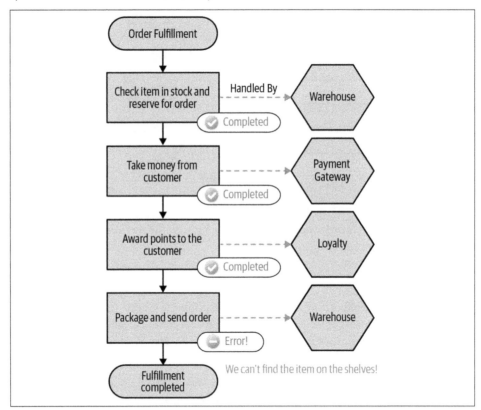

Figure 4-51. We've tried to package our item, but we can't find it in the warehouse

Now, let's assume we decide we want to just roll back the entire order, rather than giving the customer the option for the item to be placed on back order. The problem is that we've already taken payment and awarded loyalty points for the order.

If all of these steps had been done in a single database transaction, a simple rollback would clean this all up. However, each step in the order fulfillment process was handled by a different service call, each of which operated in a different transactional scope. There is no simple "rollback" for the entire operation.

Instead, if you want to implement a rollback, you need to implement a compensating transaction. A *compensating transaction* is an operation that undoes a previously committed transaction. To roll back our order fulfillment process, we would trigger the compensating transaction for each step in our saga that has already been committed, as shown in Figure 4-52.

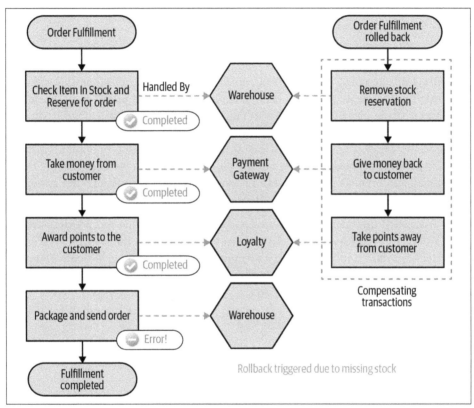

Figure 4-52. Triggering a rollback of the entire saga

It's worth calling out the fact that these compensating transactions can't have exactly the same behavior as that of a normal database rollback. A database rollback happens before the commit; and after the rollback, it is as though the transaction never happened. In this situation, of course, these transactions *did* happen. We are creating a new transaction that reverts the changes made by the original transaction, but we can't roll back time and make it as though the original transaction didn't occur.

Because we cannot always cleanly revert a transaction, we say that these compensating transactions are *semantic rollbacks*. We cannot always clean up everything, but we do enough for the context of our saga. As an example, one of our steps may have involved sending an email to a customer to tell them their order was on the way. If we decide to roll that back, you can't unsend an email![11] Instead, your compensating transaction could cause a second email to be sent to the customer, informing them that there had been a problem with the order and it had been canceled.

It is totally appropriate for information related to the rollback saga to persist in the system. In fact, this may be very important information. You may want to keep a record in the Order service for this aborted order, along with information about what happened, for a whole host of reasons.

Reordering steps to reduce rollbacks

In Figure 4-52, we could have made our likely rollback scenarios somewhat simpler by reordering the steps. A simple change would be to award points only when the order was actually dispatched, as seen in Figure 4-53. This way, we'd avoid having to worry about that stage being rolled back if we had a problem while trying to package and send the order. Sometimes you can simplify your rollback operations just by tweaking how the process is carried out. By pulling forward those steps that are most likely to fail and failing the process earlier, you avoid having to trigger later compensating transactions as those steps weren't even triggered in the first place.

These changes, if they can be accommodated, can make your life much easier, avoiding the need to even create compensating transactions for some steps. This can be especially important if implementing a compensating transaction is difficult. You may be able to move the step later in the process to a stage where it never needs to be rolled back.

Mixing fail-backward and fail-forward situations

It is totally appropriate to have a mix of failure recovery modes. Some failures may require a rollback; others may be fail forward. For the order processing, for example, once we've taken money from the customer, and the item has been packaged, the only step left is to dispatch the package. If for whatever reason we can't dispatch the package (perhaps the delivery firm we have doesn't have space in their vans to take an order today), it seems very odd to roll the whole order back. Instead, we'd probably just retry the dispatch, and if that fails, require human intervention to resolve the situation.

---

11 You really can't. I've tried!

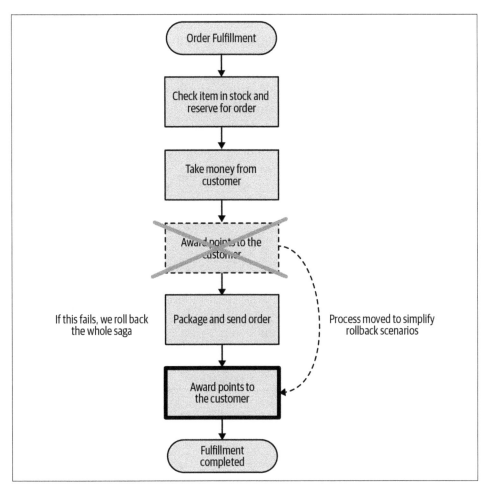

Figure 4-53. Moving steps later in the saga can reduce what has to be rolled back in case of a failure

Implementing Sagas

So far, we've looked at the logical model for how sagas work, but we need to go a bit deeper to examine ways of implementing the saga itself. We can look at two styles of saga implementation. *Orchestrated sagas* more closely follow the original solution space and rely primarily on centralized coordination and tracking. These can be compared to *choreographed sagas*, which avoid the need for centralized coordination in favor of a more loosely coupled model, but which can make tracking the progress of a saga more complicated.

Orchestrated sagas

Orchestrated sagas use a central coordinator (what we'll call an *orchestrator* from now on) to define the order of execution and to trigger any required compensating action. You can think of orchestrated sagas as a command-and-control approach: the central orchestrator controls what happens and when, and with that comes a good degree of visibility as to what is happening with any given saga.

Taking the order fulfillment process shown in Figure 4-50, let's see how this central coordination process would work as a set of collaborating services, as in Figure 4-54.

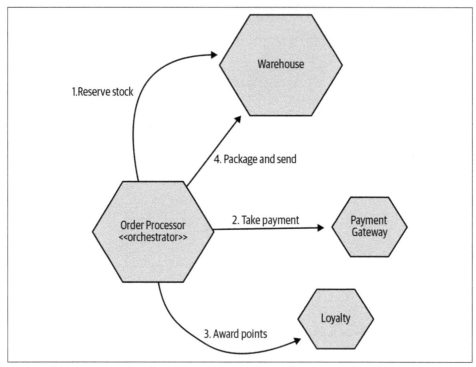

Figure 4-54. An example of how an orchestrated saga may be used to implement our order-fulfillment process

Here, our central Order Processor, playing the role of the orchestrator, coordinates our fulfillment process. It knows what services are needed to carry out the operation, and it decides when to make calls to those services. If the calls fail, it can decide what to do as a result. These orchestrated processors tend to make heavy use of request/response calls between services: the Order Processor sends a request to services (such as a Payment Gateway), and expects a response letting it know if the request was successful and providing the results of the request.

Having our business process explicitly modeled inside the Order Processor is extremely beneficial. It allows us to look at one place in our system and understand how this process is supposed to work. That can make onboarding of new people easier, and help impart a better understanding of the core parts of the system.

There are a few downsides to consider, though. First, by its nature, this is a somewhat coupled approach. Our Order Processor needs to know about all the associated services, resulting in a higher degree of what we discussed in Chapter 1 as domain coupling. While not inherently bad, we'd still like to keep domain coupling to a minimum if possible. Here, our Order Processor needs to know about and control so many things that this form of coupling is hard to avoid.

The other issue, which is more subtle, is that logic that should otherwise be pushed into the services can start to instead become absorbed in the orchestrator. If this starts happening, you may find your services becoming anemic, with little behavior of their own, just taking orders from orchestrators like the Order Processor. It's important you still consider the services that make up these orchestrated flows as entities that have their own local state and behavior. They are in charge of their own local state machines.

 If logic has a place where it can be centralized, it will become centralized!

One of the ways to avoid too much centralization with orchestrated flows can be to ensure you have different services playing the role of the orchestrator for different flows. You might have an Order Processor service that handles placing an order, a Returns service to handle the return and refund process, a Goods Receiving service that handles new stock arriving at the warehouse and being put on the shelves, and so on. Something like our Warehouse service may be used by all those orchestrators; such a model makes it easier for you to keep functionality in the Warehouse service itself to allow you to reuse functionality across all those flows.

BPM Tools?

Business process modeling (BPM) tools have been available for many years. By and large, they are designed to allow nondevelopers to define business process flows, often using visual drag-and-drop tools. The idea is developers would create the building blocks of these processes, and then nondevelopers would wire these building blocks together into the larger process flows. The use of such tools seems to line up really nicely as a way of implementing orchestrated sagas, and indeed process orchestration is pretty much the main use case for BPM tools (or, in reverse, the use of BPM tools results in you having to adopt orchestration).

In my experience, I've come to greatly dislike BPM tools. The main reason is that the central conceit—that nondevelopers will define the business process—has in my experience almost never been true. The tooling aimed at nondevelopers ends up getting used *by* developers, and they can have a host of issues. They often require the use of GUIs to change the flows, the flows they create may be difficult (or impossible) to version control, the flows themselves may not be designed with testing in mind, and more.

If your developers are going to be implementing your business processes, let them use tooling that they know and understand and is fit for their workflows. In general, this means just letting them use code to implement these things! If you need visibility as to how a business process has been implemented, or how it is operating, then it is far easier to project a visual representation of a workflow from code than it is to use a visual representation of your workflow to describe how your code should work.

There are efforts to create more developer-friendly BPM tools. Feedback on these tools from developers seems to be mixed, but they have worked well for some, and it's good to see people trying to improve on these frameworks. If you feel the need to explore these tools further, do take a look at Camunda (*https://camunda.com/*) and Zeebe (*https://zeebe.io*), both of which are open source orchestration frameworks targeting microservice developers.

Choreographed sagas

Choreographed sagas aim to distribute responsibility for the operation of the saga among multiple collaborating services. If orchestration is command-and-control, choreographed sagas represent a trust-but-verify architecture. As we'll see in our example in Figure 4-55, choreographed sagas will often make heavy use of events for collaboration between services.

There's quite a bit going on here, so it's worth exploring in more detail. First, these services are reacting to events being received. Conceptually, events are broadcast in the system, and interested parties are able to receive them. You don't send events *to* a service; you just fire them out, and the services that are interested in these events are able to receive them and act accordingly. In our example, when the Warehouse service receives that first Order Placed event, it knows its job to reserve the appropriate stock and fire an event once that is done. If the stock couldn't be received, the Warehouse would need to raise an appropriate event (an Insufficient Stock event perhaps), which might lead to the order being aborted.

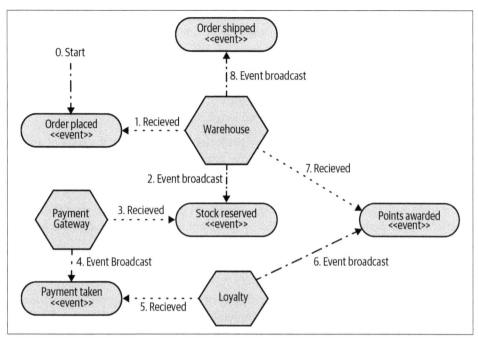

Figure 4-55. An example of a choreographed saga for implementing order fulfillment

Typically, you'd use some sort of message broker to manage the reliable broadcast and delivery of events. It's possible that multiple services may react to the same event, and that is where you would use a topic. Parties interested in a certain type of event would subscribe to a specific topic without having to worry about where these events came from, and the broker ensures the durability of the topic and that the events on it are successfully delivered to subscribers. As an example, we might have a Recommendation service that also listens to Order Placed events and uses that to construct a database of music choices you might like.

In the preceding architecture, no one service knows about any other service. They only need to know what to do when a certain event is received. Inherently, this makes for a much less coupled architecture. As the implementation of the process is decomposed and distributed among the four services here, we also avoid the concerns about centralization of logic (if you don't have a place where logic can be centralized, then it won't be centralized!).

The flip side of this is that it can now be harder to work out what is going on. With orchestration, our process was explicitly modeled in our orchestrator. Now, with this architecture as it is presented, how would you build up a mental model of what the process is supposed to be? You'd have to look at the behavior of each service in isolation and reconstitute this picture in your own head—far from a straightforward process even with a simple business process like this one.

The lack of an explicit representation of our business process is bad enough, but we also lack a way of knowing what state a saga is in, which can also deny us the chance to attach compensating actions when required. We can push some responsibility to the individual services for carrying out compensating actions, but fundamentally we need a way of knowing what state a saga is in for some kinds of recovery. The lack of a central place to interrogate around the status of a saga is a big problem. We get that with orchestration, so how do we solve that here?

One of the easiest ways of doing this is to project a view regarding the state of a saga from the existing system by consuming the events being emitted. If we generate a unique ID for the saga, we can put this into all of the events that are emitted as part of this saga-this is what is known as a *correlation ID*. We could then have a service whose job it is to just vacuum up all these events and present a view of what state each order is in, and perhaps programmatically carry out actions to resolve issues as part of the fulfillment process if the other services couldn't do it themselves.

Mixing styles

While it may seem that orchestrated and choreographed sagas are diametrically opposing views on how sagas could be implemented, you could easily consider mixing and matching models. You may have some business processes in your system that more naturally fit one model or another. You may also have a single saga that has a mix of styles. In the order fulfillment use case, for example, inside the boundary of the Warehouse service, when managing the packaging and dispatch of a package, we may use an orchestrated flow even if the original request was made as part of a larger choreographed saga.[12]

If you do decide to mix styles, it's important that you still have a clear way to understand what has happened as part of the saga. Without this, understanding failure modes becomes complex, and recovery from failure difficult.

Should I use choreography or orchestration?

Implementing choreographed sagas can bring with it ideas that may be unfamiliar to you and your team. They typically assume heavy use of event-driven collaboration, which isn't widely understood. However, in my experience, the extra complexity associated with tracking the progress of a saga is almost always outweighed by the benefits associated with having a more loosely coupled architecture.

---

12 It's outside the scope of this book, but Hector Garcia-Molina and Kenneth Salem went on to explore how multiple sagas could be "nested" to implement more complex processes. To read more on this topic, see Hector Garcia-Molina et al, "Modeling Long-Running Activities as Nested Sagas," *Data Engineering* 14, no. 1 (March 1991: 14–18.

Stepping aside from my own personal tastes, though, the general advice I give regarding orchestration versus choreography is that I am very relaxed in the use of orchestrated sagas when one team owns implementation of the entire saga. In such a situation, the more inherently coupled architecture is much easier to manage within the team boundary. If you have multiple teams involved, I greatly prefer the more decomposed choreographed saga as it is easier to distribute responsibility for implementing the saga to the teams, with the more loosely coupled architecture allowing these teams to work more in isolation.

Sagas Versus Distributed Transactions

As I hope I have broken down by now, distributed transactions come with some significant challenges, and outside of some very specific situations are something I tend to avoid. Pat Helland, a pioneer in distributed systems, distills the fundamental challenges with implementing distributed transactions for the kinds of applications we build today:[13]

> In most distributed transaction systems, the failure of a single node causes transaction commit to stall. This in turn causes the application to get wedged. In such systems, the larger it gets, the more likely the system is going to be down. When flying an airplane that needs all of its engines to work, adding an engine reduces the availability of the airplane.
>
> —Pat Helland, *Life Beyond Distributed Transactions*

In my experience, explicitly modeling business processes as a saga avoids many of the challenges of distributed transactions, while at the same time has the added benefit of making what might otherwise be implicitly modeled processes much more explicit and obvious to your developers. Making the core business processes of your system a first-class concept will have a host of benefits.

A fuller discussion of implementing orchestration and choreography, along with the various implementation details, is outside the scope of this book. It is covered in Chapter 4 of *Building Microservices*, but I also recommend *Enterprise Integration Patterns* for a deep dive into many aspects of this topic.[14]

---

13 See Pat Helland, "Life Beyond Distributed Transactions," *acmqueue* 14, no. 5.

14 Sagas are not mentioned explicitly in either book, but orchestration and choreography are both covered. While I can't speak to the experience of the authors of *Enterprise Integration Patterns*, I personally was unaware of sagas when I wrote *Building Microservices*.

Summary

We decompose our system by finding seams along which service boundaries can emerge, and this can be an incremental approach. By getting good at finding these seams and working to reduce the cost of splitting out services in the first place, we can continue to grow and evolve our systems to meet whatever requirements come down the road. As you can see, some of this work can be painstaking, and it can cause significant issues that we will need to address. But the fact that it can be done incrementally means there is no need to fear this work.

In splitting our services, we've introduced some new problems too. In our next chapter, we'll take a look at the various challenges that will emerge as you break down your monolith. But don't worry, I'll also give you a host of ideas to help you deal with these problems as they arise.

CHAPTER 5

Growing Pains

As you adopt a microservice architecture, you'll experience challenges along the way. We've looked at some of these problems in passing already, but I want to explore them further to help give you some forewarning.

What I'm hoping to do with this chapter is give you just enough information about the sorts of issues you may face. I can't solve them all in this book, and many of the problems I outline here already have a more detailed treatment in *Building Microservices*, which was very much written with these challenges in mind.

I also want to give you some signs to look for to help you spot when these issues may need addressing, as well as an indication of where along your journey these issues are most likely to arise.

More Services, More Pain

When exactly problems will occur with a microservice architecture is related to a multitude of factors. The complexity of service interactions, size of the organization, number of services, technology choices, latency, and uptime requirements are just a subset of the forces that can bring forth pain, suffering, excitement, and stress. This means it's difficult to say when, or indeed if, you'll actually encounter these issues.

In general, though, I've realized that the sorts of problems that arise in a company with ten services tend to be quite different from the ones seen at a company with hundreds of services. The number of services seems to be as good a measure as any for indicating when certain issues are most likely to manifest themselves. I should note here that when I talk about the number of services, unless otherwise specified I'm taking about different logical services. When those services are deployed into production, they may then be deployed as multiple service instances.

Don't think of adopting microservices as flipping a switch; think about it as turning a dial. As you turn that dial, and have more services, you'll hopefully have more opportunity to get the good stuff out of microservices. But as you turn up that dial, you'll hit different pain points as you go. As you do, you'll need to find ways to resolve these problems that might require new ways of thinking, new skills, different techniques, or perhaps new technology.

Figure 5-1 roughly maps the pain points we'll cover in the rest of this chapter based on where in your service growth these issues are most likely to arise. This is deeply unscientific, and based heavily on anecdotal experience, but I still think it's useful as an overview.

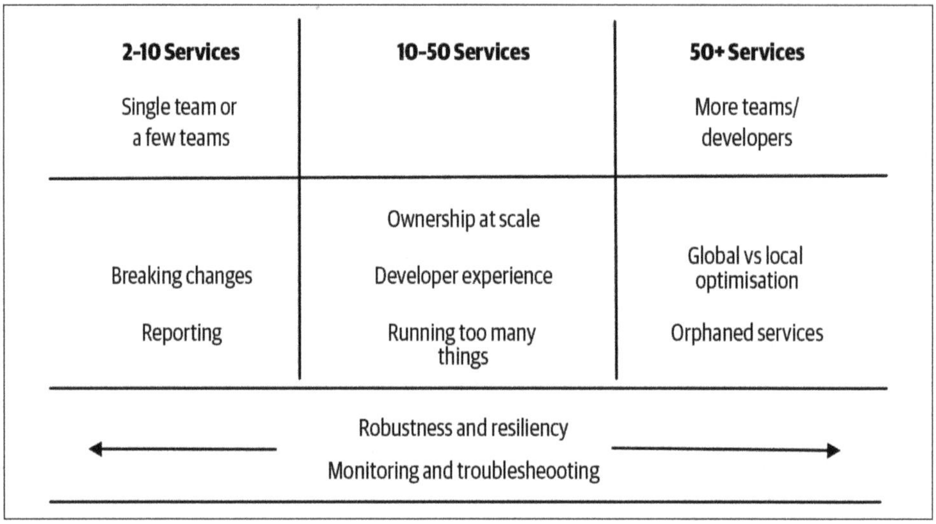

2-10 Services	10-50 Services	50+ Services
Single team or a few teams		More teams/ developers
Breaking changes	Ownership at scale	Global vs local optimisation
	Developer experience	
Reporting	Running too many things	Orphaned services
	Robustness and resiliency ← Monitoring and troublesheooting →	

Figure 5-1. Showing at a high level where some of the pain points often manifest

I'm not saying that you'll *definitely* see all of these problems at these times, or at all. There are certain variables involved that a simple diagram like this can't really articulate. One factor in particular that may change when these issues will strike is how coupled your architecture ends up being. With a more coupled architecture, issues around robustness, testing, tracing, and the like may manifest themselves earlier. All I'm hoping to do is shine a light on the potential pitfalls that might be out there.

However, keep in mind that you should use this as a general indicator. You need to make sure you're building in feedback mechanisms to look for some of the potential indicators I outline here.

Now that I've fully caveated the preceding diagram, let's take a look at each of these issues in a little more detail. I'm going to give you some pointers about which factors are likely to bring these problems to the fore, an understanding of how these issues may impact you, and some pointers for solving these challenges as they come up.

Ownership at Scale

As you have more and more developers working on your microservice architecture, you'll get to a place where you may want to reconsider how you handle ownership.

Martin Fowler has previously differentiated different types of ownership (*http://bit.ly/2n5pSAf*) from the point of view of generic code ownership, and I find that, broadly speaking, they work within the context of microservice ownership too. Here, primarily we're looking at ownership from a point of view of making code changes, not ownership in terms of who handles deployments, first-line support, and so on. Before we talk about the sorts of problems that crop up, let's first take a look at the concepts Martin outlines, and put them in the context of microservice architecture:

Strong code ownership
>All services have owners. If someone outside that ownership group wants to make a change, they have to submit that change to the owners, who decide whether it is allowed. The use of a pull request for people outside the ownership group is one example of how this could be handled.

Weak code ownership
>Most, if not all, services are owned by someone, but anyone can still directly change their modules without resorting to the need for things like pull requests. Effectively, source control is set up to still allow anyone to change anything, but there is the expectation that if you change someone else's service, you'll speak to them first.

Collective code ownership
>No one owns anything, and anyone can change anything they want.

How Can This Problem Show Itself?

As you grow your number of services and number of developers, you may start to experience problems with collective ownership. For collective ownership to work, the collective needs to be well-connected enough to have a common shared understanding of what a good change looks like, and in which direction you want to take a specific service from a technical point of view.

Left alone, at scale I've seen collective code ownership be disastrous for a microservice architecture. One fintech company I spoke to shared stories of a small team experiencing rapid growth, moving from 30–40 developers to over 100, but without any assigned responsibilities for different parts of the system or any concept of ownership other than "people know what is right."

What emerged was no clear vision for the system architecture as it evolved, and a horribly tangled "distributed monolith." One of the developers there referred to their architecture as "colander architecture" because it was so full of holes—people would just "punch a new hole" whenever they felt like it by exposing data or just making lots of point-to-point calls.[1] The reality is these sorts of challenges are easier to fix with a monolithic system, but far harder with a distributed system—the cost of detangling a distributed monolith is much higher.

When Might This Problem Occur?

For many teams starting out small, a collective code ownership model makes sense. With a small number of colocated developers (around 20), I'm happy with this model. As the number of developers increases, or those developers are distributed, it becomes harder to keep everyone on the same page regarding things like what makes for a good commit or how individual services should evolve.

For teams experiencing fast growth, a collective ownership model is problematic. The issue is that for collective ownership to work, you need time and space for the consensus to emerge, and be updated as new things are learned. This becomes harder with more people in general, and *really* hard if you're hiring new people at a rapid pace (or transferring them to the project).

Potential Solutions

In my experience, strong code ownership is almost universally the model adopted by organizations implementing large-scale microservice architectures consisting of multiple teams and over 100 developers. It becomes easier for the rules of what constitutes a good change to be decided by each team; you can view each team as adopting collective code ownership locally. This model also allows for product-oriented teams; if your team owns some services, and those services are oriented around the business domain, then your team becomes more focused on one area of the business domain. This makes it easier to maintain customer-focused teams who build domain expertise, often with embedded product owners guiding their work.

Breaking Changes

A microservice exists as part of a wider system. It either consumes functionality provided by other microservices, exposes its own functionality to other microservice consumers, or possibly does both. With a microservice architecture, we are striving for independent deployability, but for that to happen, we need to make sure that when we make a change to a microservice we don't break our consumers.

We can think of the functionality we expose to other microservices in terms of a *contract*. It's not just about saying, "This is the data I'll return." It's also about defining the

---

1 A colander is a bowl with lots of holes, used for straining pasta, for example.

---

expected behavior of your service. Whether or not you've made this contract with your consumers explicit, it exists. When you make a change to your service, you need to make sure you don't break this contract; otherwise, nasty production issues can occur.

Sooner or later, you'll need to deal with the challenges that breaking changes cause—either because you've made a conscious decision to make a backward-incompatible change, or perhaps because you made an innocent change that you thought would impact just your local service, only to find it broke other services in ways you didn't imagine.

How Can This Problem Show Itself?

The worst occurrence of this issue is when you see production outages caused by new microservices being sent live which break compatibility with existing services. This is a sign that you're not catching accidental contract breakages early enough. These issues can be catastrophic if you don't have a fast rollback mechanism in place. The only positive to take out of these failure modes is that they *normally* manifest quite quickly after a release, unless the backward-incompatible change is made to a part of a service contract that is rarely used.

Another sign is if you start seeing people try to orchestrate simultaneous deployments of multiple services together (sometimes called a *lock-step release*).This could also be a sign that this is happening due to trying to manage contract changes between client and server. The occasional lock-step release isn't too bad within a team, but if it is common, something needs to be investigated.

When Might This Problem Occur?

I find this to be a fairly early growing pain that teams encounter, especially when development is spread across more than one team. Within a single team, people tend to be a bit more aware when they make breaking changes, partly because there is a good chance the developers work on both the service being changed and the consuming service. When you get into situations where one team is changing a service that is then consumed by other teams, this problem can come up more often.

Over time, as teams become more mature, they get more diligent about making changes to avoid breakages in the first place, and also put mechanisms in place to catch problems early.

Potential Solutions

I have a set of rules for managing breaking contracts. They're pretty simple:

1. Don't break contracts.
2. See rule 1.

OK, I kid, but only slightly. Making breaking changes to the contracts you expose isn't great and is a pain to manage. You really want to keep it to a minimum if you can. That said, these are more realistic rules:

1. Eliminate accidental breaking changes.
2. Think twice before making a breaking change—can you possibly avoid it?
3. If you need to make a breaking change, give your consumers time to migrate.

Let's look at these steps in a bit more detail.

Eliminate accidental breaking changes

Having an explicit schema for your microservice can quickly detect *structural* breakages in your contract. If you expose a calculate method that is used to take two integers as parameters but now takes only a single integer, this is obviously a breaking change, which should be obvious from the new schema. Making this schema explicit to developers can help with early detection of this sort of thing; if they have to go in and make a change to the schema by hand, that becomes an explicit step that will hopefully cause them to pause for a moment and think about a change. If you have a formal schema format, there is the option to handle this programmatically too, of course, although this isn't done as much as I'd like. protolock (*http://bit.ly/2kUxvbq*) is an example of one such tool, which will actually prohibit making incompatible changes to your protocol buffers.

The default choice for many people is to use schema-less interchange formats, with JSON being the most common example. Although theoretically you can define explicit schemas for JSON, these aren't used in practice. Developers tend to curse the constraints of formal schemas initially—after they've had to deal with breaking changes across services, they'll change their minds. It's also worth noting that some of the serialization formats that make use of schemas are able to achieve performance improvements in deserializing data because of the formal types—something worth considering.

Structural breakages are only part of it, though. You also have *semantic* breakages to consider. If our calculate method still takes two integers, but the latest version of our microservice multiplies those two integers whereas it used to just add them, this is also a break in contract. In practice, testing is one of the best ways of detecting this. We'll look at that shortly.

Whatever you do, the quickest win is to make it as obvious to developers as possible when they make changes to the external contract. This may mean avoiding technology that magically serializes data or generates schemas from code, preferring to hand-roll these things instead. Trust me—making it hard to change a service contract is better than constantly breaking consumers.

Think twice before making a breaking change

If possible, prefer expansion changes to your contract if you can. Add new methods, resources, topics, or whatever that support the new functionality without removing the old. Try to find ways to support the old while still supporting the new. This may mean you end up having to support old code, but that still may be less work than handling a breaking change. Remember, if you decide to break a contract, it's on you to handle the implications of that.

Give consumers time to migrate

As I've been clear about from the beginning, microservices are designed to be *independently deployable*. When you make a change to a microservice, you need to be able to deploy that microservice into a production environment without having to deploy anything else. For that to work, you need to change your service contract in such a way that existing consumers are not impacted—so it follows that you need to allow consumers to still use the old contract even if your newer contract is available. You'll then need to give all consumers time to change their services to migrate over to your newer service version.

I've seen this done in two ways. The first is to run two versions of your microservice, as outlined in Figure 5-2: two builds of the Notifications service are available at the same time, each one exposing different incompatible endpoints that consumers can choose between. The primary challenges with this approach are that you have to have more infrastructure to run the extra services, you probably have to maintain data compatibility between the service versions, and bug fixes may need to be made to all running versions, which inevitably requires source code branching. These issues are somewhat mitigated if you are only coexisting the two versions for short periods of time, which is the only situation where I'd consider this approach.

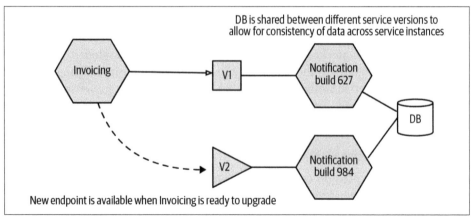

Figure 5-2. Coexisting two versions of the same microservice to support backward-incompatible changes

The approach I prefer is to have one running version of your microservice, but have it support *both* contracts, as we see in Figure 5-3. This could involve exposing two APIs on different ports, for example. This pushes complexity into your microservices implementation, but avoids the challenges of the earlier approach. I've spoken to some teams that are supporting three or more old contracts in the same service years later, due to external consumers being unable to change. That's not a fun position to be in, but if you do find yourself with consumers who won't change, I still think this is the best option.

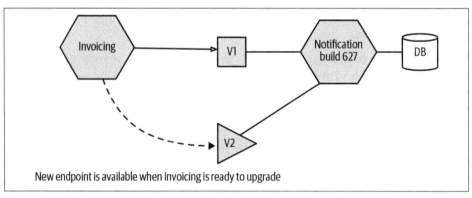

Figure 5-3. One service exposing two contracts

Of course, if the same team handles both consumer and producer, you could do a lock-step release and deploy new versions of both consumer and producer at the same time. It's not something I'd want to do often, but at least within a single team it can be easier to manage the release coordination—just don't make a habit of it!

Changes within a team are easier to manage, as you control both sides of the equation. As the microservice you want to change is used more widely, the cost of managing the change becomes greater. As a result, you can be more relaxed about making breaking changes within a team, but breaking an API you expose to third-party organizations is likely to be quite painful.

However you do it, you need good communication with the people who manage the services that consume your service. You're likely going to inconvenience them (at best), so it's a good idea to be on good terms with them. Treat consumers of your service like customers—and you should treat your customers well!

Get This Sorted—Fast!

As organizations have increasing numbers of microservices, they eventually work out how to mostly eliminate accidental breaking changes, and come up with a managed mechanism for handling purposeful changes. If they don't, the impacts become so significant that a microservice architecture is untenable. Put a different way, I highly suspect that small microservice organizations that don't sort this stuff out won't last long enough to become large microservice organizations.

Reporting

With a monolithic system, you typically have a monolithic database. This means that stakeholders who want to analyze all of the data together, often involving large join operations across data, have a ready-made schema against which to run their reports. They can just run them directly against the monolithic database, perhaps against a read replica, as shown in Figure 5-4. With a microservice architecture, we have broken up this monolithic schema. That doesn't mean that the need for reporting across all of our data has gone away; we've just made it much more difficult, as now our data is scattered across multiple logically isolated schemas.

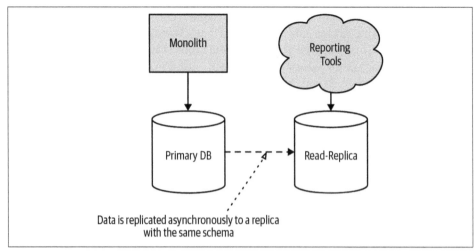

Figure 5-4. Reporting being carried out directly on the database of a monolith

When Might This Problem Occur?

This one tends to bite fairly early, and normally comes at the stage when you're start-ing to consider decomposing a monolithic schema. Hopefully, this is discovered before it becomes an issue, but I've seen more than one project where the team doesn't realize until halfway through that the architecture direction was going to cre-ate misery for stakeholders interested in reporting use cases. All too often, the needs for downstream reporting are not considered early enough, as it happens outside the realm of normal software development and system maintenance—out of sight, out of mind.

You may be able to sidestep this problem if your monolith already uses a dedicated data source for reporting purposes, like a data warehouse or data lake. Then all you need to ensure is that your microservices are able to copy the appropriate data to the existing data sources.

Potential Solutions

For many situations, the stakeholders who care about having access to all your data in one place probably also have an investment in a tool chain and processes that expect direct access to the database, normally making use of SQL. It also follows that their reporting is likely tied to the schema design of your monolithic database. This means that unless you want to change how they work, you're going to still need to present a single database for reporting, and quite possibly one that matches the old schema design to limit the impact of any changes.

The most straightforward approach for solving this problem is to first separate the need for a single database to store data for reporting purposes, from the databases your microservices use to store and retrieve data, as Figure 5-5 shows. This allows the content and design of your reporting database to be decoupled from the design and evolution of each service's data storage requirements. This also allows for this new reporting database to be changed with the specific requirements of reporting users in mind. All you then need to do is to work out how your microservices can "push" data into your new schema.

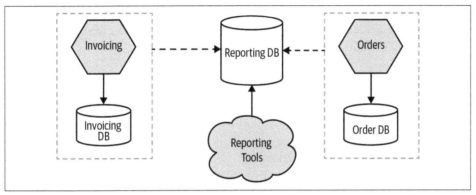

Figure 5-5. A dedicated reporting database with data being pushed to it from different microservices

We've already looked at potential solutions to this problem in Chapter 4. A change data capture system is an obvious potential solution for solving this, but techniques like views can also be useful, as you may be able to project a single reporting schema from views exposed from the schemas of multiple microservice databases. You may also consider the use of other techniques, like having the data copied to your reporting schema programmatically as part of the code of your microservices, or perhaps having intermediary components that may populate the reporting database by listening to events of upstream services.

I further explore the challenges and potential solutions around this topic in a lot more detail in Chapter 5 of *Building Microservices*.

Monitoring and Troubleshooting

> We replaced our monolith with microservices so that every outage could be more like a murder mystery.
>
> —Honest Status Page (@honest_update), *http://bit.ly/2mldxqH*

With a standard monolithic application, we can have a fairly simplistic approach to monitoring. We have a small number of machines to worry about, and the failure mode of the application is somewhat binary—the application is often either all up or all down. With a microservice architecture, we can have the failure of just one service instance, or just one type of instance to consider—can we pick those up properly?

With a monolithic system, if our CPU is stuck at 100% for a long time, we know that's a big problem. With a microservice architecture with tens or hundreds of processes, can we say the same thing? Do we need to wake someone up at 3 a.m. when just one process is stuck at 100% CPU?

Working out where you have problems, and understanding whether those problems you are seeing are actually things you need to worry about becomes much more complicated as you have more moving parts. The way you approach monitoring and troubleshooting will need to change as your microservice architecture grows. This is an area that will require constant attention and investment.

When Might These Problems Occur?

It's a bit trickier to predict exactly when you'll start having a problem with this. The simple answer can be "the first time something goes wrong in production," but trying to work out what went wrong where is something developers and testers may have to deal with before you even get to production. You could hit these limitations when you have a couple of services, or perhaps not until you hit 20 or more.

Because it can be hard to predict exactly when your existing monitoring approach will start to let you down, all I can suggest is that you prioritize implementing some basic improvements ahead of time.

How Can These Problems Occur?

This is fairly easy to spot, in a way. You'll see production issues that you can't explain or understand, you'll have alerts that trigger despite the system being apparently healthy, and it will become harder to answer the simple question "Is everything OK?"

Potential Solutions

A multitude of mechanisms—some easy to implement, others more complex—can help change how you monitor and troubleshoot problems with a microservice architecture. What follows is a nonexhaustive overview of some key things to consider.

Log aggregation

With a small number of machines, especially machines that are long-lived, when we needed to check logs, we would normally go to the machines themselves and fetch the information. The problem with a microservice architecture is that we have many more processes, often running on more machines, which can be short lived (e.g., virtual machines or containers).

A *log aggregation system* will allow you to capture all your logs and forward them to a central location where they can be searched, and in some cases can even be used to generate alerts. Many options exist, from the open source ELK stack (*https://www.elas*

tic.co/elk-stack) (Elastic search, Logstash/Fluent D, and Kibana) to my personal favorite Humio (*https://humio.com*), these systems can be incredibly useful.

 Strongly consider implementing log aggregation as the first thing you do before implementing a microservice architecture. It's incredibly useful, and is a good test of your organization's ability to implement change in the operational space.

Log aggregation is one of the simplest mechanisms to implement, and it's something you should do early on. In fact, I suggest it's the *first* thing you should do when implementing a microservice architecture. This is partly because it's so useful right from the start. In addition, if your organization struggles to implement a suitable log aggregation system, you might want to reconsider whether you're ready for microservices. The work required to implement a log aggregation system is fairly straightforward, and if you aren't ready for that as an organization, microservices are likely a step too far.

Tracing

Understanding where a sequence of calls between microservices failed, or which service caused a latency spike can be difficult if you can analyze information only from each service in isolation. Being able to collate a series of flows and look at them as a whole is incredibly useful.

As a starting point, generate correlation IDs for all calls coming into your system, as shown in Figure 5-6. When the Invoice service receives a call, it is given a correlation ID. When it dispatches a call to the Notification microservice, it passes that correlation ID along—this could be done via an HTTP header, or a field in a message payload, or some other mechanism. Typically, I'd look to an API gateway or service mesh to generate the initial correlation ID.

When the Notification service handles the call, it can log information about what it is doing in conjunction with that same correlation ID, allowing you to use a log aggregation system to query for all logs associated with a given correlation ID (assuming you put the correlation ID in a standard place in your log format). You can, of course, do other things with correlation IDs, such as managing sagas (as we discussed in Chapter 4).

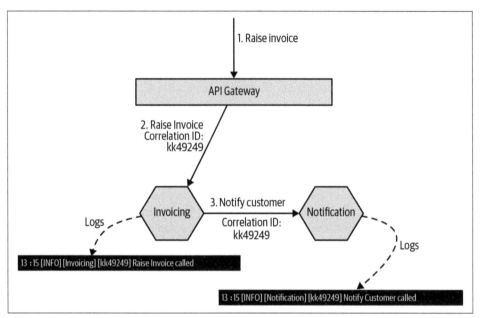

Figure 5-6. Using correlation IDs to ensure that information about a specific chain of calls can be collected

Taking this idea further, we can use tools to also trace the time taken for calls. Due to the way log aggregation systems work, where logs are batched and forwarded to a central agent on a regular basis, it isn't possible to get accurate information to allow you to determine exactly where time may be getting spent during a chain of calls. Distributed tracing systems like the open source Jaeger (*https://www.jaegertracing.io*), shown in Figure 5-7, can help.

The more latency sensitive your application is, the sooner I'd be looking to implement a distributed tracing tool like Jaeger. It's worth noting that if you've worked correlation ID generation and use into your existing microservice architectures (which in general is something I advocate for well before you need a distributed tracing tool), then you've likely already got the places in your existing service stack that can be easily changed to push data to a suitable tool. The use of a service mesh can also help, as it can at least handle inbound and outbound tracing for you, even if it can't do much about instrumenting calls inside individual microservices.

Figure 5-7. Jaeger is an open source tool for capturing information for distributed traces and analyzing the performance of individual calls

Test in production

Functional automated tests are typically used to give us feedback before deployment regarding whether or not our software is of sufficient quality to be deployed. But once it hits production, we still want that same feedback! Even if a given feature worked once in production, a new service deployment or environmental change could break that functionality later on.

By injecting fake user behavior into our system, in the form of what is often called *synthetic transactions*, we can define the behavior we expect, and alert accordingly if this isn't the case. At one of my previous companies, Atomist, we had a somewhat complex onboarding process for new customers that required authorizing our software with both their GitHub and Slack accounts. There were enough moving parts that early on this process would hit issues, with things like being rate limited against the GitHub APIs. One of my colleagues, Sylvain Hellegouarch, scripted enrollment of fake customers. On a regular basis we would trigger a sign-up process for one of these fake customers, which scripted the whole process end to end. When this failed, it was often a sign that something was wrong in our systems and it was much better catching this with a "fake" user than a real one!

A good starting point for testing in production could be to take existing end-to-end test cases and rework them for use in a production environment. An important consideration is to ensure that these "tests" don't cause unforeseen impact in production. With Atomist, we created GitHub and Slack accounts that we controlled for use in the synthetic transactions, so no real human was involved or impacted, and it was easy for our scripts to clean up these accounts afterward. On the other hand, I did hear reports of a company that ended up accidentally ordering 200 washing machines to be delivered to their head office because they hadn't properly accounted for the fact that the test orders would actually end up getting sent out. So be careful!

Toward observability

With traditional monitoring and alerting processes, we think about what might go wrong, collect information to tell us when this is the case, and use this to fire off alerts. So we are primarily setting ourselves up to handle known causes of problems—disk space running out, a service instance not responding, or perhaps a spike in latency.

As our systems become more complicated, it becomes increasingly difficult to predict all the nasty ways in which our system might let us down. What becomes important at that point is to allow us to ask open-ended questions of our systems when these issues occur, to help us in the first instance to stop the bleeding and make sure the system can continue to operate, but to also allow us to gather enough information to fix the problem going forward.

So we need to be able to gather lots of information about what our system is doing, allowing us to after the fact ask questions of the data that we didn't know we'd have to ask in the first place. Tracing and logs can form an important source of data from which we can ask questions and use real information rather than conjecture to determine what the problem is. The secret is in making this information easy to query and view in context.

Don't assume you know the answers up front. Rather, adopt the view that you can and will get surprised, so get good at asking questions of your system, and make sure you use toolchains that allow for ad hoc querying of information. If you'd like to explore this concept in more detail, I recommend *Distributed Systems Observability* as an excellent starting point.[2]

Local Developer Experience

As you have more and more services, the developer experience can start to suffer. More resource-intensive runtimes like the JVM can limit the number of microservices that can be run on a single developer machine. I could probably run four or five JVM-based microservices as separate processes on my laptop, but could I run ten or twenty? Probably not. Even with less-taxing runtimes, there is a limit to how many things you can run locally, which inevitably will start conversations about what to do when you can't run the entire system on one machine.

---

2 See Cindy Sridharan, *Distributed Systems Observability* (Sebastopol: O'Reilly Media, Inc., 2018).

How Can This Problem Show Itself?

The day-to-day development process can start to slow down, with local builds and execution taking longer, due to more services having to be stood up. Developers will start requesting bigger machines to handle the number of services they have to handle, and while that might be OK for a short-term fix, that will only buy you some time if your service estate continues to grow.

When Might This Occur?

When exactly this will manifest itself is likely a function of the number of services a developer wants running locally, combined with the resource footprint of those services. A team using Go, Node, or Python may well find they can have more services running locally before hitting resource constraints—but a team using the JVM may hit this problem earlier.

I also think teams practicing collective ownership of multiple services are more susceptible to this problem. They are more likely to require the ability to switch between different services during their development. Teams with strong ownership of a few services will mostly focus only on their own services, and will be more likely to develop mechanisms for stubbing out services that are outside their control.

Potential Solutions

If I want to develop locally but reduce the number of services that I have to run, a common technique is to "stub out" those services I don't want to run myself, or else have a way to point them against instances running elsewhere. A pure remote developer setup allows for you to develop against lots of services hosted on more capable infrastructure. However, with that comes associated challenges of needing connectivity (which can be a problem for remote workers or frequent travelers), potentially having slower feedback cycles with the need to deploy software remotely before you can see it working, and a potential explosion in resources (and associated costs) needed for developer environments.

Telepresence (*https://www.telepresence.io*) is an example of a tool that is aiming to make a hybrid local/remote developer workflow easier for Kubernetes users. You can develop your service locally, but Telepresence can proxy calls to other services to a remote cluster, allowing you (hopefully) the best of both worlds. Azure's cloud functions can be run locally too, but connected to remote cloud resources, allowing you to create services made out of functions with a fast local developer workflow, while still having them run against a potentially extensive cloud environment.

Seeing how the developer experience changes as the number of services increases is important—so you need feedback mechanisms put in place. You'll need to continually invest to ensure that developers remain as productive as possible as the number of services they are working with increases.

Running Too Many Things

As you have more services, and more service instances of those services, you have more processes that need to be deployed, configured, and managed. Your existing techniques for handling the deployment and configuration of your monolithic application may well not scale well as you increase the number of moving parts that need to be managed.

Desired state management in particular becomes increasingly important. *Desired state management* is the ability for you to specify the number and location of service instances that you require, and ensure that this is maintained over time. You may currently manage this with your monolith using manual processes—but that isn't going to scale well when you have tens or hundreds of microservices, especially if each of them has a different desired state.

How Might This Problem Show Itself?

You'll start to see an increasing percentage of time spent managing deployments and troubleshooting the issues that occur during these deployments. Mistakes will always be made if processes rely on manual activities—and the impact to distributed systems of innocent mistakes can be hard to predict.

As you add more services and service instances, you'll find yourself needing more people to manage the activities associated with deploying and maintaining your production fleet. This could result in requests for more people to support your operation team, or perhaps seeing a higher percentage of time being spent on deployment concerns by your delivery team.

When Might This Problem Occur?

This is all about scale. The more microservices you have, and the more instances you have of those microservices, the more manual processes or more traditional automated configuration management tools like Chef and Puppet no longer fit the bill.

Potential Solutions

You want a tool that allows for a high degree of automation, that can allow developers ideally to self-service provision deployments, and that handles automated desired state management.

For microservices, Kubernetes has emerged as the tool of choice in this space. It requires that you containerize your services, but once you do, you can use Kubernetes to manage the deployment of your service instances across multiple machines, ensuring you can scale to improve robustness and handle load (assuming you have enough hardware).

Vanilla Kubernetes isn't what I would consider developer-friendly. A multitude of people are working on higher-order, more developer-friendly abstractions, and I expect that work to continue. In the future, I expect that many developers who are running software on Kubernetes won't even realize, as it will just become an implementation detail. I tend to see larger organizations adopt a packaged version of Kubernetes, such as OpenShift from RedHat, which bundles Kubernetes with tooling that makes it easier to work with within a corporate environment—perhaps handling corporate identity and access management controls. Some of these packaged versions also provide simplified abstractions for developers to work with.

If you're lucky enough to be on the public cloud, you could use the many different options there to handle deployments of your microservice architecture, including managed Kubernetes offerings. Both AWS and Azure, for example, offer multiple options in this space. I'm a big fan of Function-as-a-Service (FaaS), a subset of what is called *serverless*. With a suitable platform, developers just worry about code, and the underlying platform handles most of the operational work. While the current crop of FaaS offerings do have limitations, they nonetheless offer the prospect of drastically reduced operational overhead.

For teams I work with who are already on the public cloud, I tend to not start with Kubernetes or similar container-based platforms. Instead, I've adopted an approach of serverless-first—try to make use of serverless technology like FaaS as a default choice, because of the reduction in operational work. If your problem doesn't fit the limitations of the serverless products available to you, then look for other options. Not all problem spaces are equal, obviously, but I feel that if you're already on the public cloud, you may not always need the complexity of a container-based platform like Kubernetes.

 I do see people reaching for Kubernetes and the like a bit too early in the process of adopting microservices, often assuming it is a prerequisite. Far from it—platforms like Kubernetes excel at helping you manage multiple processes, but you should wait until you have enough processes that your current approach and technology are starting to strain. You might find that you need only five microservices, and that you can happily handle this with your existing solutions—in which case, great! Don't adopt a Kubernetes-based platform just because you see everyone else doing it, which can also be said for microservices!

End-to-End Testing

With any type of automated functional test, you have a delicate balancing act. The more functionality a test executes—the broader the scope of the test—the more confidence you have in your application. On the other hand, the larger the scope of the test, the longer it can take to run, and the harder it can be to work out what is broken when it fails.

End-to-end tests for any type of system are at the extreme end of the scale in terms of functionality they cover, and we are used to them being more problematic to write and maintain than smaller-scoped unit tests. Often this is worth it, though, as we want the confidence that comes from having an end-to-end test use our systems in the same way a user might.

But with a microservice architecture, the "scope" of our end-to-end tests gets *very* large. We are now having to run tests across multiple services, all of which need to be deployed and appropriately configured for the test scenarios. We also have to be prepared for the false negatives that occur when environmental issues, such as service instances dying or network time-outs of failed deployments, cause our tests to fail. I'd argue that we are much more vulnerable to issues outside of our control when running end-to-end tests against a microservice architecture than we are with a standard monolithic architecture.

As the scope of the tests increase, you'll spend more of your time fighting the problems that arise, to the point where trying to create and maintain end-to-end tests becomes a huge time sink.

How Can This Problem Show Itself?

One sign is that your end-to-end test suite grows, taking longer and longer to complete. This is caused by multiple teams being unsure of what scenarios are covered and adding new ones "just in case." You see more failures in the end-to-end test suite that are not highlighting issues with your code—and developers often just run the tests again to see if they pass.

The amount of time being spent on end-to-end tests takes longer and longer, to the point where you start seeing pressure for more testers and perhaps even a separate test team.

When Might This Problem Occur?

This problem tends to sneak up on you, but I see it most keenly felt in situations where the work for different user journeys is handled by multiple teams. The more isolated each team is in its work, the easier it is for them to manage their own tests locally. The more you need to test cross-team flows, the more problematic end-to-end, large scoped tests become.

Potential Solutions

I outlined a number of options for helping change how you handle testing in *Building Microservices*, and in fact have a whole chapter dedicated to it, but here is a brief summary to get you started.

Limit scope of functional automated tests

If you are going to write test cases that cover multiple services, try to ensure that these tests are kept inside the team that manages these services—in other words, avoid larger-scoped tests that cross team boundaries. Keeping ownership of tests within a single team makes it easier to understand what scenarios are properly covered, ensures that developers can run and debug the tests, and more clearly articulates responsibility for who should make sure the tests run and pass.

Use consumer-driven contracts

You may want to consider the use of consumer-driven contracts (CDCs) to replace the need for cross-service test cases. With CDCs, you have the consumer of your microservice define their expectations of how your service should behave in terms of an executable specification—a test. When you change your service, you ensure that these tests still pass.

As these tests are defined from the consumer point of view, we get good coverage for picking up accidental contract breakage. We can also understand our consumer requirements from their point of view, and importantly understand how different consumers might want different things from us.

You can implement CDCs by using a simple development workflow, but this can be made easier through the use of tooling designed to support this technique. The best example is probably Pact (*https://pact.io*).

It's worth noting that I've seen some teams have huge success with this approach, but it's been difficult for others to adopt. The idea is sound, and I know it can work well, but I haven't yet fully understood the challenges that some people have had in adopting this technique. It remains a poorly underused practice for solving a really difficult problem.

Use automated release remediation and progressive delivery

With automated testing, we are typically trying to find problems before they impact production, but it can become increasingly difficult to do that as your system becomes more complex. Therefore, it can be worth spending effort in reducing the impact of production issues if they do occur.

As we touched on in Chapter 3, *progressive delivery* is the umbrella term for controlling how you roll out new versions of your software incrementally to your customers. The idea is that you can assess the impact of your new release with a smaller group of customers, deciding if and when to continue or revert the rollback. An example of a progressive delivery technique could be a canary release.

By defining acceptable measures for how your service should behave, it then becomes possible to control the progressive delivery in an automated fashion. As a simple example, you might define an acceptable threshold for 95th percentile latencies and error rates, and continue the rollout only if these measures are met. Otherwise, you may automatically roll back the latest release, giving you time to analyze what happened.

Many organizations use these automated release remediation techniques. Netflix, in particular, has spoken at length about using this idea. It developed Spinnaker as a deployment management tool partly to help control progressive delivery for its services, but there are many other ways you can put these ideas into practice.

I'm not saying you should consider automated release remediation *instead* of testing, just that you should think about where you get the best return on your effort. You may end up with a far more robust system by putting some work into catching problems if they do occur, rather than just focusing on stopping problems from happening in the first place.

It's important to note that while these techniques work well together, even if you think automated remediation isn't something you can do right now, there is still huge value to be had from implementing some form of progressive delivery. Even manually controlling progressive delivery can be a big step up from just rolling the new software out to everyone.

Continually refine your quality feedback cycles

Understanding how and where you should test is an ongoing challenge. You need people who have the context to look holistically across the development process to adapt how and where you are testing your application. This means having people who can identify the need to add new tests to cover areas of the system where they are seeing an increase in production defects, but also who can remove tests when there is already coverage in an effort to improve feedback cycles.

In short, it's about balancing the need for fast feedback with safety. You need to be just as willing to identify, and remove or replace, the wrong test as you are to add a new test.

Global Versus Local Optimization

Assuming you embrace the model of teams having more responsibility for local decision-making, perhaps owning the entire life cycle of the microservices they manage, you'll get to the point where you start to need to balance local decision-making with more global concerns.

As an example of how this problem might manifest, consider three teams who manage the Invoicing, Notifications, and Fulfillment services. The Invoicing team decides to use Oracle as a database, as they know it well. The Notifications team wants to use MongoDB because it fits their programming model well. Meanwhile, the Fulfillment team wants to use PostgreSQL, as they already have it. When you look at each decision in turn, it makes perfect sense, and you understand how that team would have made that choice.

If you step back and look at the big picture, though, you have to ask yourself whether or not as an organization you want to build skills, and pay license fees, for three databases with somewhat similar capabilities. Would you be better off adopting just one database, accepting that it isn't perfect for everyone, but is good enough for most? Without the ability to see what is happening locally, and being able to put this into a global context, how would you ever be able to make these sorts of decisions?

How Can This Problem Show Itself?

The most common way I've seen this problem come to light is when someone suddenly realizes that multiple teams have solved the same problem in different ways, but were never aware that they were all trying to fix the same issue. Over time this can be incredibly inefficient.

I remember speaking to people at REA, a real estate company in Australia. After many years building microservices, they got to the point where they realized that there were many ways that teams would deploy services. This caused problems when people moved from one team to another, as they had to learn the new way of doing things. It also became hard to justify the duplicate work that each team was doing. As a result, they decided to put some work into coming up with a common way to handle this.

You'll typically find out about these things accidentally, after a passing comment you overhear at lunch, perhaps. You can spot these problems much earlier if you have some sort of cross-team technical group, such as a community of practice.

When Might This Problem Occur?

This problem tends to arise in multiteam organizations over time, especially in organizations that give teams more freedom in how they go about their work. Don't expect to see this issue early on in your microservice journey. You'll start out probably with a clear shared understanding of how things should be done. Over time, each team will be increasingly focused on their local problems, and will optimize how they solve problems based on this, so that core shared view of "this is how we do things" will start to shift.

I often see this problem being raised and discussed after organizations have gone through a period of scaling. The influx of a lot of developers in a short space of time makes it harder for ad hoc information sharing to scale. This can lead to more information silos that may need to be bridged.

If you practice collective ownership of services, that will likely help avoid or at least limit these problems, as collective ownership of services requires a degree of consistency in terms of how problems are solved. Put another way, if you want collective ownership, you *have* to solve this problem; otherwise, your collective ownership won't scale.

Potential Solutions

We've already touched on some ideas that can help in this area. In Chapter 2, we explored the idea of irreversible and reversible decisions, as shown again in Figure 5-8. The higher the cost of change, the larger the impact, and the more you'll want a broader consensus behind decision-making. The smaller the impact, the easier it is to roll back, and the more decisions can be left to local teams.

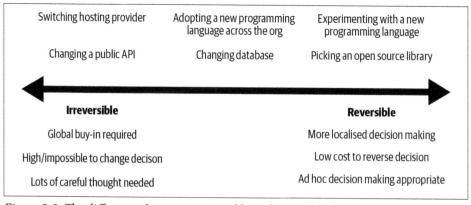

Figure 5-8. The differences between irreversible and reversible decisions, with examples along the spectrum

The trick is helping people in teams realize where their decisions might tend toward the irreversible or reversible ends of this spectrum. The more a decision tends toward irreversible, the more important it might be for them to involve other people outside their team boundary in their decision-making. For this to work well, teams need to have at least a basic understanding of the bigger-picture concerns to see where they may overlap, and they'll also need a network where they can surface these issues and get involvement from their colleagues in other teams.

As a simple mechanism, having at least one technical leader from each team being part of a technical cross-cutting group where these concerns can be addressed is a sensible approach. This group may be chaired by a CTO, chief architect, or other person who is responsible for the overall technical vision of the company.

This cross-cutting group can work both ways. In addition to offering a place where teams can surface local issues that they want to discuss in a larger forum, it is also somewhere people can pick up cross-cutting issues. Without some communication between teams, how would we realize that we're solving problems in different ways locally, and that perhaps solving them at a global level might make more sense?

Depending on the nature of your organization, you may be able to rely on a more ad hoc, informal process. At Monzo, for example, people can submit free-form documents referred to internally as "proposals." These are published into a shared space that in turn alerts the whole company via Slack that a new proposal is available. Interested parties can then discuss the proposal and help refine it. The expectation is that these proposals aren't the finished artifact, and in fact must be open to change. This seems to work well for Monzo, in part because of its culture around communication and sharing of responsibility.

Fundamentally, each organization needs to find the right balance between global and local decision-making. How much responsibility are you happy to push into the teams? How much control do you want to hold centrally? The more responsibility you push to the teams, the more you'll get the benefits of greater autonomy, but the trade-off is that you may have less consistency in how problems are solved. The more you drive things from the center, the more you'll need to build consensus and that will likely slow you down. I can't tell you how to achieve balance between these two forces in a way that is right for you; you'll need to work that out for yourself. You just need to be aware that this balance exists, and you need to make sure you're gathering the right information to make sure you can adjust this balance over time.

Robustness and Resiliency

Distributed systems can exhibit a whole host of failure modes that may be unfamiliar to you if you are more accustomed to monolithic systems. Network packets can get lost, network calls can time out, machines can die or stop responding. These situations may be rare with simple distributed systems, such as a traditional monolithic application, but as the number of services increases, rare occurrences become more commonplace.

How Can This Problem Show Itself?

These problems are, unfortunately, most likely to arise in a production setting. During traditional development and test cycles, we're re-creating production-like circumstances only for short periods of time. Those rare occurrences are less likely to emerge, and when they do, they often get dismissed.

When Might This Problem Occur?

I'll be honest here—if I could tell you in advance when your system will suffer from instability I wouldn't be writing this book, as I'd likely be spending my time on a beach somewhere drinking mojitos. All I can say is that as the number of services increases, and the number of service calls increase, you'll become more and more vulnerable to resiliency issues. The more interconnected your services are, the more likely you'll suffer from things like cascading failures and back pressure.

Potential Solutions

A good starting point is to ask yourself a couple of questions about each service call you make. First, do I know the way in which this call might fail? Second, if the call does fail, do I know what I should do?

Once you've answered these questions, you can then start looking at a host of solutions. Isolating services more from each other can help, perhaps including the introduction of asynchronous communication to avoid temporal coupling (a topic we touched on in Chapter 1). Using sensible time-outs can avoid resource contention with slow downstream services, and in conjunction with patterns like circuit breakers, you can start failing fast to avoid problems with back pressure.

Running multiple copies of services can help with instances dying, as can a platform that can implement desired state management (which can ensure that services get restarted if they crash).

To restate a point made in Chapter 2, resiliency is more than just implementing a few patterns. It's about a whole way of working—building an organization that not only is ready to handle the unforeseeable problems that will inevitably crop up, but also evolves working practices as necessary. One concrete way you can put this idea into practice is by documenting production issues when they arise and keeping a record of what you learned. All too often I see organizations move on too quickly once the initial problem has been solved or worked around—only for those same problems to come back again some months later.

To be honest, I've just scratched the surface here. For a more detailed examination of these ideas I recommend reading Chapter 11 in *Building Microservices*, or taking a look at *Release It!* by Michael Nygard (Pragmatic Bookshelf, 2018).

Orphaned Services

It seems odd, given some of the amazing technology that we have and the incredibly complex and massively scalable systems we are now building, that we also still see problems with some of the most prosaic issues. One example is that I see many organizations struggle with knowing exactly what they have, where it is, and who owns it.

As microservices become even more focused in their purpose, you'll find more and more services have been happily running for weeks, months, or perhaps years without any changes being made to them. On the one hand, this is exactly what we want; independent deployability is such an appealing concept partly because it allows the rest of the system to remain stable, and maintaining stability of the parts of our system that don't need to change is a good idea.

I refer to these services as *orphaned services*, as fundamentally no one in the company is taking ownership or responsibility for them.

How Can This Problem Show Itself?

I remember hearing (perhaps apocryphal) stories of old servers being discovered walled up in old offices. No one remembers they were there, but they are still happily running, doing whatever it is they do. As no one remembers exactly what these newly discovered computers do, people are scared to turn them off. Microservices can exhibit some of the same characteristics; they're out there and they're working (we assume), but we have the same problem that we may not know what to do with them, and that fear can put us off changing them.

The fundamental problem is that if this service does stop working, or does require a change, people are at a loss as to what to do. I've spoken to more than one team that shared stories of not knowing where the source code was for the service in question, which is a pretty big problem.

When Might This Problem Occur?

This problem typically occurs with organizations that have been using microservices for a long period of time—long enough that the collective memory regarding what this service did has long since diminished. The people involved with this microservice have either forgotten what they did to it or perhaps left the company.

Potential Solutions

I have an (untested) hypothesis that organizations that practice collective ownership of services might be less prone to this problem, primarily because they will already have to have implemented mechanisms to allow developers to move from service to service and make changes. These sorts of organizations already probably restrict language and technology choice to reduce the cost of context switching between services. They may also have common tooling around making changes to a service, testing it, and deploying it. If those common practices have changed since the service was last changed, of course this may not help.

I've spoken with a number of companies that have had these issues, and that ended up creating simple in-house registries to help collate metadata around services. Some of these registries simply crawl source code repositories, looking for metadata files to build up a list of services out there. This information can be merged with real data coming from service discovery systems like consul or etcd to build up a richer picture of what is running, and who you could speak to about it.

The Financial Times created Biz Ops to help address this problem. The company has several hundred services developed by teams all over the world. The Biz Ops tool (Figure 5-9), gives them a single place where you can find out lots of useful information about their microservices, in addition to information about other IT infrastructure services like networks and file servers. Built on top of a graph database, they have a lot of flexibility about what data they gather and how the information can be modeled.

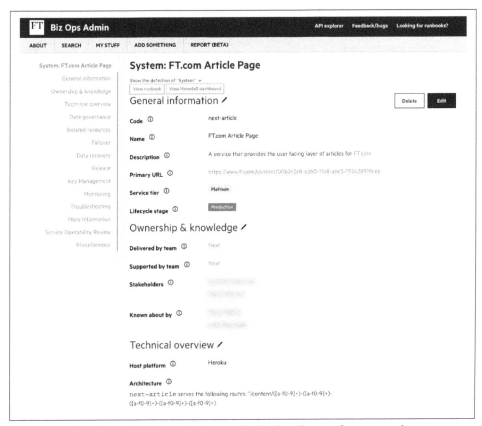

Figure 5-9. The Financial Times Biz Ops tool, which collates information about its microservices

The Biz Ops tool goes further than most I have seen, however. They calculate what they call a System Operability Score, as shown in Figure 5-10. The idea is that there are certain things that services and their teams should do to ensure the service can be easily operated. This can go from making sure the teams have provided the correct information in the registry to ensuring the services have proper health checks. These scores are calculated, allowing teams to see at a glance if there are things that need to be fixed.

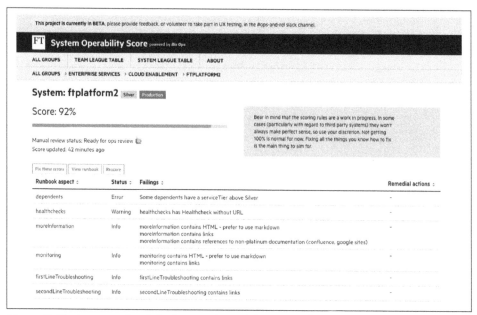

Figure 5-10. An example of the Service Operability Score for a microservice at The Financial Times

Having something like a service registry can help, but what happens if your orphaned service predates your registry? The key thing is to bring these newly discovered "orphaned" services into line with how other services are managed, and that requires you to either assign ownership to an existing team (if practicing strong ownership), or raise work items for the service to be improved (if practicing collective ownership).

Summary

What we've covered in this chapter isn't meant to be an exhaustive list of all the issues that microservices can cause, nor have I listed all the potential solutions. Instead, the focus has been on the most common problems that I see people struggle with.

I hope I've also made it clear that there isn't a hard-and-fast rule about exactly when you'll see these problems. Every situation is different, and a multitude of factors come into play. What I've tried to do is highlight that while you can't see the future, you can at least be forewarned. What is more challenging is finding the right balance between fixing problems before they occur versus spending time fixing problems you'll never have. I hope you walk away from this chapter knowing what warning to watch for.

CHAPTER 6
Closing Words

So we've come to the end of the book. Throughout it all, I've hoped to get across two key messages. First, give yourself enough space and gather the right information to make rational decisions. Don't just copy others; think instead about your problem and your context, assess the options, and move forward, while being open to change if you need to later. Second, remember that incremental adoption of microservices, and many of the associated technologies and practices, is key. No two microservice architectures are alike—while there are lessons to be learned from the work done by others, you need to take the time to find an approach that works well in your context. By breaking the journey into manageable steps, you give yourself the best chance of success, as you can adapt your approach as you go.

Microservices are definitely not for everyone. But, hopefully, after reading this book, you'll have not only a better sense of whether they are right for you, but also some ideas about how to get started on the journey.

Bibliography

Bird, Christian, Nachiappan Nagappan, Brendan Murphy, Harald Gall, and Premkumar Devanbu. "Don't Touch My Code! Examining the Effects of Ownership on Software Quality." *http://bit.ly/2p5RlT1*.

Bland, Mike. "Test Mercenaries." *http://bit.ly/2omkxVy*.

Bland, Mike. "Testing On The Toilet." *http://bit.ly/2ojpWwm*.

Brandolini, Alberto. *Introducing EventStorming*. Leanpub, 2019. *http://bit.ly/2n0zCLU*.

Brooks, Frederick P. *The Mythical Man-Month, 20th Anniversary Edition*. Addison Wesley, 1995.

Bryant, Daniel. "Building Resilience in Netflix Production Data Migrations: Sangeeta Handa at QCon SF." *http://bit.ly/2m1EwHT*.

Devops Research & Assessment. *Accelerate: State Of Devops Report 2018. http://bit.ly/2nPDNLe*.

Evans, Eric. *Domain-Driven Design: Tackling Complexity in the Heart of Software*. Addison-Wesley, 2003.

Feathers, Michael. *Working Effectively with Legacy Code*. Prentice-Hall, 2004.

Fowler, Martin. "Strangler Fig Application." *http://bit.ly/2p5xMKo*.

Fowler, Martin. "Reporting Database." *http://bit.ly/2kWW9Ir*.

Garcia-Molina, Hector, and Kenneth Salem. "Sagas." *ACM Sigmod Record* 16, no. 3 (1987): 249–259.

Garcia-Molina, Hector, Dieter Gawlick, Johannes Klein, Karl Kleissner, Kenneth Salem. "Modeling Long-Running Activities as Nested Sagas." *Data Engineering* 14, no, 1 (March 1991): 14–18.

Helland, Pat. "Life Beyond Distributed Transactions." *Acmqueue* 14, no. 5.

Hodgson, Peter. "Feature Toggles (aka Feature Flags)." *http://bit.ly/2m316zB.*

Hohpe, Gregor, and Bobby Woolf. *Enterprise Integration Patterns.* Addison-Wesley, 2003.

Humble, Jez, and David Farley. *Continuous Delivery: Reliable Software Releases through Build, Test, and Deployment Automation.* Addison-Wesley, 2010.

Humble, Jez. "Make Large-Scale Changes Incrementally with Branch by Abstraction." *http://bit.ly/2p95lv7.*

Kim, Gene, Patrick Debois, Jez Humble, and John Willis. *The Devops Handbook.* IT Revolution Press, 2016.

Kleppmann, Martin. *Designing Data-Intensive Applications.* O'Reilly, 2017.

Kniberg, Henrik, and Anders Ivarsson. "Scaling Agile @ Spotify." October 2012. *http://bit.ly/2ogAz3d.*

Kotter, John P. *Leading Change.* Harvard Business Review Press, 1996.

Mitchell, Lorna Jane. *PHP Web Services, Second Edition.* O'Reilly, 2016.

Newman, Sam. *Building Microservices.* O'Reilly, 2015.

Nygard, Michael T. *Release It!: Design and Deploy Production-Ready Software, Second Edition.* Pragmatic Bookshelf, 2018.

Parnas, David. "On the Criteria to be Used in Decomposing Systems into Modules." *Information Distributions Aspects of Design Methodology*, Proceedings of IFIP Congress '71 (1972).

Parnas, David. "The Secret History of Information Hiding." David Parnas. In *Software Pioneers*, edited by M. Broy and E. Denert. (Berlin: Springer, 2002).

Pettersen, Snow. "The Road to an Envoy Service Mesh." *https://squ.re/2nts1Gc.*

Skelton, Matthew, and Manuel Pais. *Team Topologies.* IT Revolution Press, 2019.

Smith, Steve. "Application Pattern: Verify Branch By Abstraction." *http://bit.ly/2mLVevz.*

Sridharan, Cindy. *Distributed Systems Observability.* O'Reilly, 2018. *http://bit.ly/2nPZ73d.*

Thorup, Kresten. "Riak on Drugs (and the Other Way Around)." *http://bit.ly/2m1CvLP.*

Vernon, Vaughn. *Domain-Driven Design Distilled.* Addison-Wesley, 2016.

Woods, David, "Four concepts for resilience and the implications for the future of resilience engineering." Reliability Engineering & System Safety 141 (2015): 5–9.

Yourdon, Edward, and Larry Constantine. *Structured Design: Fundamentals of a Discipline of Computer Program and Systems Design*. Prentice-Hall, 1979.

Pattern Index

Aggregate exposing monolith	Exposing domain aggregates from a monolith to allow microservices to access entities managed by the monolith.
Branch by abstraction	Coexisting two implementations of the same functionality in the same codebase at the same time, allowing for a new implementation to be incrementally developed until it can replace the old implementation.
Change data capture	Transmit changes made to an underlying datastore to other interested parties.
Change data ownership	Moving the source of truth from the monolith to a microservice.
Database as a Service interface	Using a dedicated database to provide read-only access to internal service data.
Database view	A view is projected from an underlying database, allowing for parts of the database to be hidden.
Database wrapping service	A facade service is placed in front of an existing shared database, allowing for services to migrate away from direct use of the database.
Decorating collaborator	Trigger functionality running in a separate microservice by sniffing requests sent to the monolith, and the responses that are sent back in return.
Dedicated reference data schema	A dedicated database to house all static reference data. This database can be accessed by multiple different services.
Duplicate static reference data	Copy static reference data into microservice databases.
Monolith as data access layer	Accessing data managed by the monolith via APIs rather than directly accessing the database.
Move foreign key to code	Move management and enforcement of foreign-key relationships from a single database up into your service tier.
Multischema storage	Managing data in different databases, typically while migrating from a shared database to a database-per-service model.
Parallel run	Run two implementations of the same functionality side by side, to ensure that the new functionality behaves appropriately.
Repository per bounded context	Break apart a single repository layer around different parts of the domain, making decomposition into services easier.

Shared database	A single database is shared between more than one service.
Split table	Breaking a table into two parts prior to service decomposition.
Static reference data library	Move static reference data into a library or configuration file that can be packaged with each microservice that needs it.
Static reference data service	A dedicated microservice that provides access to static reference data.
Strangler fig application	Wrap your new microservice architecture around the existing monolith. Calls to use functionality that has been migrated from the monolith to your microservices are diverted; other calls are left unchanged.
Synchronize data in application	Synchronize data between two sources of truth from inside a single application.
Tracer write	Incrementally migrate data from one source of truth to another, tolerating two sources of truth during the migration.
UI composition	Presenting a single user interface by assembling many small parts together.

Index

user interfaces (UIs)
    leaving monolithic, problems with, 7
    Music Corp example, 2
    treating microservice interfaces as, 22

V
Vault, Hashicorp, 129
verify branch by abstraction pattern, 111
vertical scaling, 38
vision, 49
    communicating the change vision, 50

W
widget composition example, UI composition
    migration pattern, 99
Woods, David, 39
Working Effectively with Legacy Code (Feath-
    ers), 77

Y
Yourdon, Edward, 17

About the Author

Sam Newman is a developer, architect, writer, and speaker who has worked with various companies in different domains across the world. He works independently, focusing mostly on the cloud, continuous delivery, and microservices. Before this book, he wrote the best-selling *Building Microservices*, also published by O'Reilly.

When not jumping from one bandwagon to the next, he can be found in the East Kent countryside, getting cross about various forms of sport.

Colophon

The animal on the cover of *Monolith to Microservices* is the stinging cauliflower jellyfish (*Drymonema dalmatinum*). This subtropical jellyfish lives in the Central Atlantic Ocean and the Mediterranean Sea. It was first identified in 1880 off the coast of Croatia (then Dalmatia). Sightings of the stinging cauliflower have been rare since WWII, but a giant specimen was photographed off the coast of Italy in 2014.

This jellyfish is also nicknamed "the big pink" because of its brownish-pink coloring and impressive size—up to three feet in diameter. The class name Scyphozoa comes from a Greek word meaning "cup," alluding to the animal's body shape. The name of the subphylum Medusozoa comes from the jellyfish's long tentacles, which resemble the snakes growing from the mythological monster's head.

Like other jellyfish, the stinging cauliflower uses both sexual and asexual reproduction. In sexual reproduction, males release sperm and females release eggs that then connect in the water. The fertilized eggs become polyps, which reproduce asexually by budding before they mature. The stinging cauliflower is believed to feed on other jellyfish, usually moon jellyfish.

Jellyfish are found only in bodies of saltwater; never in fresh water.

Many of the animals on O'Reilly covers are endangered; all of them are important to the world.

The cover illustration is by Karen Montgomery, based on a black and white image from *Medusae of the World*. The cover fonts are Gilroy Semibold and Guardian Sans. The text font is Adobe Minion Pro; the heading font is Adobe Myriad Condensed; and the code font is Dalton Maag's Ubuntu Mono.

O'REILLY®

There's much more where this came from.

Experience books, videos, live online training courses, and more from O'Reilly and our 200+ partners—all in one place.

Learn more at oreilly.com/online-learning